SYSTEM SOFTWARE

SANTANU CHATTOPADHYAY
Associate Professor
Department of Electronics and Electrical Communication Engineering
Indian Institute of Technology Kharagpur

PHI Learning Private Limited
New Delhi-110001
2008

Rs. 175.00

SYSTEM SOFTWARE
Santanu Chattopadhyay

ISBN-978-81-203-3051-1

The export rights of this book are vested solely with the publisher.

Second Printing ... ... **September, 2008**

Published by Asoke K. Ghosh, PHI Learning Private Limited, M-97, Connaught Circus, New Delhi-110001 and Printed by Rajkamal Electric Press, B-35/9, G.T. Karnal Road Industrial Area, Delhi-110033.

To
my wife, Santana
my inspiration
and
my son, Sayantan
the future

Contents

Preface .... *ix*

Acknowledgements .... *xi*

1. INTRODUCTION 1–10

1.1 Overview of System Softwares 2
  1.1.1 Operating System (OS) 2
  1.1.2 Compiler 3
  1.1.3 Assembler 4
  1.1.4 Linker 5
  1.1.5 Loader 6
  1.1.6 Text Editor 7
  1.1.7 Debugger 7
1.2 Program Development Flow 8
1.3 Conclusion 8
Exercises 10

2. ASSEMBLY LANGUAGE PROGRAMMING 11–35

2.1 Pentium Assembly Language 11
  2.1.1 Registers 11
  2.1.2 Memory Models 14
  2.1.3 Addressing Modes 19
  2.1.4 Instruction Set 22
  2.1.5 Instruction Format 25
2.2 Netwide Assembler: NASM 27
  2.2.1 Layout of NASM Source Line 28
  2.2.2 Assembler Directives 29
2.3 Conclusion 35
Exercises 35

3. ASSEMBLER DESIGN 36–62

3.1 A Simple Manual Assembler 37

3.2 Assembler Design Process 40
3.2.1 Major Data Structures Used 41
3.2.2 Two-Pass Assembler 46
3.2.3 Single-Pass Assembler 54
3.3 Load-and-Go Assembler 58
3.4 Object File Formats 60
3.5 Conclusion 62
Exercises 62

4. LINKER AND LOADER 63–83

4.1 Linking 63
4.1.1 Static vs. Dynamic Linking 65
4.1.2 Combining Object Modules 65
4.1.3 Pass I of Linking 66
4.1.4 Pass II of Linking 69
4.2 Library Linking 73
4.3 Position Independent Code (PIC) 77
4.4 Shared Library Linking 79
4.5 Loader 80
4.5.1 Binary Image 81
4.5.2 Types of Loaders 81
4.6 Conclusion 82
Exercises 82

5. MACROPROCESSOR 84–101

5.1 Macro in NASM 85
5.1.1 Local Labels in Macro Body 86
5.1.2 Nested Macros 87
5.2 Design of Macroprocessors 88
5.2.1 Major Data Structures 89
5.2.2 Macroprocessing Technique 90
5.2.3 Simple Macroprocessor without Nesting 91
5.2.4 Macroprocessing with Nested Calls 94
5.2.5 Macroprocessing with Nested Calls and Definitions 96
5.3 Conclusion 100
Exercises 100

6. COMPILER 102–165

6.1 Lexical Analysis 102
6.1.1 Specification of Tokens 104
6.1.2 Token Recognition 105
6.1.3 Regular Expression to NFA 111

6.2 Syntax Analysis 114
6.2.1 Grammar 114
6.2.2 LL(k) Parsing—Topdown Predictive Parsing 119
6.2.3 LR Parsing—Bottomup Approach 123
6.2.4 Handling Ambiguity in LR Parsers 128
6.2.5 Error Recovery in LR Parser 131
6.3 Intermediate Code Generation 132
6.3.1 Three-Address Code Generation 134
6.3.2 Translation of Boolean Expressions 135
6.3.3 Translation of Control Flow Statements 142
6.4 Target Code Generation 144
6.4.1 Code Generation for Trees 148
6.5 Optimizing Transformations 150
6.5.1 Compile-time Evaluation 151
6.5.2 Common Sub-expression Elimination 152
6.5.3 Variable Propagation 153
6.5.4 Code Movement Optimization 155
6.5.5 Strength Reduction 157
6.5.6 Dead Code Elimination 157
6.5.7 Loop Optimization 158
6.6 Conclusion 163
Exercises 163

7. TEXT EDITOR 166–179

7.1 Design of a Text Editor 167
7.1.1 Common Edit-Control Features 168
7.2 Data Structures for Text Sequences 168
7.2.1 Basic Sequence Data Structures 169
7.2.2 Recursive Sequence Data Structures 171
7.3 TextDocument Design 176
7.4 TextView Design 176
7.4.1 Scrolling 177
7.4.2 Multicoloured Text 178
7.4.3 Multifont Display 178
7.5 Conclusion 179
Exercises 179

8. DEBUGGER 180–186

8.1 Overview of Debugger Features 181
8.2 Breakpoint Mechanisms 181
8.3 Hardware Support for Debugging 182
8.4 Context of Debugger 183
8.4.1 Same-process Debugger 184
8.4.2 Separate-process Debugger 184

8.5 Checkpointing and Reverse Execution 185
8.6 Conclusion 186
Exercises 186

APPENDIX: THE NETWIDE ASSEMBLER: NASM 187–188

A.1 What is NASM 187
A.2 Installation 187
A.2.1 Under MS-DOS or Windows 187
A.2.2 Under Linux 187
A.3 Assemblying with NASM 188

Bibliography* *189–191

Index* *193–195

Preface

With the advancement of computer systems in the field of hardware, it is essential to develop the necessary software to exploit those features efficiently and provide the application developer a platform in which designing complete applications can be an easy task. This book deals with the development of such system software. The target architecture is Intel's 32-bit architecture—perhaps the most widely used system today. Designing good system software requires a thorough knowledge about the underlying hardware, its instruction set, addressing modes, etc. At the same time, it requires techniques for good data structure design and the fundamentals of language processing.

Organized into eight chapters, the book covers the unique aspects of system software in such a fashion that the students can grasp the concepts with ease. Chapter 1 gives a broad overview of the system software commonly available in today's systems, its requirements, and interfacing and illustrates the complete design flow of an application through such tools.

Chapter 2 introduces the readers to the architectural details, instruction set, and addressing modes of Intel 32-bit (IA32) architecture. It also provides a brief introduction to the freely available assembler—Netwide Assembler (NASM) and its associated commands. (Appendix gives further details.) A number of examples given in the chapter are meant to make the reader confident about writing assembly language programs.

Chapter 3 deals with the design of *assemblers*, the required data structures and their implementation strategies, followed by the design of two-pass and single-pass assemblers, along with illustrative examples and their relative merits and demerits. The assembler output is expected to be in some standard format to be compatible with other tools. Accordingly, the commonly used object-file formats are introduced.

Chapter 4 on the design of *linker* and *loader* describes associated data structures and algorithms with suitable examples. It also gives a detailed discussion on topics like *relocation* and *position independent coding (PIC)*, handling of library routines and types of loaders.

Chapter 5 covers *macros* and *macroprocessing* and explains the macro features available with NASM. Macroprocessing is dealt in increasing complexities. First, a design is presented which can handle simple macro definitions and calls. In the next stage, nested macro calls are taken up, which is followed by the design of macroprocessors capable of handling both nested macro definitions and calls. Each of these is illustrated with suitable examples.

Chapter 6 focuses on another very important system software—*compiler*. It starts with the design of *lexical analyzers* and then proceeds via other stages such as *parser*, *intermediate code generation*, *target code generation*, and *code optimization*. Since the subject of compiler designing is a vast one, only the essential concepts are explained here. For a complete discussion, readers may refer the book *Compiler Design* by the author and published by Prentice-Hall of India.

Chapter 7 concentrates on the design of *text editors*. This is one of the tools, the design of which is affected mostly by the advancement in window-based graphical user interface (GUI). The chapter provides a detailed description of the data structures used in modern text editors as well as a discussion on designing such advanced editors, their features, design challenges, and possible solutions.

Chapter 8 deals with the tool *debugger*. After establishing its necessity and illustrating its essential features, the chapter throws light on possible hardware and operating system supports that can be exploited for its efficient design. It also elaborates on different types of debuggers and their implementation philosophies.

In this book, I have attempted to cover all the topics on system software, prescribed for the undergraduate students of computer science. I will consider my efforts worthwhile if the book fully meets the needs of the students. Any constructive suggestion for improving the content is most welcome.

SANTANU CHATTOPADHYAY

Acknowledgements

I am indebted to all my teachers who taught me *Computer Science* and, particularly, topics such as System Software, Architecture, Operating Systems, and Compilers. Their discussions have helped me learn the subject and develop further interest in it. I am also thankful to all my students whose thought-provoking questions have spurred me on to learn the subject better. I acknowledge all the authors from whom I have drawn much of the material (of course, presenting it in my own style).

This book would not have seen the light of the day without the constant inspiration and support from my wife Santana, who literally compelled me to complete the study. In the process, she took charge of most of the family responsibilities and never complained for the lack of attention paid by me. However, she never allowed me to show even a little negligence in writing the book. My son, Sayantan, always trying to achieve more than myself, in some sense, forced me to write the book to set perhaps a difficult (!) target for him. At this moment, I sadly remember my mother-in-law, Mrs. Aruna Mukherjee who passed away while the manuscript was still in the process of completion. I still vividly remember how much she longed to find an achiever in me! I humbly seek her blessings!

Finally, I must thank the editorial and production team of Prentice-Hall of India who worked tirelessly to ensure timely publication of the book.

SANTANU CHATTOPADHYAY

Chapter 1

Introduction

System softwares are programs used for functioning of a computer system, its maintenance, and for providing the general user with a very user-friendly development platform for their programs. In earlier systems, the amount of such system softwares present was very small and not that efficient. This made working with such systems difficult. To understand the situation better, we may think of the bare minimum hardware, consisting of CPU and memory chips. This may still perform a lot of work in the sense that the program may be burnt into a *Read Only Memory (ROM)* and the CPU will execute the instructions one after the other from the memory. However, this needs the user to be capable of writing the program in the machine language directly, which is almost impossible for any program excepting very small and trivial ones. This shows the necessity of the existence of more user-friendly interfaces.

Historically, system software has been viewed in a number of different ways since the invention of computers. The original computers were so expensive that their use for such clerical jobs as language translation was viewed as a dangerous waste of scarce resources. Early system developers seem to have consistently underestimated the difficulty of producing working programs, but it did not take long for them to realize that letting the computer spend a few minutes on the clerical job of assembling a user program was less expensive than having the programmer hand assemble it and then spend hours of computer time debugging it. As a result, by 1960, the assembly language was widely accepted. The new high level language, FORTRAN, was attracting a growing user community, and many other languages like Algol, COBOL, LISP were coming up. In early systems, compilers and other program development tools were integrated with the operating system. This is because, such tools generally consume a lot of system resources that was scarce in those systems. However, by the mid-1960s, the resource management tools had become so powerful that they could efficiently treat the resource demands of program preparation tools the same way as any other application program. By the 1970s, it became quite common for the computer users to obtain editors, compilers, and operating systems from different vendors.

Thus, the whole gamut of softwares present in a computer system can broadly be classified into two categories.

1. *Application softwares*: Written by individual users for their particular computational requirements, e.g. scientific calculations, database applications, etc.

2. *System softwares*: Generally written by the manufacturer or the system administrator for proper and easy use of the system and its maintenance.

It is very difficult to draw the *demarcation* line between these two categories of softwares, because in most of the systems, softwares are designed following a layered approach—a software available at lower level may be used to design a higher level one. But, we can broadly say that a system software is much closer to the actual hardware than the application programs. System softwares help in the development of application programs and system maintenance. The major system softwares are listed below:

- Operating system
- Compiler
- Assembler
- Linker
- Loader
- Text editor
- Debugger

1.1 OVERVIEW OF SYSTEM SOFTWARES

In this section, an overview of the commonly used system softwares and their features are given. The individual software developments will be taken up in successive chapters.

1.1.1 Operating System (OS)

It is the system software which is responsible for resource allocation to the user programs, management of the resources, interacting with the hardware, and thus providing an environment in which programs can be executed in a smooth manner. It normally consists of the following modules:

Process management. It deals with the creation and scheduling of processes in the computer. It may be noted that a process is an executable chunk of code. OS also takes care of *interprocess communication*, (that is, interaction between processes) and *synchronization*. Process scheduling refers to the allocation of CPU for the execution of the process. It may range from simple *first-in-first-out* to *round-robin* to *multiple priority* based scheduling.

Resource management. It refers to the allocation and management of system resources. Typical resources in a computer system include CPU time, main memory, disk blocks, printers, process communication and synchronization primitives like *semaphore, monitor, shared memory*, and so on. The resource management policy must ensure that the system does not fall into a state of *deadlock* in which case none of the processes can progress due to an interlocking of resources between them.

Memory management. The policies for memory management play a vital role in determining the performance of the system. In today's *virtual memory* environment, the size of user program can be very large—several times higher than the physical memory. Thus, at a point of time, only a portion of the program is loaded into the memory. Hence, judging the portion to be kept in memory becomes a very crucial decision, as reference to missing portions needs to access the secondary storage, introducing quite some delay. Various replacement algorithms are used for this purpose.

Secondary storage management. Operating system must ensure that the secondary storage devices (like disks, tapes, etc.) are used in both space and time efficient manner, striking a proper balance between them. Depending upon the type of secondary storage, different management policies need to be used.

User management. A system may have different types of users having different levels of priorities and access to the system resources. OS must ensure that various levels of users can be created and their capabilities are maintained.

Security management. It refers to maintaining the system integrity and security. A user should not be able to modify OS data inadvertently or maliciously. At the same time, the resources allotted to particular process/user should not be made available to others unless explicitly permitted. Thus, security and permission management is a very important responsibility of OS.

1.1.2 Compiler

A compiler is a system software that converts a source language program into an equivalent target language program. It also validates the input program to be conforming to the source language specification. A compiler can be conceptually divided into a number of phases. They are as follows:

Lexical analysis. This is the interface of the compiler to the outside world. The task of this phase is to scan the input source program and identify the valid words within it. It also does the additional job of removing *cosmetics* (like extra white spaces, comments added by the user, etc.) from the program, expanding the user defined macros (like `#include` and `#define` in C), and reporting the presence of foreign words (that is, words not belonging to the language of the source program), if any. The lexical analysis phase is generally implemented as a *finite automata.*

Syntax analysis. The syntax analysis phase takes words/tokens from the lexical analyzer and checks the syntactic correctness of the input program. The syntax analysis phase is successful if it can identify a sequence of grammar rules that can be used to derive the input program from a special start symbol of the grammar. In such a case, it generates a tree representation (known as *parse tree*) to depict how the sequence of words in the program can be combined to establish the program to be grammatically correct. If it is not possible to construct such a parse tree, then the input program is syntactically incorrect, and an appropriate error message is flashed to the user. This phase is also known as *parsing.*

Semantic analysis. Once a program is found to be syntactically correct (that is, grammatically okay), the next task is to check for semantic correctness. Since the semantics of a program is dependent on the language, it is not possible to enumerate the types of semantic checks that should be included in a compiler. However, one very common check is for the types of variables and expressions occurring in the program. The second check requires determining the definition of the variables to be used as per the *scope rules.*

Intermediate code generation. This phase is an optional one towards the target code generation. In this phase, codes corresponding to the input source language program are generated in terms of some hypothetical machine instructions. The process helps retarget the compiler generating code for one processor to another one.

Target code generation. The task of target code generation from intermediate code is one of template substitution. For every statement of the intermediate language, a predefined target language template is used to generate the final code. The availability of machine instructions, addressing modes, and the number of registers (both general and special purpose) play vital roles in designing such templates. Efforts are made to pack the temporary variables of the program (some user defined and some compiler generated) into the CPU registers. This expedites the program execution.

Code optimization. This is the most vital step in target code generation to make the code efficient. Since the stages of a compiler are often automated, it generates a lot of redundant codes that can possibly be eliminated. Some important optimization methods include *loop optimization, algebraic simplifications, elimination of store-and-load* cases, in which a variable computed in the previous statement is stored in memory, while the subsequent instruction loads it again from memory. Preservence of a copy of the variable in a register removes the reloading requirement. A plenty of other code optimization strategies have been reported in the literature.

Symbol table management. The symbol table is a data structure holding information about all the symbols defined in the source program. Though it does not form a part of the final code generated, it is used as a reference table by almost all the phases of a compiler. The typical information stored in the symbol table includes the name of the variables, their types, sizes, relative offsets within the program, and so on. The generation of this table is normally carried out by the lexical analyzer and syntax analyzer phases.

Error handling and recovery. Though not related to the quality of code generated, error handling is one of the criteria for judging the quality of the compiler. In the case of a semantic error, the parser can still progress; however, in case of a syntax error, the parser reaches an erroneous state. Recovery needs to undo some processing already carried out by the parser, and perhaps discard a few more tokens to reach a descent state from which it can proceed again. In the absence of this, the parser will come out at the first error itself, and the user would need to correct it. However, since a number of such errors may be there, a lot of user's time is wasted to correct a single error at a time.

1.1.3 Assembler

Assembler is a utility to convert *assembly language program* to machine code. For the earlier CPUs, the instruction format was simple. Thus, even for moderately sized programs, the conversion from assembly language to machine language could often be done manually. This is popularly known as *hand assembly.* However, with the increase in the complexity of instruction sets and addressing modes, it is now almost impossible to generate machine code manually. Most of the compilers also use the assembly language for target code generation, which is then converted to machine language using assembler. The input to and output from an assembler is shown in Fig. 1.1.

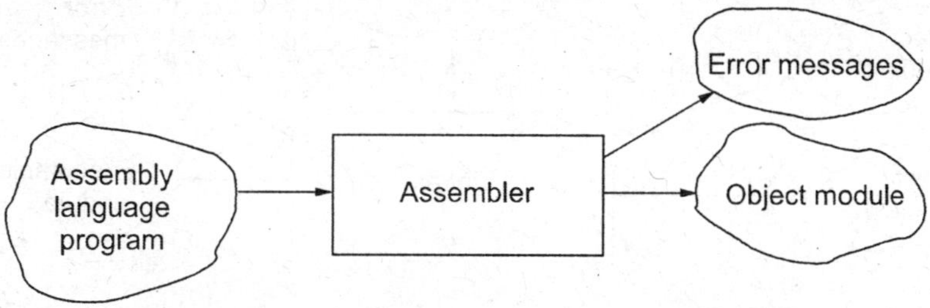

FIGURE 1.1 Input-output of an assembler.

Given an assembly language program, an assembler checks for its syntactic correctness, ensures that all the variables and labels referred to in the source program are either defined inside the program, or have been marked to be supplied later (*external definitions*) in *linking* phase. The object file produced needs to have a definite format which is often dictated by the linker input format. An assembler may support different object file formats.

Sometimes it is necessary to generate object code to be executed on a different CPU than that used in the machine for development. This is particularly true for designing new computer systems. For example, on a system that uses *Pentium* processor, we may use its assembler to generate object code for another system that uses, say *Motorolla* processor. This type of assembler is known as *cross-assembler.*

1.1.4 Linker

In a large project, generally a team of people work together to design the entire system. They may develop their modules separately. *Separate compilation* is an important feature of programming languages designed for the development of large software systems. The compiler/assembler is able to compile/assemble each module of a program by itself with little or no information from other parts of the program. It is the responsibility of the *linker* to combine all such object files produced by the compiler/assembler and produce the executable form of the program. In the process of combining object modules, the linker needs to *relocate* them, since the codes are generated by the compiler/assembler assuming the same fixed start address for all modules. The address sensitive portions within the code need to be modified properly. Another important responsibility of the linker is to adjust *external references.* As pointed out earlier, in a collaborative development environment, one module may use a variable/function which is defined in some other module. Thus, the undefined entity in the first module is an external symbol, which gets defined when the modules are combined together at the time of linking. The linker needs to fill up the blanks left by the assembler/compiler regarding all these external references. Some of the external symbols may need some library elements to be included for resolving them. For example, the basic input/output routines, mathematical functions, etc. come in the form of libraries. Thus, to produce the executable version, these libraries also need to be included. Finally, the linker should produce *error messages* if some external reference could not be resolved even after consulting all object modules and libraries. The operation of the linker can thus be depicted as in Fig. 1.2.

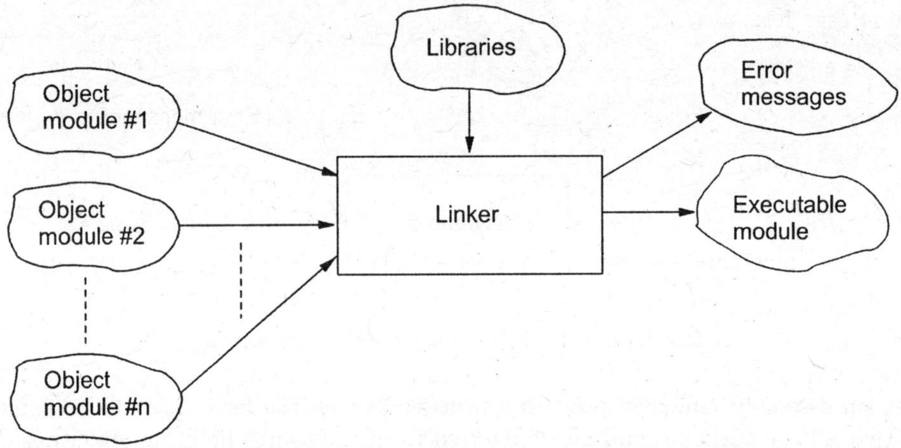

FIGURE 1.2 Input-output of a linker.

1.1.5 Loader

Loading is the process of bringing an executable file produced by the linker from the secondary storage to the primary storage in such a way that it can be executed by the operating system. In most of the modern systems, *loader* is a part of the operating system itself, making it invisible to the common users. It may be noted that the executable module produced by the linker is assumed to start from a fixed memory location. However, the process of loading may necessitate it to start from a different start address depending upon the availability of memory locations. Thus, all address sensitive portions within the code need to be modified again to reflect the change. Thus, loading is essentially the same as the relocation performed by a static linker, except that it applies to just a single file (the executable module) instead of a number of object files. The objective of loading is to bring a binary image into memory and bind relocatable addresses to absolute ones. Input-output of the loader is shown in Fig. 1.3.

It may be noted that a number of executable files may be using the same set of libraries (for example, the input/output routines of the system are used by all executables). Hence, instead of loading the libraries several times, it is advisable to share the loaded library between the processes. The library routines, being *read-only* code, are not affected by multiple programs using them simultaneously.

Modern operating systems use *virtual memory* to enable programs to transparently access more memory than the machine actually has. Thus, loading in these operating systems typically reduces to setting up the appropriate mappings between virtual and physical addresses and the program can pretend that its address space always starts at a standard place (for example, address zero). Thus, if the linker has produced an executable under this assumption, no further relocation needs to be done to the program.

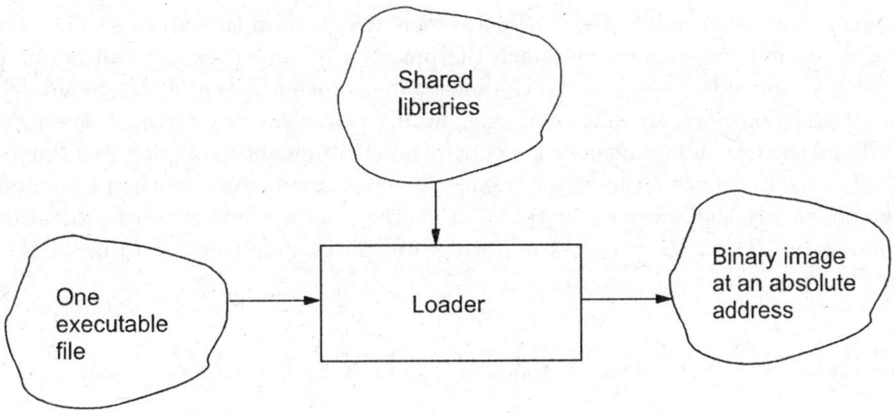

FIGURE 1.3 Input-output of a loader.

1.1.6 Text Editor

Editor is the utility used most by the program developers. The user creates the program using editor. Thus, a very simple editor should do the bare minimum job of taking the characters from the user and store it in the same order in a file. However, this basic operation needs to be augmented in many ways. First of all, the files may become too large to allow a number of users to do editing simultaneously. Thus, the portions of the file need to be stored in the secondary storage and brought back to memory when the user wants to edit those portions. The first generation of editors was known as *line editors* as their unit of editing was a full line. That is, even to modify a single character, one had to re-enter the entire line. The *EDLIN* available with *DOS* operating system is an example of this category. The next generation of editors is *screen editors* that allow the use of cursor keys to go to any desired location in the file and modify it. The *vi* editor of *Unix* is an example of screen oriented text editor. Since most of the modern operating systems are windows based, the editors have also gone through another advancement. The window based editors possess a mouse interface through which any segment of the program can be selected for necessary operation (for example, copy, delete, move, etc.). They also provide very convenient and powerful *search-and-replace* strategy to make editing easy. *Language-sensitive* editors have made the life of the programmer much easier with their ability to display language keywords and variables in different colours for ready identification, automated parentheses matching to reduce the burden of checking balanced parentheses, and many other language dependent features.

1.1.7 Debugger

The tools that we have described so far help in writing grammatically correct programs, satisfying syntactic and semantic requirements of a language. However, these tools cannot catch any logical mistakes in the program. In fact, it is the responsibility of the programmer to ensure that the idea of the algorithm is correctly coded into the program. In the case of logical bugs, it is necessary to run the program step-by-step, and check the program variables at these intermediary stages. For a normal program under execution, the user does not have any control on it to stop the execution at any arbitrary point, do some checks, and resume the program again from that point. *Debuggers* are tools that help in this process. They provide a controlled execution environment in which the program is run, so that it can be interrupted or suspended at some desirable point. The most important facility provided by all debuggers is to set a few *breakpoints*, so that when execution reaches any one of these, the program is suspended and the user is provided with a controlled environment to check/set variable values, check *stack trace* to find out the call sequence showing how control reached that point, etc. The breakpoints may be specified in terms of source program line numbers, function entry points, and so on. Thus, the progress of a program can be monitored in terms of the source program's line numbers.

1.2 PROGRAM DEVELOPMENT FLOW

Figure 1.4 shows the total design process for programs. Given a problem, it is first broken down into a set of modules with well-defined interfaces between them. Depending upon the nature of a module, a suitable language is chosen for its coding. The language can be a high-level language or the assembly language for the target processor. For modules coded in high-level languages, corresponding *compilers* are used to generate the object modules. For modules using assembly language, an *assembler* is used to get the object code. All these object modules are linked together along with necessary library modules using *linker* to generate an executable module. Next, the *loader* is used to load this executable module into memory which, along with shared libraries, is now ready for execution. Once the loaded module is allocated CPU, it starts executing. If the program executes correctly, we are through. However, in case of logical bugs, the program will either produce an *exception* (a situation in which execution cannot continue, like division by zero, accessing illegal memory locations, etc.) or generate erroneous results. In such cases, the reason needs to be traced out, which is done using step-by-step execution of the program in a controlled environment provided by the *debugger*. Once the reason behind the logical bug is understood, the corresponding source modules are modified and the whole cycle is repeated till we get the desired correct execution of the program.

1.3 CONCLUSION

System softwares are utilities required for the development and execution of user programs and system maintenance. We have seen a broad overview of such tools in this chapter. In the chapters to come, we will look in detail the design of such tools. However, discussions on *operating system* have been kept outside the scope of this book, since a good treatment of the topic will need a separate volume. Readers may follow some relevant text accordingly. To understand the remaining tools and challenges in designing them, we first need to have a fair idea about the structure of a CPU and its assembly language. In Chapter 2, we have discussed the assembly language programming for the *Pentium* processors.

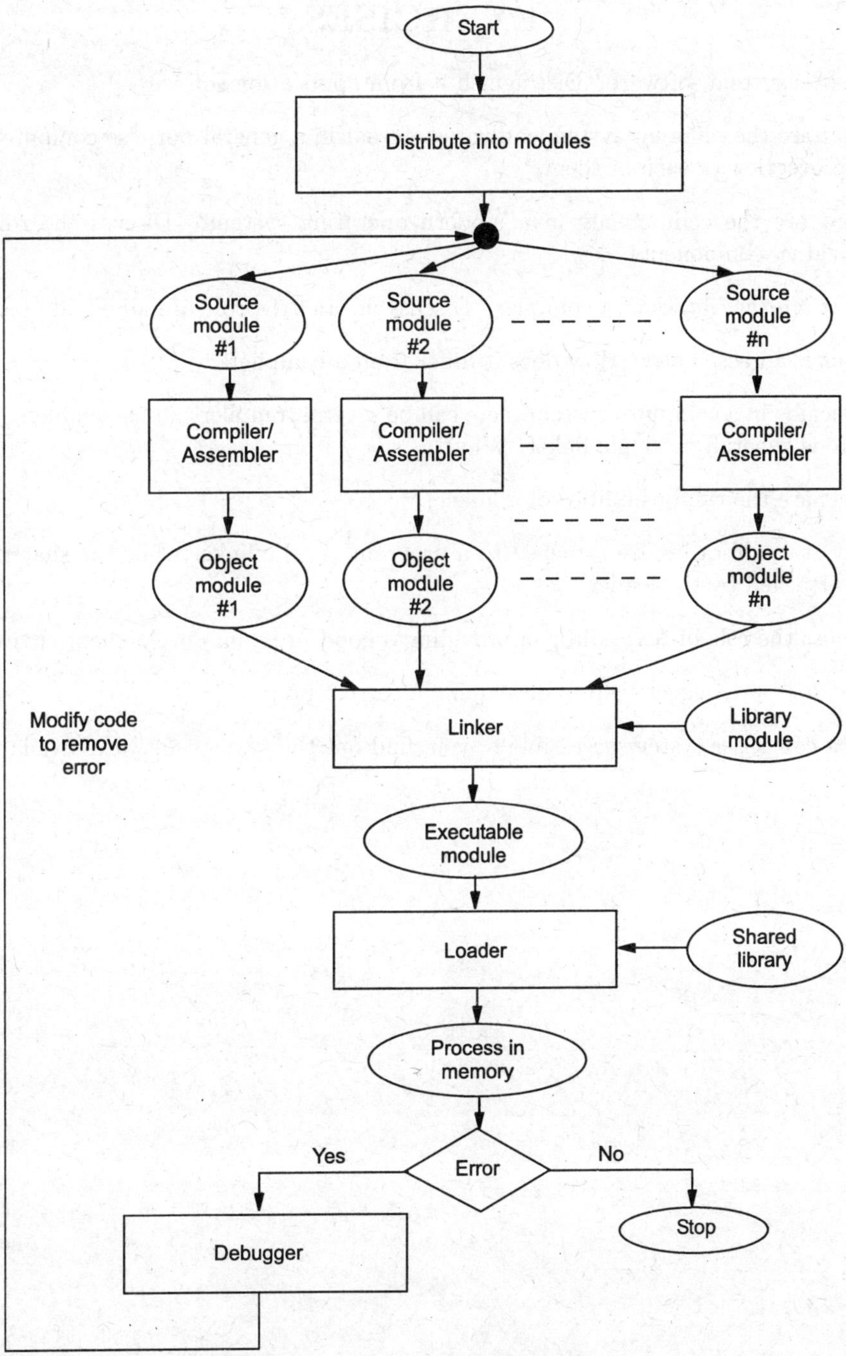

FIGURE 1.4 Program development flow.

EXERCISES

1.1 What is system software? Distinguish it from application software.

1.2 What are the different system softwares present in a general purpose computer? Give a brief overview of each of them.

1.3 What are the components in a modern operating system? Discuss the roles of the individual components.

1.4 What are the phases of a compiler? Discuss in brief the role of individual phases.

1.5 What is an assembler? How does it differ from a compiler?

1.6 Typically, in a computer system there can be several compilers and assemblers. However, there is generally a single linker. Why?

1.7 What are the responsibilities of a linker?

1.8 Why static libraries are attached to a program via the linker while the shared libraries are attached by the loader?

1.9 Discuss the role of text editor in providing a good program development environment.

1.10 How does a debugger help in developing a correct program?

1.11 For a computer system accessible to you, find out the system softwares available in it.

Chapter 2

Assembly Language Programming

The design of an assembler needs a detailed knowledge about the underlying processor and its instruction set. To make the concepts about system softwares clear, we will provide an overview of *Pentium* assembly language in this chapter. It may be noted that the instruction set of Pentium is really huge; hence, we will be discussing only a subset of it, rich enough to serve most of the programming purposes. Because of its backward compatibility with other *Intel* processors, lots of extra instructions are still supported which we have excluded here. The program written in the assembly language needs to be converted into machine code by means of an *assembler*. Though there exist a large number of assemblers, namely, *a86, gas, as86, MASM, TASM*, etc., these are either not freely available, or not good enough to support the requirements of today's programmers. Some of these assemblers do not port easily to different operating systems. In this direction, a *Netwide Assembler, NASM* has come up for *80x86* assembly designed for portability and modularity. The details of availability and installation of NASM have been given in *Appendix A*. It supports a wide range of object file formats, including *Linux* and *NetBSD/FreeBSD a.out, ELF, COFF,* Microsoft 16-bit *OBJ* and *Win32.* Its syntax is designed to be simple and easy to understand. It supports *Pentium, P6, MMX, 3DNow!, SSE,* and *SSE2* opcodes and has *macro* capability. The details of this assembler with examples illustrating the usages are given in the later part of this Chapter.

2.1 PENTIUM ASSEMBLY LANGUAGE

In this section, we provide an overview of the assembly language of *Pentium.* However, the details presented are not specific to just Pentium architecture. They are applicable to the *486, Pentium II,* and *Pentium Pro* as well.

2.1.1 Registers

The Intel 32-bit architecture provides 16 basic program execution registers for use in general system and application programming. A grouping of these registers has been shown in Fig. 2.1.

- *General purpose registers:* Eight general purpose registers are available storing operands and pointers as explained later.
- *Segment registers:* Six segment registers hold up to six *segment selectors.*
- *EFLAGS register:* It holds the program status and allows limited control of the processor to the application program.
- *EIP:* It is the 32-bit instruction pointer pointing to the next instruction to be executed.

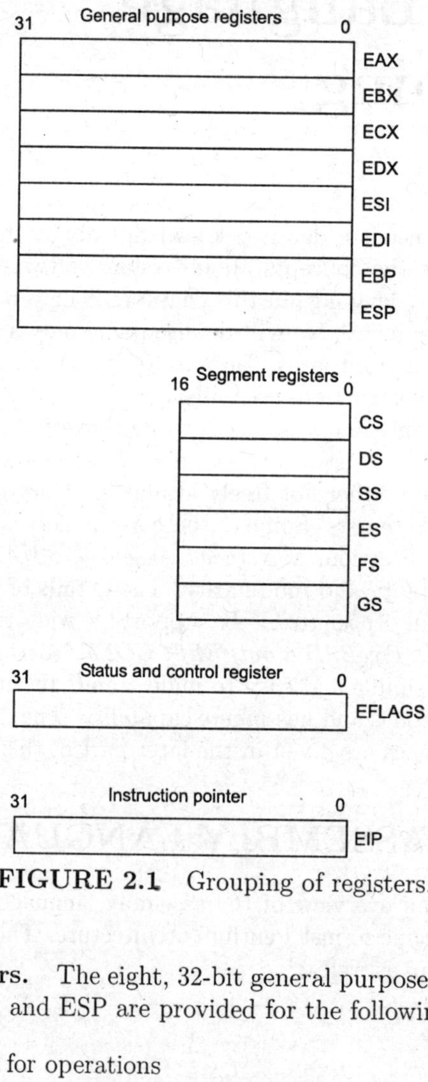

FIGURE 2.1 Grouping of registers.

General purpose registers. The eight, 32-bit general purpose registers EAX, EBX, ECX, EDX, ESI, EDI, EBP, and ESP are provided for the following operations:

- to hold operands for operations
- to hold operands for address calculations
- for memory pointers

The special uses of general purpose registers by instructions are as follows:

- EAX — Accumulator for operands and results data.
- EBX — Pointer to data in the data segment.
- ECX — Counter for string and loop operations.
- EDX — I/O pointer.
- ESI — Pointer to data in the segment pointed to by the DS segment register (introduced later); source pointer for string operations.
- EDI — Pointer to data (or destination) in the segment pointed to by the segment register ES (introduced later); destination pointer for string operations.
- EBP — Pointer to data on the stack (in the SS segment).
- ESP — Stack pointer in the segment pointed to by the segment register SS.

The lower order 16 bits of the general purpose registers map directly to the register set found in the earlier *Intel* processors, like 8086. These 16-bit registers can be referenced with the names AX, BX, CX, DX, BP, SP, SI, and DI. The 8-bit portions of AX, BX, CX, and DX can be accessed as a collection of 8-bit registers. The higher order 8-bits of AX is referred to as AH, while the lower order 8-bits can be accessed as AL. Similarly, BX, CX, and DX can be accessed as BH and BL, CH and CL, and DH and DL registers. This is shown in Fig. 2.2.

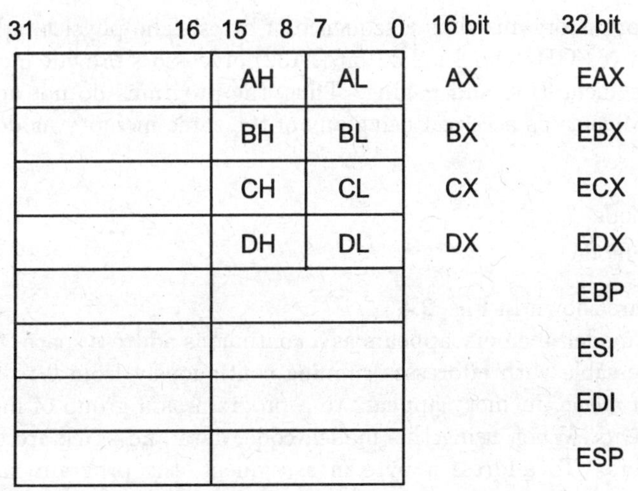

FIGURE 2.2 General purpose registers.

Segment registers. The segment registers (CS, DS, SS, ES, FS, and GS) hold 16-bit segment selectors. A segment selector is a special pointer that identifies a segment in memory. To access a particular segment in memory, the segment selector for that segment must be present in the appropriate segment register. The structure of segment selector has been illustrated later in Section 2.1.2. Each of the segment registers is associated with one of the three types of storage: *code, data,* or *stack.* For example, the CS register contains the segment selector for the code segment, where the instructions being executed are stored. The processor fetches instructions from the code segment, using a logical address that consists of the segment selector in the CS register and the contents of the EIP register holding the offset of the next instruction to be executed. The CS register cannot be loaded explicitly by an application program. Instead, it is loaded implicitly by instructions or internal processor operations that change the program control (such as procedure calls, interrupts, etc.). The DS, ES, FS, and GS registers point to four data segments. The availability of four data segments permits efficient and secure access to different types of data. To access additional data segments, the application program must load segment selectors for these segments into the corresponding segment register. The SS register contains the segment selector for a stack segment. Unlike CS register, SS register can be loaded explicitly, permitting application programs to set up multiple stacks and switch between them.

EFLAGS register. The 32-bit EFLAGS register contains a group of status flags, a control flag, and a group of system flags. Some of the flags in the EFLAGS register can be modified directly, using special purpose instructions. However, there are no instructions that allow the whole register to be examined or modified directly. The format of the EFLAGS register has been shown in Fig. 2.3.

2.1.2 Memory Models

The physical memory is organized as a sequence of bytes. The physical address space ranges from zero to $2^{36} - 1$ (64 GBytes). Intel 32-bit (IA32) processors provide memory management facilities such as segmentation and paging. Thus, the programs do not address the physical memory directly. Memory is accessed using any of the three memory models:

1. Flat mode
2. Segmented mode
3. Real address mode

The three models are shown in Fig. 2.4.

In *flat* memory model, memory appears as a continuous address space. This linear address space is byte addressable with addresses running continuously from 0 to $2^{32} - 1$. With the *segmented memory model*, memory appears to a program as a group of independent address spaces called *segments*. When using this model, code, data and stack are typically contained in separate segments. To address a byte in a segment, the program must issue a logical address, which consists of a *segment selector* and an offset. The segment selector identifies the segment to be accessed and the offset identifies a byte in the address space of the segment. The programs can address up to 16,383 segments of different sizes and types, and each segment can be as large as 2^{32} bytes. The *real address mode* memory model uses the memory model for Intel 8086 processor. Individual segments can be up to 64 KBytes in size, and maximum size of the linear address space is 2^{20} bytes. The linear address is obtained by multiplying the segment register by 16 and adding offset to it.

Modern operating systems and applications use the *flat* (that is, unsegmented) memory mode: all the segment registers are loaded with the same segment selector (zero) so that

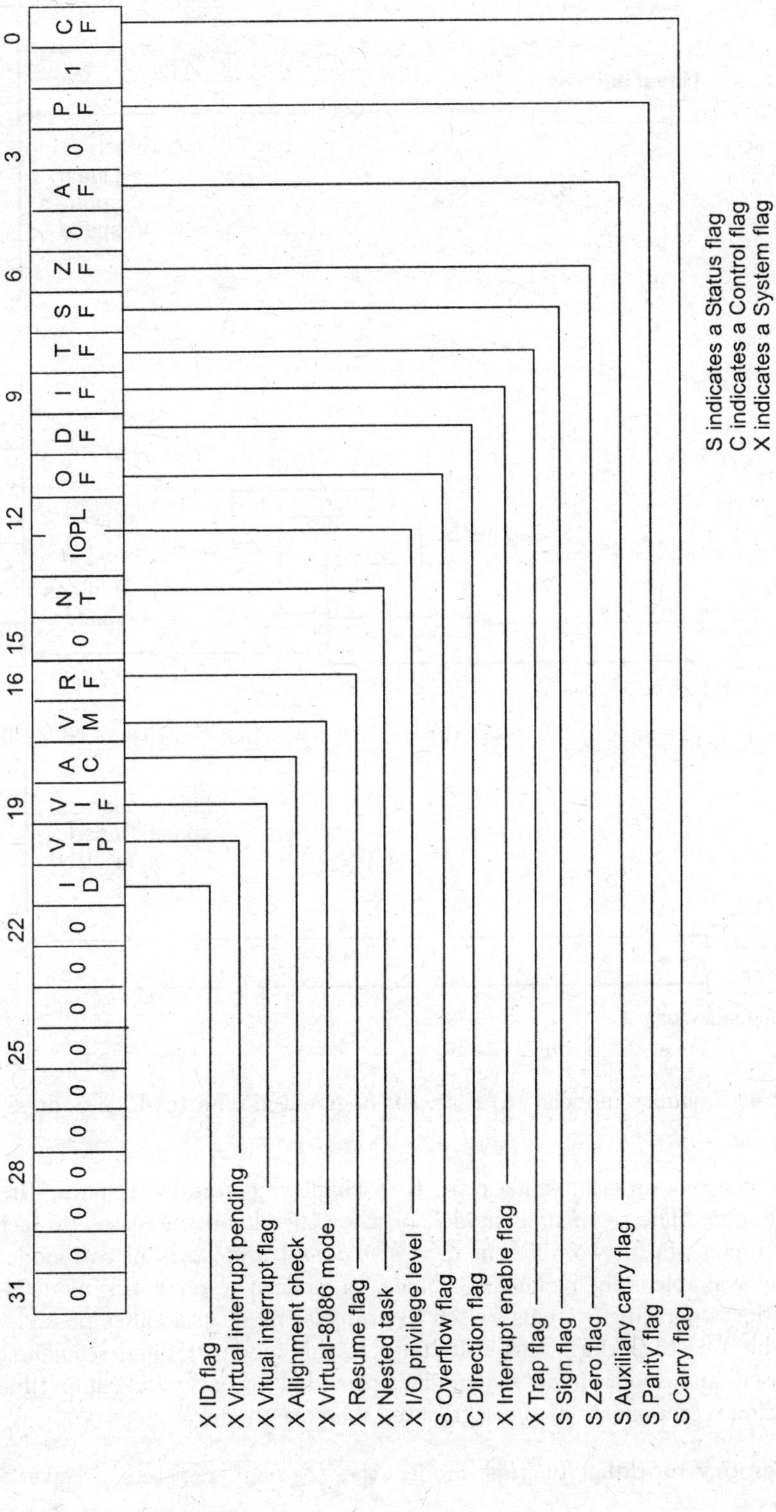

FIGURE 2.3 EFLAGS register.

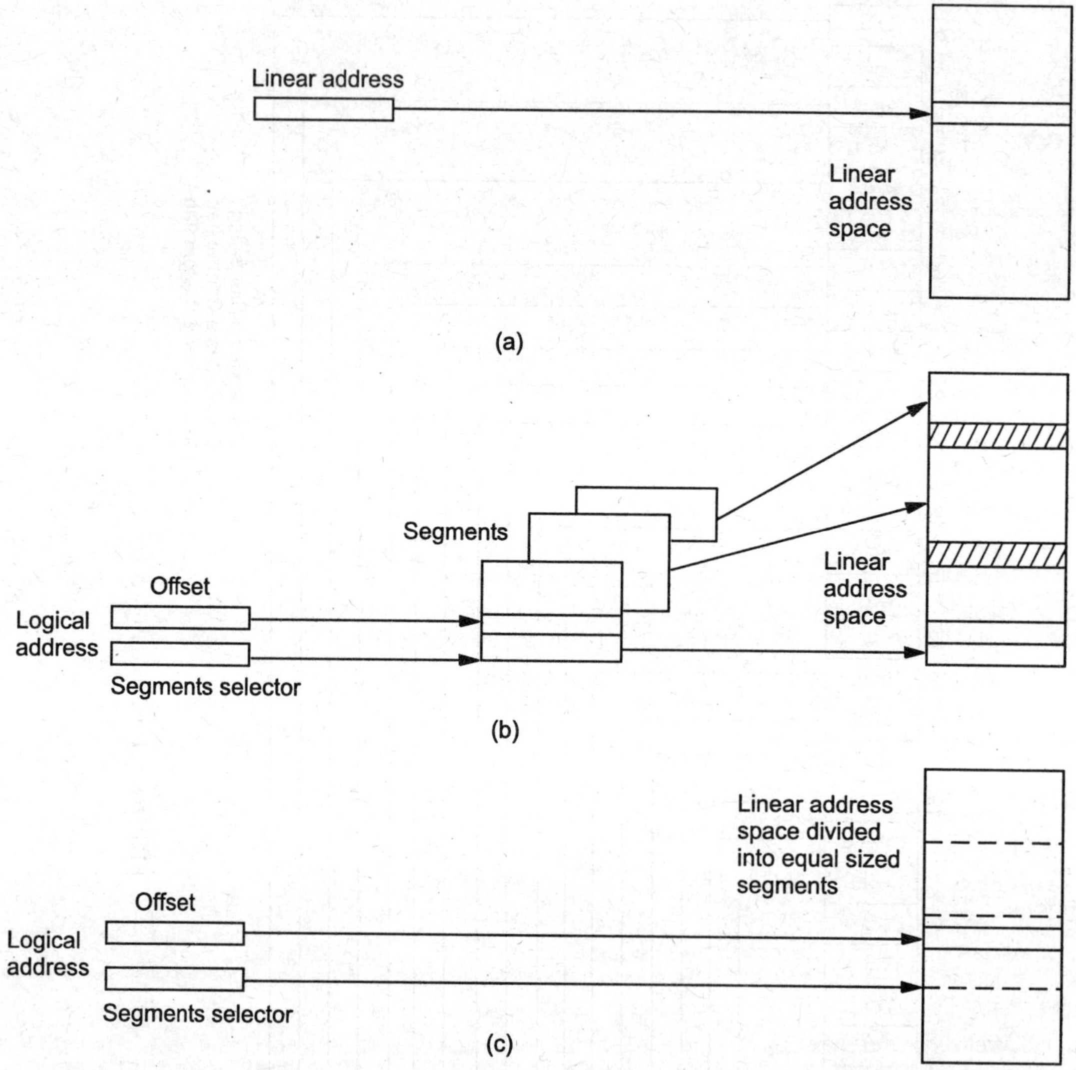

FIGURE 2.4 Memory models: (a) Flat, (b) Segmented, and (c) Real address mode.

all memory references a program makes are to a single linear-address space. It has been explained in Fig. 2.5. The segmented model, on the other hand, increases protection. The IA32 architecture can run in two different modes, *real* and *protected*. In *real* mode, the only addressing model available is the *real address mode*. In modern systems, this mode is only used when booting. Most operating systems switch to *protected* mode as soon as possible. A single instruction can be used to perform this switching. In this mode, *flat* and *segmented* memory models can be used, and also a *virtual real* mode is provided for backward compatibility. Here, we deal with various components of the segmented memory model.

Segmented memory model. In this mode, the segment registers receive the name

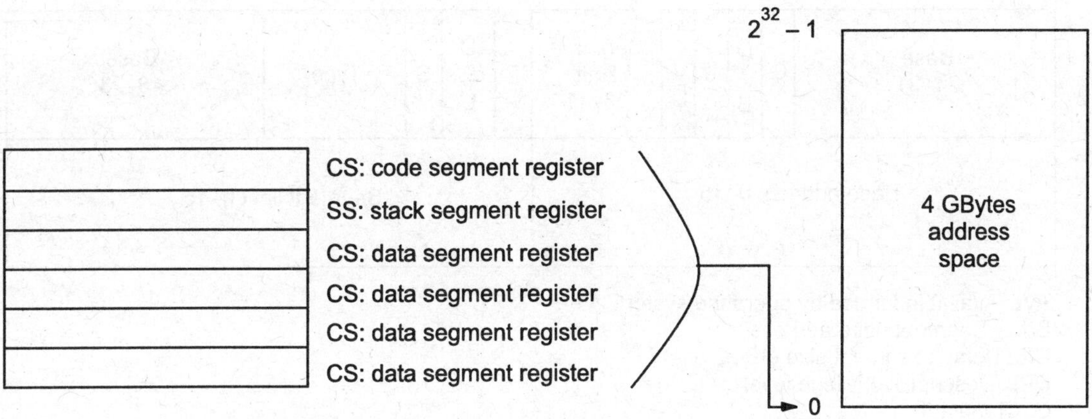

FIGURE 2.5 Segment registers in flat memory model.

selectors. Although the segment registers are still 16-bit in size, their interpretation by the processor is different. The structure of a *selector* has been shown in Fig. 2.6. Instead of using the segment registers to extend it to 20 bits, the processor treats each selector as an index to a *Descriptor Table.*

FIGURE 2.6 Internal composition of a selector.

Descriptor tables. *Descriptor tables* reside in system memory and are used by the processor to perform address translation. Each entry in a descriptor table is 8 bytes long and represents a single segment in memory. It contains a pointer to the first byte in the associated segment and a 20-bit value representing the size of the segment in memory. Figure 2.7, represents the exact structure of a descriptor table entry. The individual fields are as follows:

1. *Base:* This 32-bit *segment base address* field points to the segment's starting location in the 4GB linear address space.

2. *D/B:* It is called *segment size bit.* When the descriptor entry describes a code segment, this bit is used to specify the default length of operands and addresses. If the bit is set, the processor assumes a 32-bit segment, else a 16-bit segment is assumed.

3. *DPL: Descriptor privilege level* (2-bit) field defines the segment privilege level. It is used by the protection mechanism built into the processor to restrict access to the segment.

4. *G: Granularity bit* controls the resolution of the segment limit field. When this bit is clear, the resolution is set to one byte. When this bit is set, the resolution is 4KB.

<table>
<tr><td>Base 24–31</td><td>G</td><td>D / B</td><td>0</td><td>A V L</td><td>Segment limit 16–19</td><td>P</td><td>D P L</td><td>S</td><td>Type</td><td>Base 16–23</td></tr>
<tr><td colspan="6">Base address 0–15</td><td colspan="5">Segment limit 0–15</td></tr>
</table>

AVL: Available for use by operating system
Base: Segment base address
D/B: Default segment size (16/32 bits)
DPL: Descriptor privilege level
G: Granularity
Limit: Segment limit
P: Present bit
S; Descriptor type (system/application)
Type: Segment type

FIGURE 2.7 Descriptor entry.

5. *Limit:* The *segment limit* field (20-bit) determines the size of the segment in units of one byte or 4KB (depending on the G-bit).

6. *P:* The *segment present bit* specifies whether the segment is present in memory.

7. *S:* The *descriptor type bit* determines whether this is a normal segment or a system segment.

8. *Type:* The *segment type bit* (4-bit) determines the type of the segment, for example, *execute-only, execute-read, read-only, read-write,* and so on.

Two types of descriptor tables are used by the processor when working in the protected mode. The first one is known as the *Global descriptor table (GDT)* and is used mainly for holding descriptor entries of operating system segments. The second type is known as the *Local descriptor table (LDT)*. It contains entries of normal application segments. During initialization, the kernel creates a single GDT which is kept in memory until either the operating system terminates or the processor is switched to the *real-mode.* Whenever the user starts an application, the operating system creates a new LDT to hold the descriptor entries, which represent the segments used by the new task. When looking into a specific descriptor entry, the addressing unit in the processor uses the *TI* bit to decide which descriptor table be used—the GDT or the currently active LDT. The linear address and size of the GDT are stored in a special processor register called *GDTR*. Similarly, *LDTR* register contains the size and position of the currently active LDT in memory. The process is illustrated in Fig. 2.8.

The logical address generated by the CPU consists of two parts—a *selector* part and an *offset* part. The segment selector points to a segment descriptor, which contains the base address of a memory segment. The 32-bit offset from the logical address is added to the segment's base address, generating 32-bit linear address. It has been illustrated in Fig. 2.9.

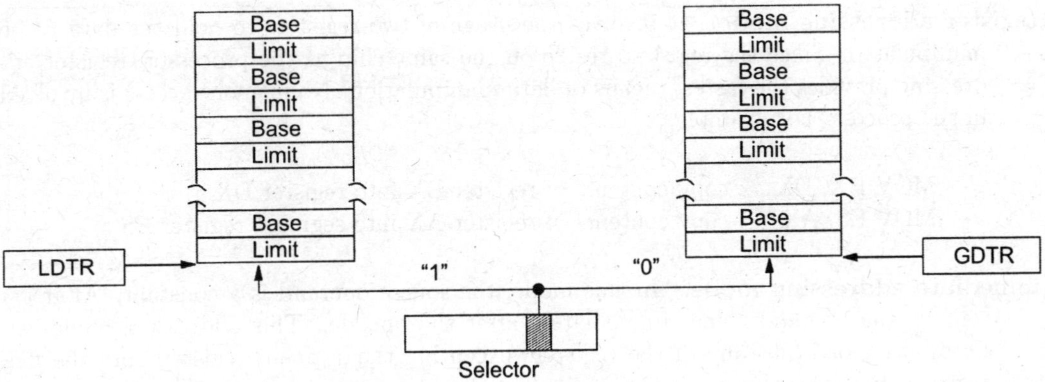

FIGURE 2.8 Table indicator bit.

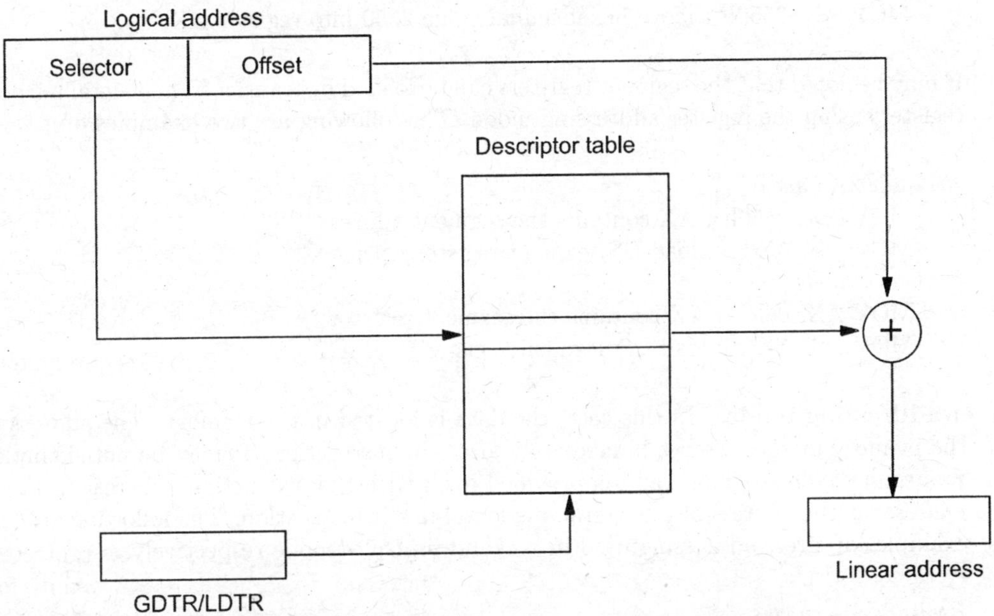

FIGURE 2.9 Logical to linear address translation.

2.1.3 Addressing Modes

The IA-32 architecture provides a total of seven distinct addressing modes, namely,

1. Register
2. Immediate
3. Direct
4. Register indirect
5. Based relative
6. Indexed relative
7. Based indexed relative.

Register addressing mode. It involves the usage of two registers to hold the data to be manipulated. Since the registers reside on the same chip as the processor, register addressing provides the fastest means of data manipulation. No memory access is involved in the process. For example,

```
MOV BX, DX    ; copy contents of register BX into register DX
MOV ES, AX    ; copy contents of register AX into segment register ES
```

Immediate addressing mode. In this mode, the source operand is a constant. After assembly, the operand comes immediately after the opcode. This addressing mode can be used to load into any of the registers excepting the segment registers and the flag register. For example,

```
MOV AX, 2550h ; move hexadecimal value 2550 into register AX.
```

It may be noted that the segment registers can be loaded by transfer from general purpose registers using the register addressing mode. The following are two examples of it.

Real-address mode:

```
MOV AX, 2550h ; AX contains the segment address
MOV DS, AX    ; load DS segment register with AX
```

Protected mode:

```
MOV AX, 08h   ; AX contains the segment selector
MOV DS, AX    ; load DS segment register with AX
```

Direct addressing mode. In this case, the data is located in the memory. The address of the memory location comes immediately after the instruction. It may be noted that in *immediate addressing*, operand is provided itself with the instruction, whereas in *direct addressing*, the address of the operand is found in the instruction. The following are two examples of direct addressing used in *real* and *protected* mode respectively.

Real-address mode:

```
MOV DL, [2400h]          ; moves content of memory location 16*DS + 2400h to DL
```

Protected mode:

```
MOV EAX, [12345678h];segment selector in DS indexes into the descriptor table to
                     get the base of the data segment to which 12345678h is
                     added to obtain the logical address – content of this location
                     is transferred to EAX
```

Register indirect addressing mode. The address of the memory location where the operand resides is held in a register. In *real-address mode*, the register SI, DI, and BX can be used for this purpose. In the *protected mode*, any of the registers EAX, EBX, ECX, EDX, ESI, or EDI can be used. These register values are combined with DS segment register to generate the physical address. For example,

Real-address mode:

MOV AL, [BX] ; moves into AL contents of memory location pointed to by DS:BX

Protected mode:

MOV AL, [EAX]; moves into AL the contents of the memory location pointed to by DS:EAX

Based relative addressing mode. In this case, in *real-address mode*, the base registers BX and BP, as well as a displacement value are used to compute an *effective address*, which, combined with the segment register value, gives the address of the operand. The default segment registers used for the calculation of physical address are DS for BX and SS for BP. For example,

MOV CX, [BX + 10h] ; moves 16-bit word at memory location DS:BX + 10h into CX register

MOV [BP + 22h], CX ; moves contents of CX into memory location SS:BP + 22h

In case of protected mode, registers EAX, EBX, ECX, EDX, ESI, EDI, EBP, and ESP can be used as base registers. The default segment registers used for the calculation of physical address are DS for EAX, EBX, ECX, EDX, ESI, and EDI and SS for EBP and ESP. For example,

MOV EAX, [EBX + 10h] ; moves 32-bit quantity at memory location DS:EBX + 10h into EAX register

MOV [EBP + 22h], EDX ; moves contents of EDX into memory location SS:EBP + 22h

Indexed relative addressing mode. In *real-address mode*, index registers SI and DI, as well as a displacement value are used to calculate effective address. The default segment register is DS. For example,

MOV CX, [SI+10h] ; moves 16-bit word at memory location DS:SI + 10h into CX register

In case of *protected mode*, registers EAX, EBX, ECX, EDX, ESI, EDI, EBP, and ESP can be used as index registers. The default segment registers used are DS for EAX, EBX, ECX, EDX, ESI and EDI, and SS for EBP and ESP. For example,

MOV EAX, [ESI+10h] ; moves 32-bit quantity at memory location DS:ESI + 10h into EAX register

Based indexed relative addressing mode. It is the combination of *based* and *indexed* addressing modes. In this mode, one base register and one index register are used. For example,

Real-address mode:

```
MOV AL, [BX + SI + 8h]      ; moves into AL contents of memory location
                              pointed to by DS:BX + SI + 8h
MOV AL, [BP + SI + 8h]      ; moves into AL contents of memory
                              location pointed to by SS:BP + SI + 8h
```

Protected mode:

```
MOV AL, [EAX + EBX + 10h] ; moves into AL the contents of the memory
                            location pointed to by DS:EAX + EBX + 10h
MOV AL, [EBP + EBX + 10h] ; moves into AL the contents of the memory
                            location pointed to by SS:EBP + EBX + 10h
```

Segment overrides. As noted earlier, each of the addressing modes has a default segment register associated with it. However, it is possible to explicitly mention in the statement some other segment register to be used to access the operands. It is called *segment overrides.* For example, the following instruction asks to use ES as the segment register, though the default segment register is DS.

```
MOV AL, ES:[SI + 8h]   ; moves into AL contents of memory location pointed to
                         by ES:SI + 8h
```

Scaling factors. For 32-bit instructions, a scaling factor can be specified in any of the *based, indexed,* or *based indexed* addressing modes. The scaling factor is 1, 2, 4, or 8. For example,

```
MOV EAX, [ESI + EAX*4]   ; moves into EAX the 32-bit quantity at
                           DS:ESI + EAX * 4
```

Thus in the protected mode, the *effective address* can be viewed as,

$$\text{effective address} = \text{base register} + (\text{index register} \times \text{ scaling factor}) + \text{ displacement}$$

2.1.4 Instruction Set

It may be noted that the *Pentium* instruction set is very large. Here, we will discuss about some representative instructions to understand how those can be used to write simple programs. Most of the instructions have exactly two operands, in which case one of the operands must be a register, while there is no restriction on the other one—it can be another register, memory location, or immediate value, etc. Most of the instructions are available in 8-, 16-, and 32-bit operands. However, for the sake of brevity we will present only 8- and 32-bit versions. We will also omit the floating-point instructions. The detailed instruction set can be found in the *Intel reference manual.* We use the following abbreviations while presenting the instruction set.

reg	: register mode operand, 32-bit register
reg8	: register mode operand, 8-bit register
r/m	: general addressing mode, 32-bit
r/m8	: general addressing mode, 8-bit

immed : 32-bit immediate along with instruction
immed8 : 8-bit immediate along with instruction
m : symbol (label) in the instruction is the effective address

The set of instructions can be classified into a number of groups based on their functionality. These are:

1. Data movement
2. Integer arithmetic
3. Logical
4. Floating point
5. Control transfer.

As mentioned earlier, we will exclude floating point instructions from our discussion. The remaining instructions are as follows.

1. **Data Movement:**

```
MOV     reg,   r/m        ; copy data
        r/m,   reg
        reg,   immed
        r/m,   immed
MOVSX   reg,   r/m8       ; sign extend and copy data
MOVZX   reg,   r/m8       ; zero extend and copy data
LEA     reg,   m          ; get effective address
```

EXAMPLE 2.1 Let us consider the following.

(a) MOV EAX, 23 – places 32-bit 2's complement immediate 23 into register EAX.

(b) MOVSX ECX, AL – sign extends the 8-bit quantity in AL to 32-bits and places it in ECX.

(c) MOV [ESP], -1 – places -1 into memory, address given by contents of ESP.

(d) LEA EBX, loop_top – put the address assigned to label loop_top into register EBX.

2. **Integer Arithmetic:**

```
ADD     reg,   r/m        ; 2's complement addition
        r/m,   reg
        reg,   immmed
        r/m,   immmed
INC     reg               ; add 1 to operand
        r/m
SUB     reg,   r/m        ; 2's complement subtraction
        r/m,   reg
        reg,   immmed
        r/m,   immmed
```

```
DEC     reg                  ; subtract 1 from operand
        r/m
NEG     r/m                  ; get additive inverse of operand
MUL     EAX, r/m             ; unsigned multiplication, EDX || EAX ← EAX * r/m
                             ; 64-bit result is stored in the EDX, EAX pair
IMUL    r/m                  ; 2's complement multiplication
                             ; EDX || EAX ← EAX * r/m
        reg,  r/m            ; reg ← reg * r/m
        reg,  immed          ; reg ← reg * immed
DIV     r/m                  ; unsigned division, does EDX || EAX / r/m
                             ; EAX ← quotient, EDX ← remainder
IDIV    r/m                  ; 2's complement division, does EDX || EAX / r/m
                             ; EAX ← quotient, EDX ← remainder
CMP     reg,  r/m            ; sets EFLAGS based on
        r/m,  immed          ; second operand – first operand
        r/m8, immmed8
        r/m,  immmed8        ; sign extends immed8 before subtract
```

EXAMPLE 2.2 Consider the following statements.

(a) NEG [EAX + 4] – takes the double word at the address EAX + 4 and finds its additive inverse, then places the additive inverse back at that address.

(b) INC ECX – adds one to the contents of register ECX, and result is stored in ECX.

3. **Logical:**

```
NOT     r/m                  ; logical NOT
AND     reg,  r/m            ; logical AND
        reg8, r/m8
        r/m,  reg
        r/m8, reg8
        r/m,  immed
        r/m8, immed8
OR      reg,  r/m            ; logical OR
        reg8, r/m8
        r/m,  reg
        r/m8, reg8
        r/m,  immed
        r/m8, immed8
XOR     reg,  r/m            ; logical exclusive OR
        reg8, r/m8
        r/m,  reg
        r/m8, reg8
        r/m,  immed
        r/m8, immed8
```

```
TEST    r/m,  reg             ; logical AND to set EFLAGS
        r/m8, reg8
        r/m,  immed
        r/m8, immed8
```

4. **Control instructions:**

```
JMP     m                     ; unconditional jump
JG      m                     ; jump if greater than 0
JGE     m                     ; jump if greater than or equal to 0
JL      m                     ; jump if less than 0
JLE     m                     ; jump if less than or equal to 0
```

There are many such control transfer instructions. The most important is the CALL instruction to be used for procedure call. It is similar to the JMP instruction.

2.1.5 Instruction Format

The instructions in an Intel processor vary in size—from one byte up to fourteen bytes. However, all these instructions follow a six-part structure noted below.

1. Prefixes – 0 to 4 bytes
2. Opcode – 1 to 2 bytes
3. ModR/M – 1 byte
4. SIB – 1 byte
5. Displacement – 1 byte or word
6. Immediate – 1 byte or word

Except for the opcode, all other parts are optional. Simple instructions such as NOP (No Operation) require just the opcode. Complicated instructions, such as ADD [GS:mem_data+EBX+ESI*8], WORD 1003H, require all of the fields. Here, we explain the subparts.

Prefixes. The optional prefixes modify the behaviour of instructions in several ways. Each prefix adds one byte to the instruction. An instruction can have one prefix from each of the four prefix groups, for a maximum of four prefix bytes.

- Group 1: LOCK, REPE/REPZ, REP, REPNE/REPNZ—the prefix bytes for these are F0H through F3H. The REP prefixes are used only with string instructions.
- Group 2: Segment overrides prefixes. The hexadecimal codes 2E, 36, 3E, 26, 64, and 65 are used to override the default segment registers by CS, SS, DS, ES, FS, and GS respectively.
- Group 3: Operand-size override (16-bit vs. 32-bit)—the prefix byte is 66H.
- Group 4: Address-size override (16-bit vs. 32-bit)—the prefix byte is 67H.

Opcode. The *operation code* or opcode comes after at the most four number of prefix bytes. The opcode field is one or two bytes. The code tells the processor which instruction to execute. Apart from the operation, it also contains bit-fields identifying the type and size of operands expected. For example, the NOT operation has an opcode 1111011w. Here, the 'w' bit determines whether the operand is a byte or a word. Similarly, the OR instruction has the format 000010dw. Here the 'd' bit determines the direction of dataflow—that is, which operand is the source and which one is the destination.

ModR/M: It is 0 or 1 byte long and is put if the instruction requires it. If present, the *ModR/M* field comes just after the opcode. This byte tells the processor which registers or memory locations to use as the instruction's operands. The byte has the structure shown in Fig. 2.10. Both *reg1* and *reg2* fields take three-bit register codes, indicating which registers to be used as operands. By default, *reg1* is the source operand and *reg2* is the destination. However, it may be overridden by some instructions like *OR*, using the *direction* bit there. If an instruction requires only one operand, the unused *reg2* field holds extra *opcode* bits.

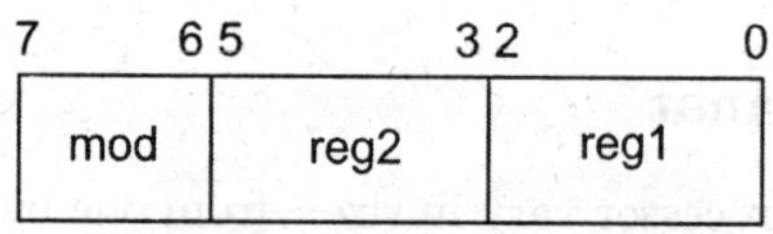

FIGURE 2.10 ModR/M.

The *mod* field determines the meaning of the *reg1* field as shown in Table 2.1.

Table 2.1: *mod* field values

Code	Meaning
00	Operand's memory address is in *reg1*
01	Operand's memory address is *reg1* + a byte-sized displacement
10	Operand's memory address is *reg1* + a word-sized displacement
11	Operand is *reg1* itself

SIB. In 32-bit addressing, for *mod* = 00, 01, or 10, when *reg1* field indicates ESP register, an additional byte follows the ModR/M byte—known as *SIB byte.* SIB is the acronym for Scale ∗ Index + Base. It provides a powerful addressing mode in 32-bit that uses a combination of two registers and a scaling factor instead of *reg1* for the operand address. The SIB byte structure is shown in Fig. 2.11.

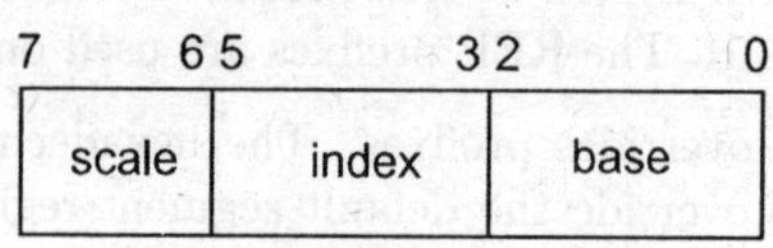

FIGURE 2.11 SIB.

In the SIB byte, both *index* and *base* are three-bit register codes, and *scale* is a two-bit number. To compute the SIB value, the processor uses the formula: $(index * 2^{scale}) + base$.

This value is used instead of *reg1* field to access the memory. For example, the ModR/M and SIB bytes for the memory address such as "[EBX*4 + ESI + disp1]" is as follows.

- ModR/M.mod = 10 (that is [reg1 + word1])
- ModR/M.reg2 = the destination register
- ModR/M.reg1 = ESP
- SIB.scale = 2
- SIB.index = EBX
- SIB.base = ESI

Displacement. When *mod* = 01 or 10, a displacement is a part of the operand's address. The displacement may be a byte or a word. For example, the full machine code for the 32-bit instruction OR EAX, [ECX + EDX*2 + 406080A0h] is shown in Fig. 2.12.

Opcode	ModR/M	SIB	Displacement
00001011	10 000 100	01 010 001	10100000 10000000 01100000 01000000

FIGURE 2.12 Instruction OR EAX, [ECX + EDX*2 + 406080A0h].

Immediate. If an instruction uses an immediate value as an operand, the immediate value is the last part of the instruction. The machine code for a 16-bit instruction, AND SI, 0420h is as shown in Fig. 2.13.

Opcode	ModR/M	Immediate
10000001	11 100 110	00100000 00000100

FIGURE 2.13 Instruction AND SI, 0420h.

2.2 NETWIDE ASSEMBLER: NASM

The *Netwide Assembler, NASM*, is a portable modular, freely available 80x86 assembler. It supports a wide range of object file formats including Linux and NetBSD/FreeBSD *a.out, ELF, COFF,* Microsoft 16-bit *OBJ* and *Win32.* It can also output plain binary files, supports a good number of Intel processors, and has *macro capability* (discussed in Chapter 5). The details about the availability of NASM and the commands and options to run it have been given in Appendix A. In this section, we will view NASM as a model assembler to understand the features an assembler should possess. Chapter 3 will use this model to design the assembler. However, we will not elaborate the full power of NASM inorder to concentrate on the most important features of an assembler.

2.2.1 Layout of NASM Source Line

Each line of an input file to the NASM assembler can be one of the following:

1. A machine instruction
2. A macro (similar to subprogram detailed in Chapter 5)
3. A pseudo-instruction
4. An assembler directive

The *machine instruction* consists of a combination of the following four fields:

label: *instruction* *operands* *; comment*

The *label* field is optional; if specified, may be used as target of some jump/call instruction in the program. The type and number of *operands* depend upon the *instruction*. The *comment* field is again optional and is used for documentation purpose only. Though NASM allows quite a good number of options for the characters that can appear in the *label*, it can be conveniently restricted to the set of letters, numbers, _, $, and ?. The *instruction* field may be prefixed by LOCK, REP, REPE/REPZ or REPNE/REPNZ.

Pseudo-instructions are some special instructions created by the assembler designer to facilitate mainly memory initialization and space reservation. NASM supports a number of pseudo-instructions like DB (define byte), DW (define word), DD (define double-word/float), DQ (define double-precision float), and DT (define extended-precision float), their uninitialised counterparts RESB (reserve byte), RESW (reserve word), RESD, RESQ, and REST. It also supports the EQU command to declare constants and the TIMES prefix to instruct the assembler to assemble the line several times, thus creating a data block.

Declaring initialised data. The pseudo-instructions DB, DW, etc. are used for this purpose. The following are a few examples of this:

```
db 0x55                  ; just the byte 0x55
db 0x55, 0x56, 0x57      ; three bytes in succession
db 'a', 0x55             ; character constant 'a' and byte 0x55
db 'hello', 13, 10, '$'  ; string "hello" terminated by <CR>, <LF>, and a '$'
dw 0x1234                ; 0x34 0x12 (higher order byte in higher order location)
dw 'a'                   ; 0x41 0x00
dw 'ab'                  ; 0x41 0x42
dw 'abc'                 ; 0x41 0x42 0x43 0x00
dd 0x12345678            ; 0x78 0x56 0x34 0x12
dd 1.234567e20           ; floating-point constant
dq 1.234567e20           ; double-precision float
dt 1.234567e20           ; extended-precision float
```

Declaring uninitialised data. This class of pseudo-instruction is used for reserving space without initializing them explicitly. The following are a few examples of this category.

```
buffer:      resb 64     ; reserve 64 bytes
wordvar:     resw 1      ; reserve a word
realarray:   resq 10     ; reserve an array of ten reals
```

Defining constants. The pseudo-instruction EQU defines a symbol to a given constant value. This definition is absolute and cannot be changed later. Thus,

```
message:    db 'hello, world'
msglen:     equ $ – message
```

defines *msglen* to be the constant 12. *msglen* may not then be redefined later. The value of *msglen* is evaluated only once, using the value of $ (evaluating to assembly position at the beginning of the line will be clarified while discussing on the assembly process).

Repeating instructions or data. The TIMES prefix causes the instruction to be assembled multiple times. For example, consider the instruction,

```
zerobuf:    times 64 db 0
```

Here, the subcommand "db 0" is assembled 64 times creating a buffer of 64 memory locations, all initialized to 0. The structure can be referred to by *zerobuf.* The following example will store exactly enough white spaces to make the total length of *buffer* up to 64.

```
buffer:     db 'hello, world'
            times 64 – $ + buffer db ' '
```

2.2.2 Assembler Directives

NASM has got a number of assembler directives that help organize the program better. Some of them are described here.

1. **BITS.** It specifies the target processor mode. The directive can be used to instruct NASM to generate code targeting 16-bit mode or 32-bit mode of the processor. The syntax is,

   ```
   BITS 16
   BITS 32
   ```

2. **Section.** It changes the section of the output file into which the assembled code will be written. Typical examples are,

   ```
   SECTION .text    ; corresponds to the code section
   SECTION .data    ; corresponds to the data section
   SECTION .bss     ; corresponds to the uninitialized-data section
   ```

   It may be noted that certain object file formats may not support arbitrary names and/or number of sections.

3. **Extern.** This directive is used to import symbols from other modules. The symbols declared as *extern* are not defined anywhere in the source module being assembled. The definitions come when the module is later on linked with another module having the corresponding definition. For example, the declaration

```
extern printf
```

declares the symbol `printf` to be external to the current module.

4. **Global.** It is used to export symbols to other modules. Naturally, global is the other end of extern. If one module declares a symbol as extern and refers to it, then, in order to prevent linker errors, some other module must actually define the symbol and declare it as global. The global directive applying to a symbol must appear before the definition of the symbol. For example, the declaration

   ```
   global main
   ```

   declares the symbol `main` to be global for any other module to use it.

5. **Common.** This directive is used to declare *common variables* between the modules. A common variable is much like a global variable declared in the uninitialized data section, so that

   COMMON intvar 4

   is similar in function to

   GLOBAL intvar
   SECTION .bss
   intvar RESD 1

   The difference is that if more than one module defines the same common variable, then at the time of linking, all these variables are merged and all references to the common variable will point to the same memory location. But global declaration can be present in only one module.

EXAMPLE 2.3 Let us consider a program to find the maximum in an array having 10 integers. Program 2.1 shows how to find the maximum in an array. The array has been initialized in the *data* section having entries 10, 20, 30, 100, 200, 56, 45, 67, 89, and 77. The C-library routine *printf* has been used to print the largest number. For this, the C-compiler *gcc* is needed to produce the executable version of the program. If the name of this file be *max.asm*, the commands used to generate the executable file are as follows.

nasm -felf max.asm -l max.lst
gcc max.o

The first command, apart from producing the object file *max.o*, also produces the *list* file *max.lst*. The list file has been shown in Program 2.2. This file, apart from the original source code, also shows the assembled object code corresponding to each of the source lines. Each line in the *list* file has the format < *line no.*, *offset*, *object code*, *source statement* >. Each *section* is assembled from offset zero. It may be noted that at line no. 31, there is a reference to the external symbol *printf*. The assembler leaves it with some special value (0 in this case), so that it can be corrected later by the linker and/or loader.

PROGRAM 2.1: To find the maximum in an array.

```
global main
extern printf

section .data
my_array:
            dd 10, 20, 30, 100, 200, 56, 45, 67, 89, 77
format:
            db '%d', 10, 0
section .text
main:
            MOV ECX, 0
            MOV EAX,  [my_array]
L2:
            INC ECX
            CMP ECX, 10
            JZ over

            CMP EAX, [my_array + ECX*4]
            JGE L1
            MOV EAX, [my_array + ECX*4]
L1:
            JMP L2

over:
            PUSH EAX
            PUSH dword format
            CALL printf
            ADD ESP, 8


            RET
```

PROGRAM 2.2: List file of the program to find the maximum.

```
 1                                        global main
 2                                        extern printf
 3
 4                                        section .data
 5                                        my_array:
 6 00000000 0A000000140000001E-              dd 10, 20, 30, 100, 200, 56, 45,
 7 00000009 00000064000000C800-              67, 89, 77
 8 00000012 0000380000002D0000-
 9 0000001B 00430000005900000-
10 00000024 4D000000
```

```
                                 format:
00000028 25640A00                    db '%d', 10, 0
                                 section .text
                                 main:
00000000 B900000000                  MOV ECX, 0
00000005 A1[00000000]                MOV EAX,  [my_array]
                                 L2:
0000000A 41                          INC ECX
0000000B 81F90A000000                CMP ECX, 10
00000011 7412                        JZ over
00000013 3B048D[00000000]            CMP EAX, [my_array + ECX*4]
0000001A 7D07                        JGE L1
0000001C 8B048D[00000000]            MOV EAX, [my_array + ECX*4]
                                 L1:
00000023 EBE5                        JMP L2
                                 over:
00000025 50                          PUSH EAX
00000026 68[28000000]                PUSH dword format
0000002B E8(00000000)                CALL printf
00000030 81C408000000                ADD ESP, 8
00000036 C3                          RET
```

EXAMPLE 2.4 Next we look into a program to sort a set of integers in an array. Program 2.3 shows how to sort a set of numbers. The corresponding list file produced by the assembler is shown in Program 2.4.

PROGRAM 2.3: A program to sort a set of numbers.

```
global main
extern printf
extern scanf

section .data
my_array: dd 10, 20, 30, 100, 200, 56, 45, 67, 89, 77
num: dd 10
format: db '%d ', 0
read_format: db '%d', 0
newline: db 10, 0
section .text
main:
```

```
            PUSH dword num
            PUSH dword read_format
            CALL scanf
            ADD ESP, 8
            MOV ESI, 0
loop1:
            MOV EDI, ESI
loop2:
            MOV EAX, [my_array + ESI * 4]
            CMP EAX, [my_array + EDI * 4]
            JLE no_change
            MOV EBX, [my_array + EDI * 4]
            MOV [my_array + ESI * 4], EBX
            MOV [my_array + EDI * 4], EAX
no_change:
            INC EDI
            CMP EDI, [num]
            JL loop2

            INC ESI
            CMP ESI, [num]
            JL loop1
            MOV ESI, 0
print_num:
            PUSH dword [my_array + ESI * 4]
            PUSH dword format
            CALL printf
            ADD ESP, 8
            INC ESI
            CMP ESI, [num]
            JL print_num
            PUSH dword newline
            CALL printf
            ADD ESP, 4
            RET
```

PROGRAM 2.4: List file for the sorting program.

```
    1                                     global main
    2                                     extern printf
    3                                     extern scanf
    4
    5                                     section .data
    6 00000000 0A000000140000001E-        my_array: dd 10, 20, 30, 100, 200, 56,
    7 00000009 00000064000000C800-                  45, 67, 89, 77
```

```
00000012 0000380000002D0000-
0000001B 00430000059000000-
00000024 4D000000
00000028 0A000000             num: dd 10
0000002C 25642000             format: db '%d ', 0
00000030 256400               read_format: db '%d', 0
00000033 0A00                 newline: db 10, 0
                              section .text
                              main:

00000000 68[28000000]             PUSH dword num
00000005 68[30000000]             PUSH dword read_format
0000000A E8(00000000)             CALL scanf
0000000F 81C408000000             ADD ESP, 8
00000015 BE00000000               MOV ESI, 0
                              loop1:
0000001A 89F7                     MOV EDI, ESI
                              loop2:
0000001C 8B04B5[00000000]         MOV EAX, [my_array + ESI * 4]
00000023 3B04BD[00000000]         CMP EAX, [my_array + EDI * 4]
0000002A 7E15                     JLE no_change
0000002C 8B1CBD[00000000]         MOV EBX, [my_array + EDI * 4]
00000033 891CB5[00000000]         MOV [my_array + ESI * 4], EBX
0000003A 8904BD[00000000]         MOV [my_array + EDI * 4], EAX
                              no_change:
00000041 47                       INC EDI
00000042 3B3D[28000000]           CMP EDI, [num]
00000048 7CD2                     JL loop2

0000004A 46                       INC ESI
0000004B 3B35[28000000]           CMP ESI, [num]
00000051 7CC7                     JL loop1
00000053 BE00000000               MOV ESI, 0
                              print_num:
00000058 FF34B5[00000000]         PUSH dword [my_array + ESI * 4]
0000005F 68[2C000000]             PUSH dword format
00000064 E8(00000000)             CALL printf
00000069 81C408000000             ADD ESP, 8
0000006F 46                       INC ESI
00000070 3B35[28000000]           CMP ESI, [num]
00000076 7CE0                     JL print_num
00000078 68[33000000]             PUSH dword newline
0000007D E8(00000000)             CALL printf
00000082 81C404000000             ADD ESP, 4
00000088 C3                       RET
```

2.3 CONCLUSION

In this chapter, we have seen the assembly language of IA32 processors and the assembler *nasm* to produce object code for them. Since all the new operating systems support 32-bit architecture with flat memory model, in our future discussions on the design of *assembler, linker, loader*, etc., we will concentrate on this particular model only.

EXERCISES

2.1 List the different registers available in IA32 processor and explain their roles.

2.2 Discuss the memory models of IA32 architecture.

2.3 List the different addressing modes of IA32 architecture with examples of each kind.

2.4 Make a complete study of the instruction set of *Pentium*.

2.5 Find out the machine instructions for the following assembly language statements.

```
MOV EAX, ECX
MOV AX, [ESI]
ADD EAX, ES:[ESI + 10]
```

2.6 Write an assembly language program to compute the GCD of two numbers.

2.7 Generate the list file for program in *Exercise 2.6* and check for its correctness manually.

2.8 Write a program to check if a given string is a palindrome or not. A palindrome is a string that remains same on reversal also. Generate the list file and check it.

2.9 Write a subprogram to check whether a number is prime or not. Use this subprogram to generate first 100 primes.

2.10 Write a program to perform sorting using *insertion sort.* Extend the program to read inputs from the keyboard and print sorted sequence on the screen.

Chapter 3

Assembler Design

Assembler is the tool to convert an assembly language program into the machine language one, understandable by the processor that executes it. The complexity of the process depends upon various factors, including the size of the *instruction set*, different *addressing modes* supported, *length of program* being translated, and so on. For the simplest case, the assembly may be done manually, aptly named as *hand assembly.* However, the job becomes difficult and error-prone for complex processors, like the *Intel's 32-bit* architectures discussed in Chapter 2. For this type of machines, the automation of the assembly process is a must.

Ideally, an assembler can be viewed as a tool that looks at each statement of the assembly language program and generates the corresponding machine language counterpart. This has been depicted in Fig. 3.1. However, apart from producing code in the machine language, some more information is needed to facilitate loading of program at arbitrary start address in the memory. It needs corrections to the address sensitive values, like *operand addresses, jump targets*, etc. The assemblers normally generate code starting at offset zero. For multi-section programs (that is, programs with multiple code and/or data sections), each section is assembled starting at offset zero, so that maximum flexibility exists regarding their loading into the memory for execution. Thus, information about all the sections and their attributes is also needed to produce the final executable version of the program.

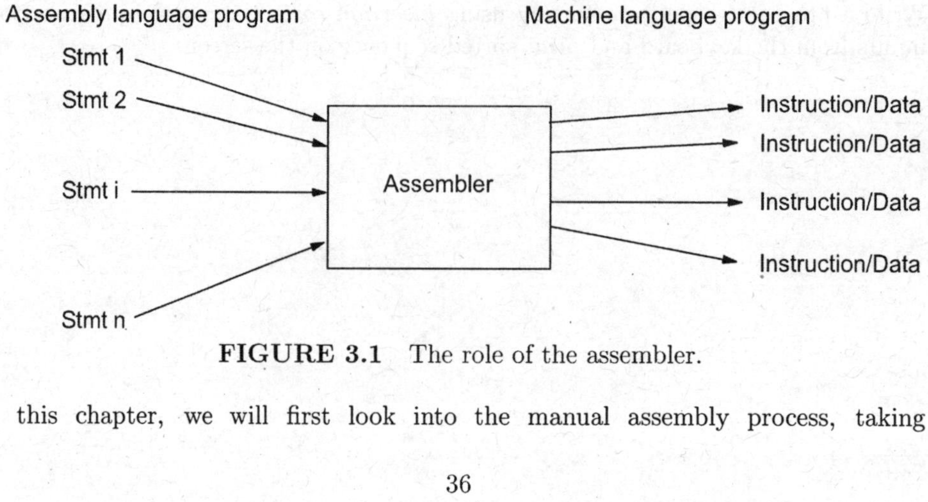

FIGURE 3.1 The role of the assembler.

In this chapter, we will first look into the manual assembly process, taking into consideration a very simple assembly language. Then, we will look into the important data structures needed in the assembly process. This will be followed by a detailed discussion on the design of assemblers.

3.1 A SIMPLE MANUAL ASSEMBLER

Consider a simple hypothetical accumulator based processor. All memory *load* and *store* operations are through the *accumulator* register (call it A). Arithmetic and logic operations mostly use A as a source register and also the destination register. Assume that there are two more 32-bit general purpose registers B, C, and an *index* register I. Arithmetic is permitted on I also. The addressing modes supported are the *immediate* and *indirect* through the index register. All memory addresses are 32-bit wide. Register-to-register data movement is also supported. The instructions and the associated codes are as shown in Table 3.1. This table depicting the machine instructions, is called the *Machine Opcode Table (MOT)*.

Table 3.1: Machine opcode table for the simple processor.

Instruction	Size (in bytes)	Format	Meaning
MVI A, <*constant*>	5	<0, 4 byte constant>	$A \leftarrow$ *constant*
MVI B, <*constant*>	5	<1, 4 byte constant>	$B \leftarrow$ *constant*
MVI C, <*constant*>	5	<2, 4 byte constant>	$C \leftarrow$ *constant*
MVI I, <*constant*>	5	<3, 4 byte constant>	$I \leftarrow$ *constant*
LOAD <*constant*>	5	<4, 4 byte constant>	$A \leftarrow$ memory[<*constant*>]
STORE <*constant*>	5	<5, 4 byte constant>	memory[<*constant*>] $\leftarrow A$
LOADI	1	< 6 >	$A \leftarrow$ memory[I]
STORI	1	< 7 >	memory[I] $\leftarrow A$
ADD B	1	< 8 >	$A \leftarrow A + B$
ADD C	1	< 9 >	$A \leftarrow A + C$
MOV A, B	1	< 10 >	$A \leftarrow B$
MOV A, C	1	< 11 >	$A \leftarrow C$
MOV B, C	1	< 12 >	$B \leftarrow C$
MOV B, A	1	< 13 >	$B \leftarrow A$
MOV C, A	1	< 14 >	$C \leftarrow A$
MOV C, B	1	< 15 >	$C \leftarrow B$
INC A	1	< 16 >	$A \leftarrow A + 1$
INC B	1	< 17 >	$B \leftarrow B + 1$
INC C	1	< 18 >	$C \leftarrow C + 1$
CMP A, <*constant*>	5	<19, 4 byte constant>	compare A to *constant*
CMP B, <*constant*>	5	<20, 4 byte constant>	compare B to *constant*
CMP C, <*constant*>	5	<21, 4 byte constant>	compare C to *constant*
ADDI <*constant*>	5	<22, 4 byte constant>	$I \leftarrow I +$ *constant*
JE <*label*>	5	<23, 4 byte address>	jump on equal to <*label*>
JMP <*label*>	5	<24, 4 byte address>	jump to <*label*>
STOP	1	< 25 >	stop the processor

We assume that our assembler supports only one pseudo-opcode *dd* to reserve and initialize four byte memory locations. In a general assembler, there may be a number of pseudo-opcodes supported which are stored in another table known as *Pseudo Opcode Table (POT)*.

Next, we consider a simple program (Program 3.1) written in this language to sum ten numbers stored in the memory. The assembly process starts at *offset* zero. To keep track of the next offset in which the generated code is to be placed, the assembler maintains a variable called *location counter*, which is analogous to the *offset* and is also initialized to zero. Since *line 1* contains a declaration of variable X having 10, 32-bit numbers, the assembler reserves

PROGRAM 3.1: A program to add 10 numbers.

```
1           X dd 10, 20, 40, 5, 7, 9, 53, 8, 11, 13
2           sum dd 0
3           MVI I, X
4           MVI B, 0
5           MVI C, 0
6     L1:   LOADI
7           ADD C
8           MOV C, A
9           INC B
10          CMP B, 10
11          JE L2
12          ADDI 4
13          JMP L1
14    L2:   STORE sum
15          STOP
```

space for the same and the locations are initialized accordingly. Next, *location counter* is incremented to 40, as the 40 locations are occupied by X. The variable X along with its attributes is entered into the *symbol table* as shown in Table 3.2. It may be noted that *symbol table* contains all variables and labels defined in the program. The table helps in the assembly process and is also is needed by later tools like *linker* and *loader*. Next four locations are used to store *sum* as specified in the program. Thus, the assembler reserves the space and initializes it to zero. The variable *sum* is also entered into the *symbol table*. Current *location counter* is 44. Next, the instruction

MVI I, X

Table 3.2: The symbol table of the program.

Name	Type	Offset
X	*variable*	0
sum	*variable*	40
$L1$	*label*	59
$L2$	*label*	83

is assembled into five bytes as depicted by the MOT. The location 44 contains the opcode 3, while 45 through 48 hold the offset of X, which is zero in this case. *Location counter* is updated accordingly. When the assembler reaches the instruction,

$L1$: LOADI

the label $L1$ is entered into the symbol table along with its offset from the beginning of the program. So that, when we assemble the instruction,

JMP $L1$

we already know the offset of $L1$ and the code can be generated accordingly. However, when we try to assemble the instruction,

JE $L2$

we have not yet seen the label $L2$. Thus, the offset of $L2$ is not known. There are several ways of handling this type of situation, that we will discuss later. For the time being, we assume that we know the offset of $L2$ to be 83 (53 hexadecimal), and accordingly generate the machine code. The code generated corresponding to each line of the program has been shown in the form of a list file in Program 3.2. The first column of the table notes the source line number, and the second column gives the *location counter* value in hexadecimal. The next column contains the code generated. The source line is noted in the last column. There are several address sensitive points in the code that need to be corrected if the program is to be loaded starting from a memory address other than zero. These have been listed in Table 3.3. If the program is loaded from location l (for example), the value l should be added to all these locations to ensure correct execution of the program. This process is known as *program relocation*, and will be discussed in detail while dealing with linking and loading techniques.

PROGRAM 3.2: The list file of the program to add to numbers.

```
 1 00000000 0A00000014000000        X dd 10, 20, 40, 5, 7, 9, 53, 8, 11, 13
            2800000005000000
            0700000009000000
            3500000008000000
            0B0000000D000000
 2 00000028 00000000                sum dd 0
 3 0000002C 03000000                MVI I, X
 4 00000031 01000000                MVI B, 0
 5 00000036 02000000                MVI C, 0
 6 0000003B 06                 L1:  LOADI
 7 0000003C 09                      ADD C
 8 0000003D 0E                      MOV C, A
 9 0000003E 11                      INC B
10 0000003F 140A000000              CMP B, 10
11 00000044 1753000000              JE L2
12 00000049 1604000000              ADDI 4
13 0000004E 183B000000              JMP L1
```

```
14 00000053 0528000000        L2:    STORE sum
15 00000058 1900000000               STOP
```

Table 3.3: Address sensitive places for the code.

Address	Reason
0000002D	X needs correction
00000044	jump target $L2$ modified
0000004E	jump target $L1$ modified
00000054	*sum* needs correction

3.2 ASSEMBLER DESIGN PROCESS

In this section, we will discuss in detail the various issues and techniques involved in the design of the assembler. To understand the process better, we can think of a program written in the assembly language to be consisting of a few components as follows:

Machine instructions. Machine instructions are the heart of the program that tells the processor the exact operations to be performed as desired by the programmer. These include all the machine opcodes like MOV, ADD, SUB, JMP, and so on.

Variable declarations. Variable declarations are the declaration of the storage space (both initialized and non-initialized). The machine instructions specified in the program will modify these data to achieve the task of the program. The common examples of this category are db, dw, dd, resb, etc.

Assembler directives. Assembler directives direct the assembler to produce code in a structured manner so that different sections of the program can be handled efficiently and perhaps independently. For example, the *section* directive in *NASM* allows the programmer to demarcate different code and data segments of the program. Another very useful directive is *END* that tells the assembler to terminate the assembly process. It is useful because there may be some portion in the file in which the user is not interested for the time being. For example, some error-handling routines may not be included in the initial versions of the program during the developmental stage. These may be excluded from the assembly process simply by terminating the assembly before those. There can be many other such directives depending upon the facilities provided to the programmer by the assembler designer.

Comments. These are used by the programmer for documentation purposes. Most assemblers allow the user to put a comment by prefixing it with a ';' symbol. For example,

```
MOV AX, 39      ;move constant 39 to AX
```

Since the comments are not useful for program execution, the assembler simply discards all comments while doing the translation.

3.2.1 Major Data Structures Used

The major tables involved in the assembly process are:

- Machine Opcode Table (MOT)
- Pseudo Opcode Table (POT)
- Symbol Table (SYMTAB).

Out of these, the *Machine Opcode Table (MOT)* and *Pseudo Opcode Table (POT)* are static in nature, in the sense that their content does not change during the lifetime of the assembler, until and unless a new processor with different opcodes is targeted, or new pseudo-opcodes are added to facilitate storage allocation. On the other hand, content of the *Symbol. Table (SYMTAB)* depends upon the program being assembled—the variables and labels declared within it. Thus, *Symbol Table* is dynamic in nature.

Machine Opcode Table (MOT): As noted earlier, the machine opcode table holds the opcodes used by the processor for different instruction mnemonics. Typical entries of this table have been shown in Fig. 3.2. The *Mnemonic* field holds various instruction mnemonics. The *Size* field contains the size of the instructions (typically in bytes). The *Opcode* field contains the machine code corresponding to the mnemonic.

Mnemonic	Size	Opcode

FIGURE 3.2 Machine opcode table structure.

The basic structure of the MOT may be varied significantly based upon the instruction set and also on the designer of the assembler. For simple machines, (like the one in Section 3.1), the *Opcode* field is quite simple. However, as noted in Chapter 2, Section 2.1.5, the *Opcode* field may also depend upon the operand type, direction of data movement etc. This makes the design of *MOT* complex. A very simplistic approach may be to just include the portion of the opcode that is independent of these sorts of variations. On the other hand, one can put all the alternative entries into the MOT and the assembler will just search out the correct combination.

Organization of MOT: Organization of any table is determined by the set of operations, namely, *insertion, deletion, search, update*, etc. to be performed on the table entries. The frequency of these operations often dictates the organization to be used. For MOT, *insertions* are not there, since the table is static in nature. Similarly, *deletion* is also absent. The only operation that is done is *searching.* In fact, the assembler needs to refer to this table to translate each line of the source file. Thus, the structure of MOT be such that the *search* operation can be carried out very fast. A very good data structure providing *constant time O(1)* searching is the *hash table.* A suitable choice of hash function has to be made to convert a mnemonic into an integer value to be used as the index to the table. A detailed discussion on such hashing functions and the general hashing scheme is beyond the scope of this book. Readers may consult some book on *Data Structures* for the same. A basic problem with hash table is the collision of data items, that is, two or more mnemonics mapping to the same location in the MOT. Good *collision resolution strategies* are needed to take care of this situation. Table 3.4 shows the calculation of hash indexes for a set of mnemonics using the hash function $h(s)$ (where s is the mnemonic) given by,

$$h(s) = (\text{Sum of ASCII values of the characters of } s) \; mod \; 23$$

It may be noted that there is a collision in the indexes computed for the mnemonics ADD and CMP, for the mnemonics LOAD and MOV, and for the mnemonics MVI and STORE.

Table 3.4: Hash table index calculation.

Mnemonics	Sum of ASCII values	hash index ($h(s)$)
ADD	201	17
ADDI	274	21
CMP	224	17
INC	218	11
JE	143	5
JMP	231	1
LOAD	288	12
LOADI	361	16
MVI	236	6
MOV	242	12
STOP	326	4
STORE	397	6
STORI	401	10

Some other alternative data structures can be,

- Binary Search Tree
- Link Lists indexed by the first alphabet of the mnemonic.

For the *binary search tree* organization, the mnemonics are sorted in the alphabetical order and then inserted into a binary search tree to ensure the worst case access time to be equal to the depth of the tree. With proper *height balancing*, a tree with n nodes provides the worst case access time of $O(\log n)$. For example, for a processor with mnemonics MVI, LOAD, STORE, LOADI, STORI, ADD, MOV, INC, CMP, JE, JMP, ADDI, STOP, a binary search tree may be as shown in Fig. 3.3. Readers may refer to some book on *Data Structures* for further details.

Alternatively, an array of link lists structure may be used. The array is indexed by the first letter of the mnemonic. For example, corresponding to the set of mnemonics used in Fig. 3.3, an array of link lists structure has been shown in Fig. 3.4. Since the number of mnemonics starting with an alphabet is expected to be small, it may provide a reasonably good access mechanism.

Pseudo Opcode Table (POT): *Pseudo opcode table* contains the pseudo opcodes supported by the assembler. These are used to reserve memory space and possibly initialize it.

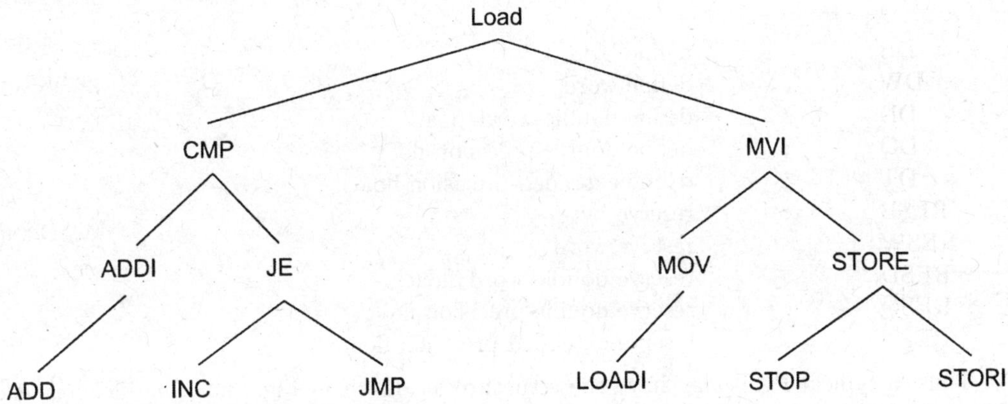

FIGURE 3.3 Binary search tree organization of MOT.

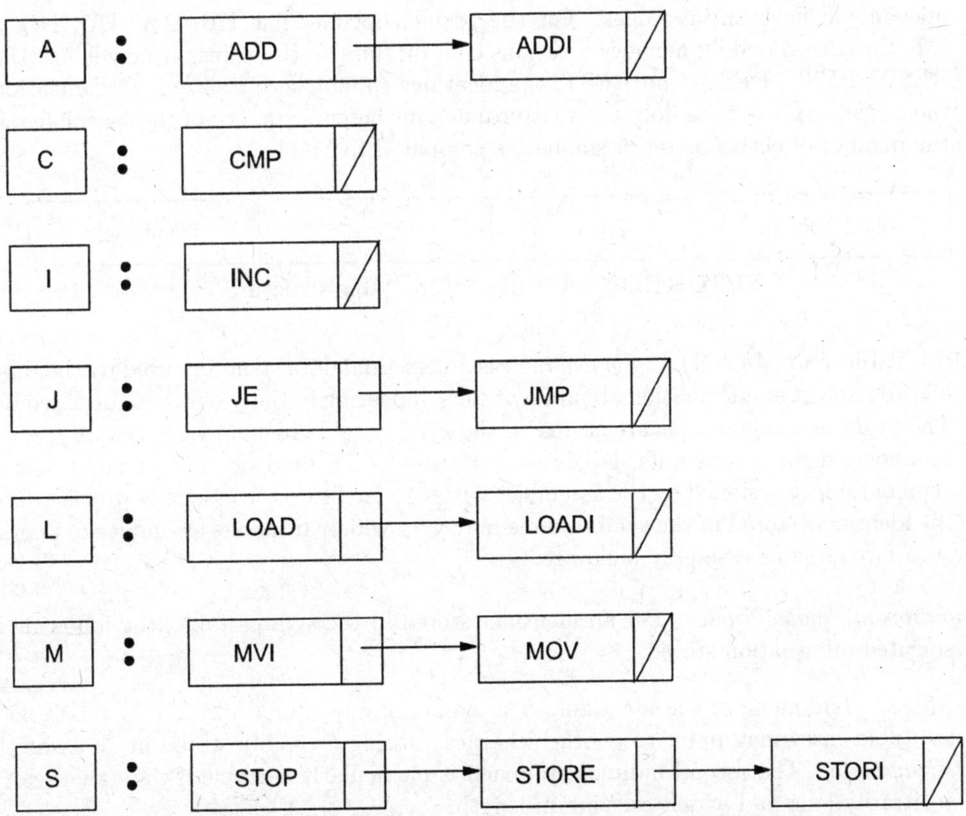

FIGURE 3.4 Array of link lists organization of MOT.

There can be several pseudo opcodes as envisaged by the assembler designer. The following is a list of such items supported in *NASM*.

DB	:	define byte
DW	:	define word
DD	:	define double-word/float
DQ	:	define double-precision float
DT	:	define extended-precision float
RESB	:	reserve byte
RESW	:	reserve word
RESD	:	reserve double word/float
RESQ	:	reserve double-precision float
REST	:	reserve extended-precision float

Thus, a typical POT may have the structure as shown in Fig. 3.5. The field *pseudo-opcode* holds the name of the pseudo opcode. The *type* field identifies type of data it can contain. *Size* field holds the size of the field (typically in bytes). The field *Initializable* is boolean, specifying whether the memory locations corresponding to the pseudo opcode can have initial values. For the pseudo opcodes like DB, DW, DD, DQ, and DT, the corresponding memory locations contain some initial values, whereas for RESB, RESW, RESD, RESQ, and REST, the locations cannot be initialized. Organization of the *Pseudo-opcode table* does not matter much in the performance of the assembler since the number of entries is much smaller as compared to MOT.

Pseudo-opcode	Type	Size	Initializable

FIGURE 3.5 Pseudo-opcode table structure.

Symbol Table (SYMTAB): *Symbol table* is an essential data structure used by the assembler to remember information about identifiers appearing in the program to be assembled. The types of symbols that are stored in the symbol table include variables, procedures, functions, defined constants, labels, etc. However, it should be kept in mind that the symbol table is designed by the assembler writer to facilitate the assembly process. Thus, the identifiers stored in the symbol table may vary widely from one assembler to another, even for the same assembly language.

Information in Symbol Table: For an identifier stored in the symbol table, the following are the associated information stored.

- *Name*: The *name* of the identifier. The name may be stored directly in the table, or the table entry may point to another character string (possibly stored in an associated *string table*). The second indirect approach is particularly suitable if the names can be arbitrarily long and widely varying in length.

- *Type*: The *type* of the identifier. It defines, for example, whether the identifier is a variable, a label, a procedure name, and so on. For variables, it will further identify the type—the basic types like *byte, word, double word, etc.*

- *Location*: This is an offset within the program where the identifier is defined.

The fundamental operations on such a table are:

- Enter a new symbol in the table.
- Lookup for a symbol
- Modify information about a symbol stored earlier in the table.

There exist several alternative data structures to choose from to create such a table. The commonly used techniques are:

- Linear table
- Ordered list
- Tree
- Hash table.

Linear Table: This is a simple array of records with each record corresponding to an identifier of the program. The entries are made in the same order in which they appear in the program.

EXAMPLE 3.1 Consider the following definitions.

x : RESB
y : RESW
z : RESD
...
procedure *abc*
...
$L1$: ...
...

The linear table will store the information as shown in Table 3.5.

Table 3.5: Symbol table.

Name	Type	Location
x	byte	offset of x
y	word	offset of y
z	double word	offset of z
abc	procedure	offset of *abc*
$L1$	label	offset of $L1$

If the language puts no restriction on the length of the string representing the name of an identifier, it may be convenient to store the names in a string table with the name field holding pointers to it. With this type of organization, the *lookup, insert* and *modify* operations are going to take $O(n)$ time, n being the number of identifiers stored. Of course, *insertion* can be made $O(1)$ by remembering the pointer to the next free index of the table where an entry can go. Also, if we can scan most recent entries first, it can probably speed up the access. This is because of program locality—a variable defined just inside a block is expected to be referred to more often than some earlier variable.

Ordered List: This is a variation of linear tables in which a list organization is used. The list may be sorted in some fashion, and then binary search can be used to access the table in $O(\log n)$ time. However, an insertion needs to be done at an appropriate place to preserve the sorted form. Thus, insertion becomes costly.

Tree: Tree organization of the symbol table may be used to speed up the access. Each entry is represented by a node of the tree. Based on string comparison of names, the entries lesser than a reference node are kept in the left-subtree of it, whereas the entries greater than the reference node are put into the right subtree. The individual nodes, apart from having the regular information related to the symbol, also hold two more pointer fields to the left and right subtrees. Moreover, each lookup operation, apart from the equality check, also needs to be followed by a *less-than/greater-than* check for each node of the tree where a match is not found, and the search must proceed further. A possible tree representing the entries of *Example* 3.1 has been shown in Fig. 3.6.

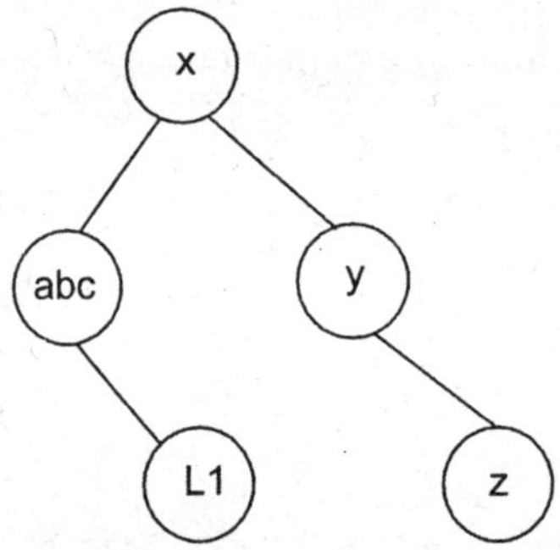

FIGURE 3.6 Tree symbol table.

The average lookup time for an entry in the tree is $O(\log n)$; however, it could degrade to a single long branching, requiring $O(n)$ search time. Proper *height balancing* strategies may be used (for example, *AVL trees*) to keep the tree balanced.

Hash Table: As discussed earlier, hash table provides the fastest mechanism to access the symbols. The techniques used can be similar to those for MOT. However, since the set of symbols appearing in a program are not fixed (unlike the MOT content which is fixed), designing a good hash function with lesser number of collisions may be difficult. Thus, good collision resolution strategies are needed to handle such situations.

3.2.2 Two-Pass Assembler

The two-pass assembly process scans the input assembly language program twice. These scans are normally called *Pass I* and *Pass II*. In *Pass I*, different data structures (tables) are filled up with the information pertaining to the symbols and sections defined in the program, whereas the second pass generates the actual code. Both the passes use a variable, *location counter* (*lc* in short) to compute current offset from the beginning of a *section* while traversing the input file.

Pass I The main task of this pass is to scan the input file and compute the offsets of all symbols appearing in the program. In the process, it fills up a number of tables as mentioned below:

- *Section table:* It holds detailed information regarding all sections appearing in the input program. The typical entries in this table are *section name, size, attributes* and a *pointer* to the translated content of the section. The table is as shown in Fig. 3.7(a). *Section name* is the name of the section, *size* is the total size. The *section* declaration may have several attributes associated with them, which we will discuss in Chapter 4, Section 4.1.2. At the end of *Pass II*, *pointer* will point to the content of the section after translation.
- *Symbol table:* As explained earlier, symbol table holds information about the symbols defined in the program. The entries are *name, type, location, size,* and *section-id.* The *name* contains the name of the symbol, *type* stores the type such as *variable, label,* etc., *location* is the offset of the symbol from the start of the section containing it, *size* stores the size of the symbol in bytes, *section-id* identifies the section to which the symbol belongs. The field *Is-global* is Boolean, identifying whether the symbol has been declared as global. The symbol table structure is shown in Fig. 3.7(b).
- *Common table:* It holds information about the variables declared *COMMON.* The structure has been shown in Fig. 3.7(c).

Name	Size	Attributes	Pointer to content

(a)

Name	Type	Location	Size	Section-id	Is-global

(b)

Name	Size

(c)

FIGURE 3.7 Structure of the (a) section table, (b) symbol table, and (c) common table.

The flowchart corresponding to the first pass of a two-pass assembler has been shown in Fig. 3.8. In the beginning, it initializes the *Global list* into which all *global* declarations will be stored. The location counter *lc* is also initialized to zero. The process then continues by reading the next line and updating one or more tables as needed, till the *end-of-file* marker is reached, which may be the physical end of the file or some special symbol marking the end of

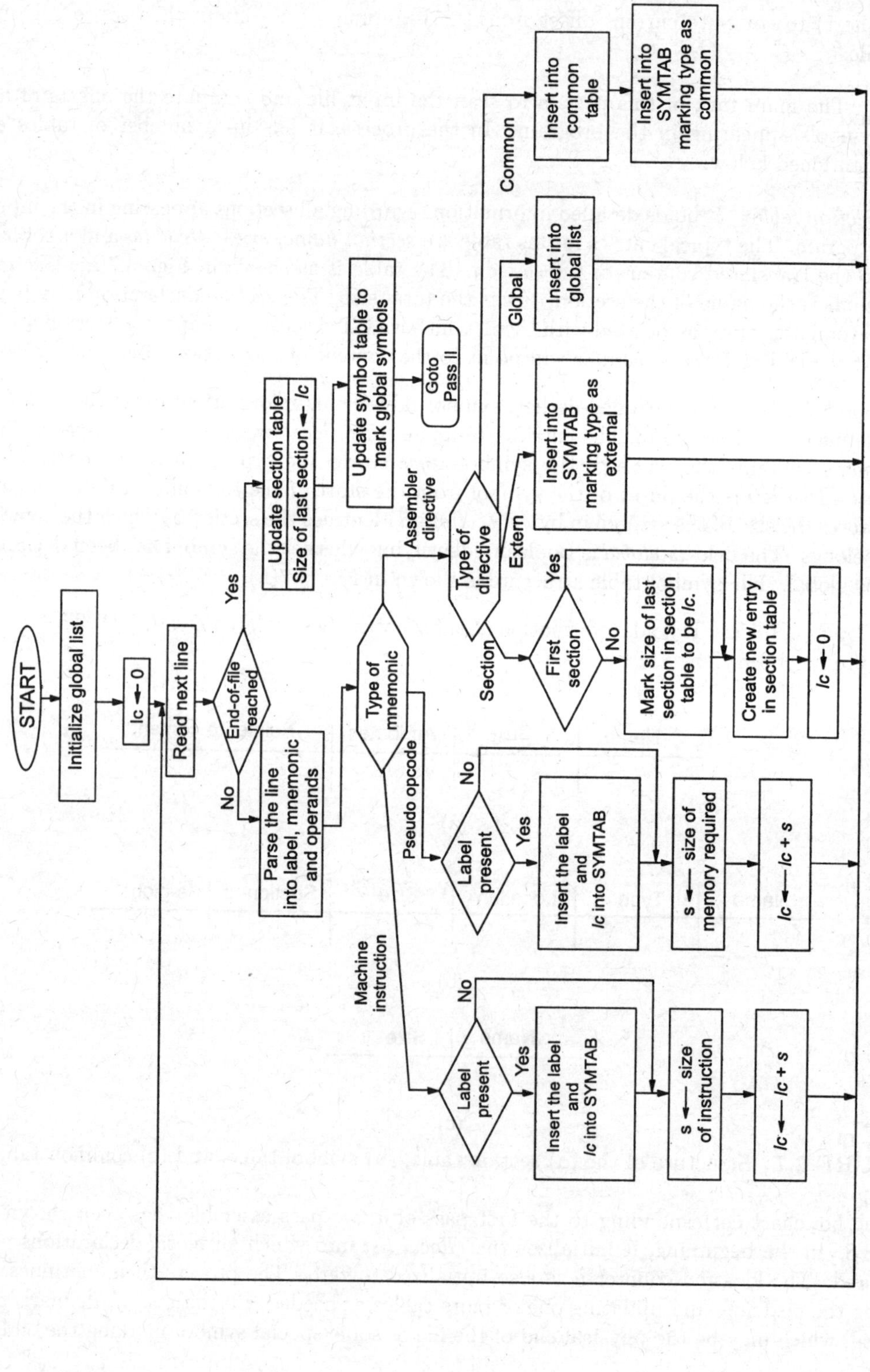

FIGURE 3.8 Pass I of the two-pass assembler.

the portion of the file to be assembled. The process *Read next line* scans the input file and returns the line to be assembled next skipping over the comments. The line is then parsed into components like a possible *label*, *mnemonic*, and *operands*. The mnemonic can be a machine instruction, a pseudo opcode, or an assembler directive. If a label is present in the line, it is put into the symbol table along with the current *lc* value as the *location*. *Type* field is set as *label* for machine instruction. For pseudo opcode, *type* field is set as *variable*. *Size* is not required for a label, whereas for a variable, it is set to the amount of memory required to store the variable. *Section-id* is set to the index of the current segment in the *Segment* table. The field *Is-global* is set to *false* for the time being. Next, *lc* is updated by the size of the instruction as computed by consulting Section 2.1.5 for IA32 processor, or similar information for other processors. For pseudo opcodes, *lc* is updated by the amount of memory required. For assembler directives, the course of action depends upon the type of the directive. For a *Section* directive indicating the beginning of a new section, the size of the last section in *Section* table is set to the current *lc* value. A new entry is created in the *Section* table and *lc* is reset to zero, as the new offsets will be calculated starting from this segment declaration. For an *external* symbol defined via an *extern* declaration, it is put into the symbol table, marking its type as *external*. For *global* symbols, it is put into the *global list*. Similarly, the common symbols are put into the *common* table and are also inserted into the *symbol* table marking its type as *common*. When the *end-of-file* is reached, *section* table is updated to mark the size of the last section as *lc*. *Symbol* table is updated to set the *Is-global* field to *true* for all entries corresponding to the symbols in the global list. Control then transfers to *Pass II*.

EXAMPLE 3.2 To understand the assembly process, let us consider the program shown in Program 2.1, reproduced in Program 3.3 for the sake of easy reference. To start with, *Global list* is initialized and *lc* is set to zero. In the first line, the statement `global main` puts the entry *main* into the *Global list*. The next line `extern printf` puts the entry `printf` into symbol table with type set as*external*. Next, the new *section declaration* `section .data` is encountered. An entry is made into the *Section table* and *lc* is reset to zero. In the next line, label *my_array* is found and entered into the *Symbol* table with *Type* as variable, *Size* as 40 bytes (as there are 10 double words, each of 4 bytes), *Location* as zero (current *lc* value), *Section-id* as 1 and *Is-global* set to *false*. *lc* is incremented to 40 (28 hexadecimal). Next, the variable *format* is found and entered into the *Symbol* table with *Type* as variable, *Location* 40, *Size* 3 bytes, *Section-id* 1, and *Is-global false*. *lc* is incremented to 43. A new section declaration `section .text` is encountered next. Thus, the current *lc* value 43 is entered as *Size* of *Section* 1 in the *Section* table. A new entry is created for section *.text* in the *Section* table and *lc* is reset to zero. The next instruction has the label *main* associated with it. Thus, *main* is entered into the *Symbol* table. Size of the instruction is 5 bytes. Thus, *lc* is incremented to five. This way, the *Pass I* continues by computing the length of the instructions and incrementing *lc* accordingly. The labels *L2, L1,* and *over* are entered into the *Symbol* table in the process. At the end, after processing the RET instruction, *end-of-file* is reached. The current *lc* value 55 (37 hexadecimal) is entered as *Size* of the section *.text*. *Global list* is consulted to mark the label *main* as global in the *Symbol* table. This is done by setting *Is-global* to *true*. The *Section* table and *Symbol* table created through *Pass I* for the program are shown in Fig. 3.9(a) and (b) respectively. The *Common* table is empty in this case, and hence, it is not shown.

PROGRAM 3.3: Program to find the maximum in an array.

```
global main extern printf

section .data
my_array:
              dd 10, 20, 30, 100, 200, 56, 45, 67, 89, 77
format:
              db '%d', 10, 0
section .text
main:
              MOV ECX, 0
              MOV EAX,  [my_array]
L2:
              INC ECX
              CMP ECX, 10
              JZ over

              CMP EAX, [my_array + ECX*4]
              JGE L1
              MOV EAX, [my_array + ECX*4]
L1:
              JMP L2

over:
              PUSH EAX
              PUSH dword format
              CALL printf
              ADD ESP, 8


              RET
```

Pass II This phase is responsible for generating the code. It uses the tables created in Pass I and writes the generated code into an object file. A flowchart of the entire Pass II has been shown in Fig. 3.10. To start with, the *obj-file-offset* and *lc* are initialized to zero. The source program lines are now read one by one sequentially and the corresponding code is generated. The source line is parsed into its components to separate out the mnemonic and operands. If the mnemonic is a machine instruction, the operand addresses are found via the symbol table. If the operand types noted in the symbol table are acceptable for the instruction, code is generated else an error message is flashed. If an operand's type is *external*, the operand address cannot be determined by the assembler. Thus, it puts the address as zero and makes an entry into the *external reference list* as shown in Fig. 3.11. The actual code generation will definitely depend upon the target processor. For example, for the IA32 processor, the translation process will be as depicted in Section 2.1.5. Generated code is written into the object file which automatically updates the *obj-file-offset*. *lc* value is also updated. It may be noted that the *lc*

Name	Size	Attributes	Pointer to content
.data	43		
.text	55		

(a)

Name	Type	Location	Size	Section-id	Is-global
printf	external				
my-array	variable	0	40	1	false
format	variable	40	3	1	false
main	label	0		2	true
L2	label	10		2	false
L1	label	35		2	false
over	label	37		2	false

(b)

FIGURE 3.9 (a) Section table, and (b) Symbol table for the example.

value will be needed to generate code for *relative JMP/CALL* instructions as explained in the following Example 3.3. For pseudo-opcodes, like *DB, DW*, etc., the corresponding initialization values are written into the object file, whereas for *RESB, RESW* etc., only the *obj-file-offset* is updated reserving their space in the object file. Among the assembler directives, the *section* directive is of particular interest. It updates the *Section* table, so that its *pointer-to-content* field holds the *obj-file-offset*, and thus point to the code corresponding to this section.

EXAMPLE 3.3 Let us look into the code generated in the program shown in Program 2.2, which is reproduced in Program 3.4 for easy reference. To start with, *obj-file-offset* and *lc* are reset. On reaching line 4, it gets a new `section` declaration. Thus, the *Section* table is updated as shown in Fig. 3.12. Next, the `dd` pseudo-opcode is found for *my_array*. Accordingly, the assembler generates code and writes into the object file. The `db` declaration for *format* is processed similarly. On getting the line `section .text`, the *Section* table is updated (Fig. 3.12). For the next few lines, code is generated and written into the file. For the instruction `JZ over` at line 20, the assembler looks into the symbol table to see the offset of *over* to be 37. Now, the value of *lc* after this instruction is 19. Thus, the distance of *over* from the current position is $(37 - 19) = 18 = 12$ (in hex) bytes. In the generated code for `JZ over`, the first byte contains the opcode for `JZ`, that is 74 (hex), and the second byte contains 12. During execution of this instruction on an IA32 processor, this 12 will be added to the instruction pointer to compute the jump target. This facilitates program relocation as explained in Chapter 4. For the instruction `JMP L2` at line 26, a similar strategy is followed; however, the distance is negative in this case as the jump target `L2` occurs earlier in the program. For the instruction `CALL printf` at line 31, the address is put as zero, since *printf* is external to the module. An entry is made accordingly in the *external reference list* as shown in Fig. 3.13.

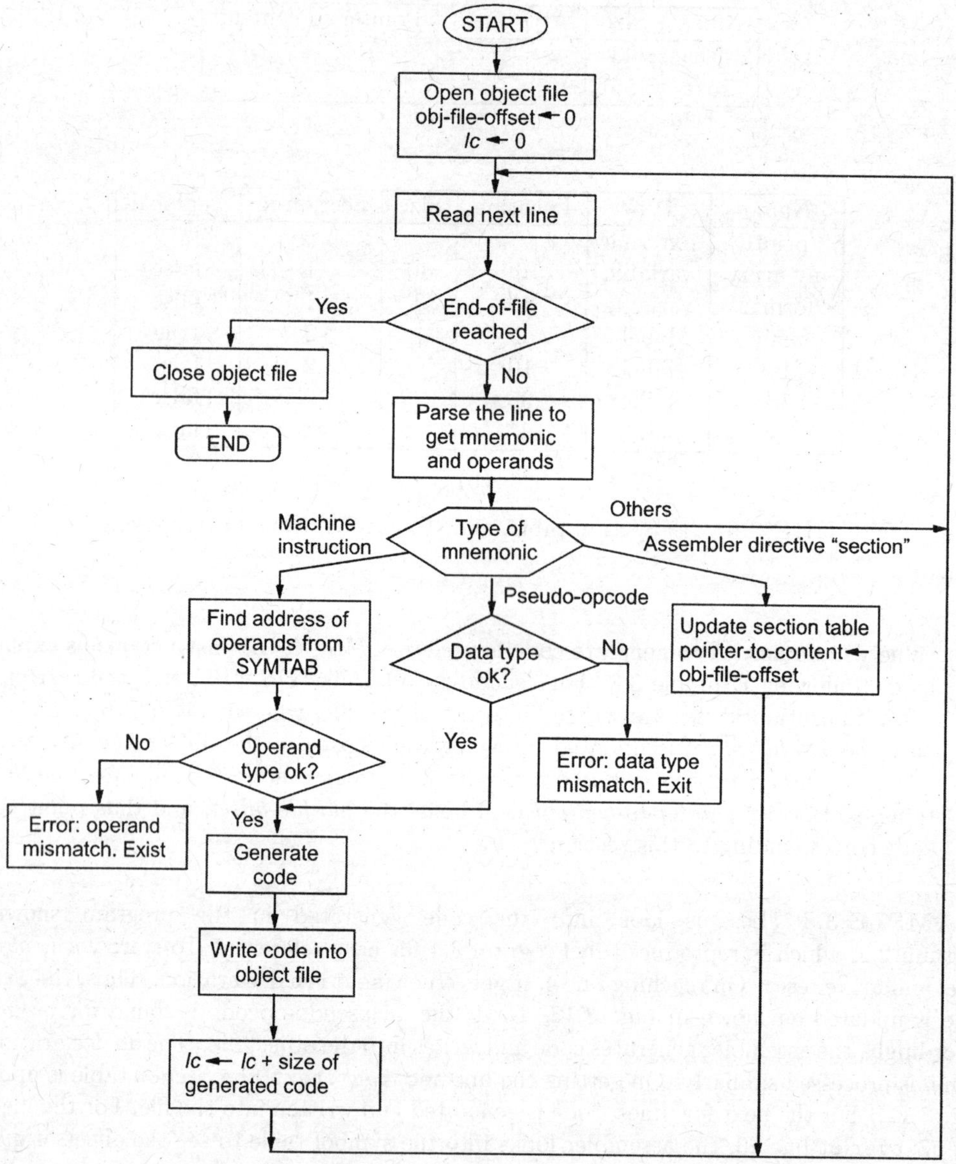

FIGURE 3.10 Pass II of a two-pass assembler.

Name	Offsets to be corrected

FIGURE 3.11 External reference list.

PROGRAM 3.4: Code generated for the program to find the maximum.

```
                                        global main
                                        extern printf

                                        section .data
                                        my_array:
00000000 0A000000140000001E-                dd 10, 20, 30, 100, 200, 56, 45,
00000009 000000640000000C800-                   67, 89, 77
00000012 0000380000002D0000-
0000001B 00430000059000000-
00000024 4D000000

                                        format:
00000028 25640A00                           db '%d', 10, 0
                                        section .text
                                        main:
00000000 B900000000                         MOV ECX, 0
00000005 A1[00000000]                       MOV EAX,  [my_array]
                                        L2:
0000000A 41                                 INC ECX
0000000B 81F90A000000                       CMP ECX, 10
00000011 7412                               JZ over

00000013 3B048D[00000000]                   CMP EAX, [my_array + ECX*4]
0000001A 7D07                               JGE L1
0000001C 8B048D[00000000]                   MOV EAX, [my_array + ECX*4]
                                        L1:
00000023 EBE5                               JMP L2

                                        over:
00000025 50                                 PUSH EAX
00000026 68[28000000]                       PUSH dword format
0000002B E8(00000000)                       CALL printf
00000030 81C408000000                       ADD ESP, 8


00000036 C3                                 RET

```

Name	Size	Attributes	Pointer to content
.data	43		0
.text	55		44

FIGURE 3.12 Updated *Section* table.

Name	Offsets to be corrected
printf	43

FIGURE 3.13 External reference list.

3.2.3 Single-Pass Assembler

A *single-pass* assembler scans the input file only once. Thus, it is generally faster than a two-pass assembler. It uses the same set of data structures as the two-pass assembler. However, it needs some extra data structures and processing to handle the references to symbols defined in the later part of the program (that is, references to symbols occurring before their definitions). For example, consider the following piece of code.

```
        ⋮
X: db 10
        ⋮
MOV AL, X
MOV Y, AL
        ⋮
Y: resb
```

Here, when the assembler reaches the line "X: db 10", it makes entry into the symbol table and simultaneously generates code to reserve one byte initialized to 10. Thus, when the assembler reaches the line "MOV AL, X", the address of X is already available in the symbol table which can be used to generate code. However, at the very next line, "MOV Y, AL" is not simple to process as the type and address of Y is not known at this point of time. These information will only be available when the line "Y: resb" is seen. This type of situation is known as *forward reference.* Similar conditions will arise for branch targets, which are not yet seen by the assembler.

It may be noted that for a two-pass assembler, forward referencing is not a problem, since the entire *Pass I* is dedicated to find the symbols defined in the input program. At the end of *Pass I*, information about all the symbols are available in the *Symbol* table. *Pass II* simply uses these values to generate code.

To resolve the problem of *forward referencing*, the assembler, upon seeing a symbol not yet defined, should make an entry into the *Symbol* table. The value of the *type* field for the symbol should be inferred from the context. The entry should also be marked as *undefined.* Later on, when the symbol gets defined, it should be checked with the entry already present in the *Symbol* table. Any discrepency may be resolved accordingly, or reported as an error. However, there exists another potential problem regarding the code generation. An instruction containing forward reference cannot be translated entirely at the time it is encountered. This is because the address of the operand symbol is not available at that time. The address will be known only after the definition has been seen. At that time, all the locations corresponding to the reference of the symbol can be fixed. This process is known as *backpatching.* For this purpose, corresponding to each such forward referenced symbol, we need to maintain the list of locations requiring correction. As and when a symbol gets defined, the corresponding list be traversed and the locations corrected. This list may conveniently be called *forward reference list.* The structure of this list has been shown in Fig. 3.14.

Name	Offsets to be corrected

FIGURE 3.14 Forward reference list.

A flowchart of the single pass assembler has been shown in Fig. 3.15. As observed from it, the flow of logic combines both *Pass I* and *Pass II* of a two-pass assembler. However, the following extra processings are needed.

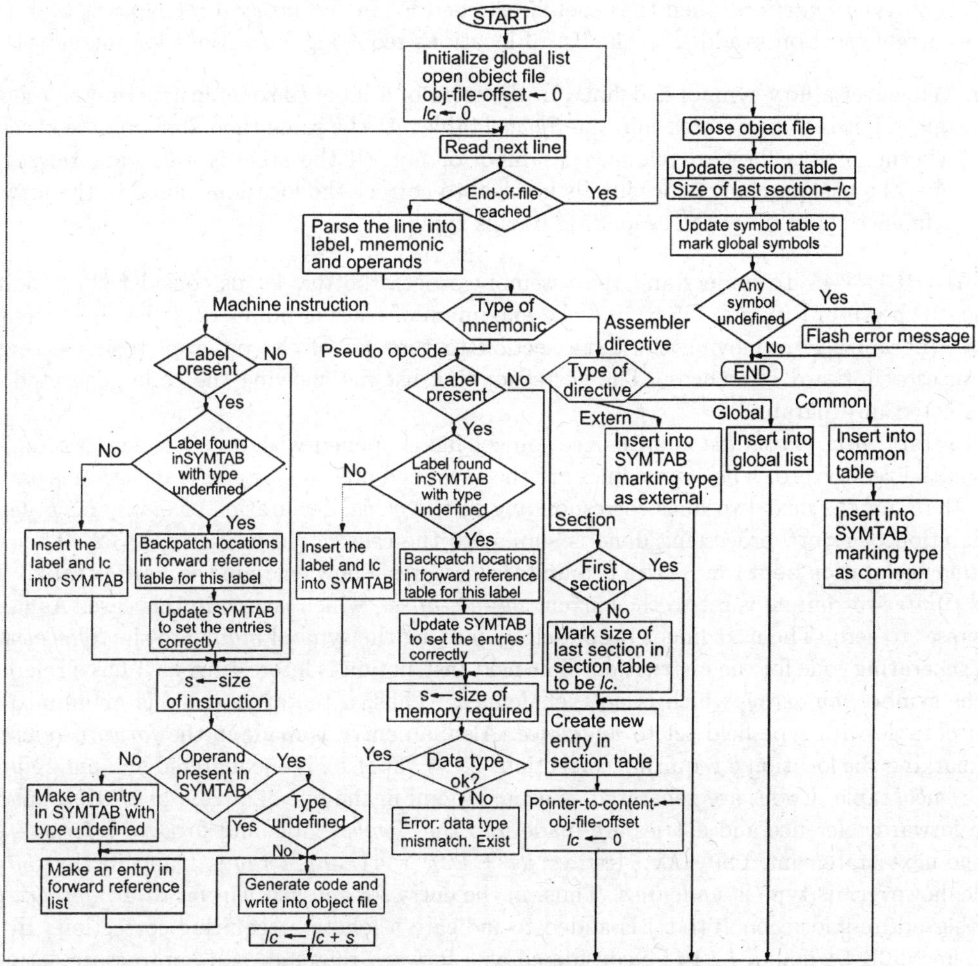

FIGURE 3.15 Single-pass assembler.

1. On reaching the end-of-file marker, apart from closing the object file, updating *Section* and *Symbol* tables, it also needs to check whether some forward referenced symbol is still left undefined. The situation may occur if some symbol is referred to in the program but never defined. At the point of referencing, the assembler assumes it to be a forward referenced symbol and expects it to appear in the later part of the program. An entry is made into the *Symbol* table with *type* left as *undefined*. Thus, at the end of assembly process, if some symbols are still undefined, it is an error and should be reported to the programmer.

2. In the code generation process, while translating an instruction, its operands are looked for in the *Symbol* table. If the operand is not found, a new entry is made into the *Symbol* table with type *undefined*, assuming that it is a forward reference. Also, an entry is created in the *forward reference list* for this label along with the location requiring correction. On the other hand, if the operand is already present in the *Symbol* table with type *undefined*, then the label is searched for in the *forward reference list*, and the current location is added to the list of locations requiring corrections for this label.

3. Whenever a new symbol is defined in the form of a label to some instruction or pseudo-opcode, it is to be entered into the *Symbol* table. At the same time, it should be checked, whether it is a forward referenced symbol or not. If the label is a forward referenced one, the backpatching procedure is invoked to correct the locations noted in the forward reference table entry corresponding to this symbol.

EXAMPLE 3.4 To understand the assembly process better, let us consider the modified program shown in Program 3.5 to find the maximum of a set of numbers. It has been created from Program 2.1 by moving the `data` section to the end of the program to make several instances of forward references. The corresponding list file showing the code generated has been noted in Program 3.6.

To start with, *Global list* is initialized, object file is opened with its offset set to zero, *lc* is also initialized to zero. The source lines are then scanned one-by-one and translation is carried out. Here, for the next two lines corresponding to the *global* declaration of *main* and *External* declaration of *printf*, processing done is similar to the case noted in Example 3.2. Then the *Section* declaration `section .text` is found that creates a new entry in the *Section* table. The field *pointer-to-content* is set to the current *obj-file-offset*, which is zero in this case. As usual, *lc* is reset to zero. The next line is processed by putting the symbol *main* into the *Symbol* table and generating code for the instruction. The next instruction is interesting, as it has a reference to the symbol *my_array*, which is not yet defined. Thus, a tentative entry is made into the *Symbol* table with type field set to *undefined*. Also, an entry is made in the *forward reference list* marking the location 6 requiring correction. Next, label *L2* is encountered and entered into the *Symbol* table. Codes are generated as usual. Again in the line `JZ over`, *over* is assumed to be a forward reference and entries are made into the *Symbol* table and *forward reference list*. In the next statement, `CMP EAX, [my_array + ECX * 4]`, *my_array* is found in the *Symbol* table; however, its type is *undefined*. Thus, in the entry for *my_array* in *forward reference list*, another address location 16(hex) is added to indicate a location requiring correction. In the next line, `JGE L1` makes *L1* to be considered as a forward reference and appropriate action is taken to update *Symbol* table and *forward reference list*. The statement `MOV EAX, [my_array + ECX * 4]` puts the address 1F(hex) in the *forward reference list* for symbol *my_array*. The entries in the *Symbol* table and *forward reference list* upto this point has been shown in Fig. 3.16. Next, label *L1* gets defined. Corrections are made in the *Symbol* table. Consulting the *forward reference list*, code location 1B(hex) is corrected to contain 07(hex). This is because, the *lc* value after the instruction at location 1B(hex) is 1C(hex) and the offset of *L1* is 23(hex) – a distance of 07(hex). Similarly, when the symbol *over* is found, *Symbol* table is corrected and the code location 12(hex) corresponding to the reference of *over* is set to 12(hex) (again by computing the distance). Next, in the statement `PUSH dword format`, *format* is entered into the *Symbol* table and *forward reference table.* Later on, when *my_array* and *format* are defined, *Symbol* table entries are corrected and backpatching is carried out to correct all code locations noted in *forward reference list.* Figure 3.17 shows the final content of the *Symbol* table and the *forward reference list.*

PROGRAM 3.5: Program to find maximum in an array.

```
global main extern printf

section .text
main:
    MOV ECX, 0
    MOV EAX,  [my_array]
L2:
    INC ECX
    CMP ECX, 10
    JZ over

    CMP EAX, [my_array + ECX*4]
    JGE L1
    MOV EAX, [my_array + ECX*4]
L1:
    JMP L2

over:
    PUSH EAX
    PUSH dword format
    CALL printf
    ADD ESP, 8


    RET
section .data
my_array:
    dd 10, 20, 30, 100, 200, 56, 45, 67, 89, 77
format:
    db '%d', 10, 0
```

PROGRAM 3.6: List file showing code generated of the program to find the maximum.

```
                                   global main
                                   extern printf

                                   section .text
                                   main:
00000000 B900000000                    MOV ECX, 0
00000005 A1[00000000]                  MOV EAX,  [my_array]
                                   L2:
0000000A 41                            INC ECX
0000000B 81F90A000000                  CMP ECX, 10
00000011 7412                          JZ over

00000013 3B048D[00000000]              CMP EAX, [my_array + ECX*4]
0000001A 7D07                          JGE L1
0000001C 8B048D[00000000]              MOV EAX, [my_array + ECX*4]
                                   L1:
00000023 EBE5                          JMP L2

                                   over:
00000025 50                            PUSH EAX
00000026 68[28000000]                  PUSH dword format
0000002B E8(00000000)                  CALL printf
00000030 81C408000000                  ADD ESP, 8


00000036 C3                            RET
                                   section .data
                                   my_array:
00000000 0A000000140000001E-           dd 10, 20, 30, 100, 200, 56, 45,
00000009 00000064000000C800-              67, 89, 77
00000012 0000380000002D0000-
0000001B 004300000059000000-
00000024 4D000000

                                   format:
00000028 25640A00                      db '%d', 10, 0
```

3.3 LOAD-AND-GO ASSEMBLER

The assemblers producing the object code directly into the memory and the code is ready for execution are of *Load-and-go* type. This is particularly suitable for small programs in their developmental stages, where after every small modification, it is desirable to check the result. Often, an editor is also clubbed with it to provide an integrated program development

Name	Type	Location	Size	Section-id	Is-global
printf	external				
main	label	0		1	-
my_array	undefined				
L2	label	10		1	-
over	undefined				
L1	undefined				

(a)

Name	Offsets(hex) to be corrected
my_array	06, 16, 1F
over	12
L1	1B

(b)

FIGURE 3.16 Partial (a) symbol table, and (b) forward reference list.

Name	Type	Location	Size	Section-id	Is-global
printf	external				
main	label	0		1	true
my_array	variable	0	40	2	false
L2	label	10		1	false
over	label	37		1	false
L1	label	35		1	false
format	variable	40	3	2	false

(a)

Name	Offsets(hex) to be corrected
my_array	06, 16, 1F
over	12
L1	1B
format	27

(b)

FIGURE 3.17 (a) Symbol table, and (b) Forward reference list.

environment. The total software development time is reduced since after every modification, the object file need not be stored into the secondary storage and loaded again from there for execution. However, it has a number of drawbacks also as enumerated below.

1. The user program needs to be reassembled each time it is run.

2. The memory occupied by the load-and-go assembler is unavailable for use by the program they process.

3. As an extreme result, a load-and-go assembler cannot be used to reassemble itself!

To avoid these problems, most of the assemblers are equipped with the capability to write their output into a file in the secondary storage. The format of this *object file* should be acceptable to many other system softwares present in the system, particularly the linker. In the following, we discuss about some of the widely accepted object file formats.

3.4 OBJECT FILE FORMATS

There are several object file formats reported in the literature, out of which the following are the widely used ones.

- Intel hex format
- obj – Microsoft OMF object files
- win32 – Microsoft Win32 object files
- coff – Common object file format
- elf – Executable and linkable format
- aout – Linux a.out object files

Intel hex format: It is a very common *blocked object code* still in widespread use. In a blocked object code, each sequence of values to be loaded in consecutive addresses is placed in a separate block, along with the address of the first item in the sequence. Intel hex code is a textual code, with each line holding one block of load data, where all of the information on the line is encoded in hexadecimal. Each line must begin with a colon, followed by a 2-digit count of the number of data bytes on the line, a 4-digit address where the data should be stored, and a 2-digit block-type indicator; type 0 is loadable data, and type 1 is used for an end-of-file marker. Following the type-marker comes the data bytes, and then a 2-digit checksum, which is always the last item on the line. The checksum serves to make it possible to detect malformed object files. The checksum is the two's complement of the least significant 8 bits of the sum of all other bytes on the line. Figure 3.18 demonstrates an example of the Intel hex format.

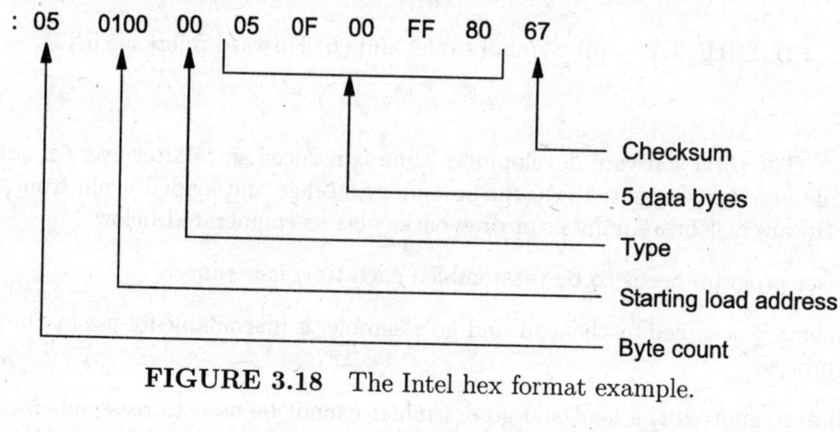

FIGURE 3.18 The Intel hex format example.

Obj format: The *obj* file format is the one used in assemblers like MASM, TASM, etc., which is typically fed to 16-bit DOS linkers to produce .EXE files. It is also used in OS/2. The default output file extension is *.obj*.

Win32 format: This format is used in Microsoft Win32 object files, suitable for passing to Microsoft linkers such as Visual C++. The default output file-name extension is again *.obj*.

Coff format: The coff object files are suitable for linking with DJGPP linker.

Elf format: This format is used by Linux as well as Unix System V, including Solaris x86, UnixWare and SCO Unix. The default output filename extension is *.o*. It allows the program to be viewed as a collection of *Sections* as shown in Fig. 3.19. An *ELF header* resides at the beginning and holds a description regarding the file organization. *Sections* hold the bulk of object file information, that is, instructions, data, symbol table, *relocation*(to be explained later) information, and so on. It also allows to specify *Position-Independent Code (PIC)* that does not need any modification if loaded at different portions of the memory, and thus useful for the libraries. The concept will be clarified in Chapter 4.

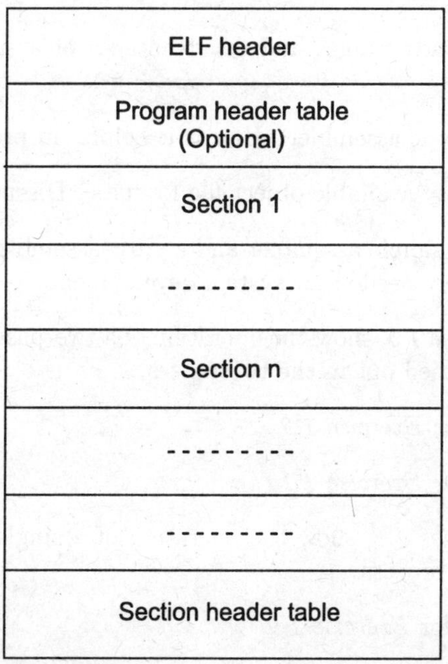

FIGURE 3.19 Elf object file format.

Aout format: The *aout* format generates *a.out* object files, in the form used by early Linux systems. It is a very simple object format, supporting no special directives or symbols. It supports only three standard section names *.text, .data,* and *.bss*.

3.5 CONCLUSION

In this chapter, we have discussed the assembler design process. The major data structures along with their possible organization have been introduced. A detailed discussion has been carried out on both two-pass and single-pass assembler design. In the next chapter, we will see how the object files created through an assembler can be combined along with the library modules to create the executable version of a program using the tools like *linker* and *loader*.

EXERCISES

3.1 Discuss the role of the assembler in program development.

3.2 Using the Machine Opcode Table shown in Table 3.1, write a program to find the maximum of ten numbers stored in memory. Hand-assemble the program and show the list file along with the symbol table.

3.3 Discuss the major data structures used and their organization in an assembler.

3.4 What is forward reference? Explain why the problem of forward reference does not occur in a two-pass assembler, but comes in a single-pass one. How is it solved in the single-pass assembler?

3.5 Compare the relative advantages and disadvantages of a single-pass assembler over a two-pass assembler.

3.6 What is load-and-go type assembler? How is it helpful in program development?

3.7 What are the commonly available object file formats? Discuss their structures in brief.

3.8 Distinguish between a simple assembler and a cross-assembler. Do you think that cross-assemblers are definitely needed for system development?

3.9 For program in *Exercise 1.8*, show the operation of a two-pass assembler clearly, bringing out the operations carried out in the two passes.

3.10 Repeat *Exercise 3.9* for *Exercise 1.9*.

3.11 Repeat *Exercise 3.9* for *Exercise 1.10*.

3.12 For program in *Exercise 1.8*, show the operation of a single-pass assembler clearly explaining the assembly process.

3.13 Repeat *Exercise 3.12* for *Exercise 1.9*.

3.14 Repeat *Exercise 3.12* for *Exercise 1.10*.

Chapter 4

Linker and Loader

Linking is the process of combining different object modules (developed in different files, probably by different people) into one executable file. As seen in the last chapter, an assembler produces code assuming the start address of each section to be zero. Now, when all these sections are put together into one file, the offsets of the symbols in the program may need recomputation. This is because at assembly time, all offsets were calculated from the start of the sections. However after linking, the offsets should be calculated starting from the beginning of the program. Apart from that, sections may have a set of attributes identifying their placement requirements in the memory. Symbols defined in a section of some object module may be used as an external reference in some other module. The assembler could not resolve these external references due to the non-availability of information about these symbols at assembly time. Now it is the responsibility of the linker to *fill up* these blanks left by the assembler. *Symbol* table produced by the assembler holds necessary information regarding the external symbols used in a module and the global symbols defined in it. Thus, the linker produces the executable version of the program. *Loader* is responsible for introduction of a program into physical memory or virtual memory. A major problem here is the conversion of logical program addresses to physical machine addresses.

4.1 LINKING

As pointed out earlier, the objectives of linking are as follows:

- To combine several object modules
- Resolve external references

The inputs of a linker are the following:

1. *Object files:* These are the modules to be combined to create the executable version of the program. As noted in Section 3.4, the object modules are specified in some standard format.
2. *Static libraries:* These are the standard pre-compiled libraries often distributed as an archive file containing individual object files for the library modules. Libraries are

handled by a recursive searching process. If an object module refers to an external symbol of a library module, then that object file for the library module is included in the set of files that need to be linked. In turn, other library modules containing symbols referred to by the first library module are also included. The process continues until a complete set of required library modules have been determined.

3. *Shared library stubs:* Shared libraries contain the common set of functions to be used by almost all the programs running in a system. Thus, instead of loading the same set of routines several times, they are loaded at a single place in the memory. These routines are written as *Position Independent Code (PIC)* to be explained later. Now, in the individual programs, some stub routines are placed that will call these routines in turn, if required.

The outputs of a linker are the following:

1. *Executable file:* The program is now ready for execution, that is, it may be loaded into the memory and start executing.
2. *External tables:* These correspond to the shared library routines. The linker cannot resolve these references as the position where these libraries are loaded is not known at the time of linking the program. Moreover, this position may vary from one execution of the program to another. Thus, the linker leaves a table of all such external references for the loader to fill up and make the program fully ready for execution.

Figure 4.1 shows the inputs and outputs of the linker.

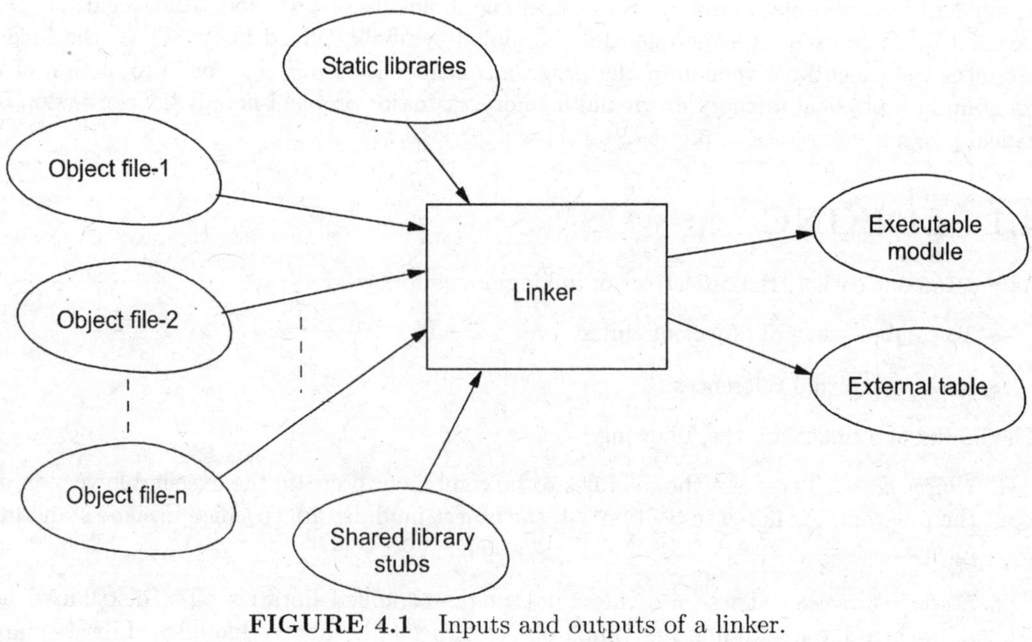

FIGURE 4.1 Inputs and outputs of a linker.

4.1.1 Static vs. Dynamic Linking

Most of the linking that we have discussed so far and that we will be discussing in this chapter pertains to *static linking*, in which all addresses are resolved before the program is loaded into the memory for execution. On the other hand, *dynamic linking* or *deferred linking* links modules on demand. In this case, when an address exception occurs, the *exception handler* is called which does the following.

- The logical address is checked to determine if it refers to a routine or variable that must be dynamically linked. The information regarding the dynamically linkable objects are kept in a *link table*.
- If the address referred to is a valid one, the memory management state of the program is adjusted to reflect the allowed address range for the program.
- The instruction causing exception is then restarted.

4.1.2 Combining Object Modules

The *sections* of object modules are combined to produce a single executable module. In the discussion to follow, we assume the *flat* or *unsegmented* memory model, as this model is followed in almost all the modern operating systems. However, the *SECTION* directive can have some associated attributes specified. All object file formats like *elf, obj*, etc. discussed in the last chapter have their corresponding similar set of attributes. To carry out our discussion, we assume the *elf* format for the object files. *NASM* allows the following qualifiers to the SECTION declaration:

- **alloc** defines the section to be one which is loaded into memory when the program is run. **noalloc** defines it to be one which is not, such as an informational or comment section.
- **exec** defines the section to be one which should have execute permission when the program is run. **noexec** defines it as one which should not.
- **write** defines the section to be one which should be writable when the program is run. **nowrite** defines it as one which should not.
- **progbits** defines the section to be one with explicit contents stored in the object file: an ordinary code or data section, for example, **nobits** defines the section to be one with no explicit contents given, such as a BSS section.
- **align=** used with a trailing number, gives the alignment requirements of the section. *align* $= x$ means that the segment can start only at an address divisible by x.

The defaults assumed by NASM if none of the above qualifiers are specified, are:

```
section   .text     progbits  alloc  exec    nowrite  align=16
section   .rodata   progbits  alloc  noexec  nowrite  align=4
section   .data     progbits  alloc  noexec  write    align=4
section   .bss      nobits    alloc  noexec  write    align=4
section   other     progbits  alloc  noexec  nowrite  align=1
```

It may be noted that any section name other than `.text`, `.rodata`, `.data` and `.bss` is treated by default like `other` as shown above.

All the information is added to the *section table* by the assembler and used by the linker to combine the sections into executable file. The process of this combining can be divided into two passes. In the first pass, the relative position of all sections is computed, assuming the start offset of the file to be zero. The second pass actually puts the code into the file.

4.1.3 Pass I of Linking

Pass I computes the start addresses of different sections in the input object modules and collects the symbols defined *public*. It looks into the *section* tables and *symbol* tables to construct a *Combined Section Table (CST)* and a *Public Definition Table (PDT)*. The structure of these tables is shown in Fig. 4.2 (a) and (b) respectively. The procedure followed in this pass has been explained in Fig. 4.3 in the form of a flowchart. Here *lc* is used to keep track of how much of the output file (executable module) is already occupied and thus the place where a new segment can be stored. It is initialized to zero assuming that the executable module will start at offset zero. Now the sections are read from the object files one after the other. Possible start address of the section in the executable module is computed. If a section with the same name as the one just read does not exist in the CST, that is, this section is a new one, its start address is computed by considering the current *lc* value and *alignment* requirements of the section. If *lc* does not satisfy the *align* specification, the immediate next address satisfying it is selected as the start address. On the other hand, if the section is already present in the CST, the possible start address is computed as the current start address (of the section) in the CST plus the current size of the section as noted in CST. This is because the section that has just been read will be concatenated to the end of the section with the same name as in CST. Next, the current size of the section in CST is added to the offsets of all *public* symbols defined in this section. It may be recalled that the assembler had noted the offsets of symbols assuming a start address of zero for the section, which is no more valid when the sections are getting combined in the executable module. All *public* definitions are now put into the *Public Definition Table (PDT)*. The *Combined Section Table (CST)* is updated next. If a new section is being considered, entries are made into CST and *lc* is updated by the start address plus the size of the section. No other modification is needed for the CST. However, if the section name is already present in the CST, only the *size* field needs to be increased for that entry. For subsequent entries, the start addresses are to be increased by the size of the current section being considered. It may be noted that the alignment requirements of the sections should be considered while modifying the start addresses of subsequent entries. The process continues till all sections in all object files have been considered. Then control passes to Pass II of linking producing the executable file. Next, we consider an example to understand the process.

Section name	Start address	Size	Align

(a)

Symbol name	Section name	Offset

(b)

FIGURE 4.2 (a) Combined section table (CST), and (b) Public definition table (PDT).

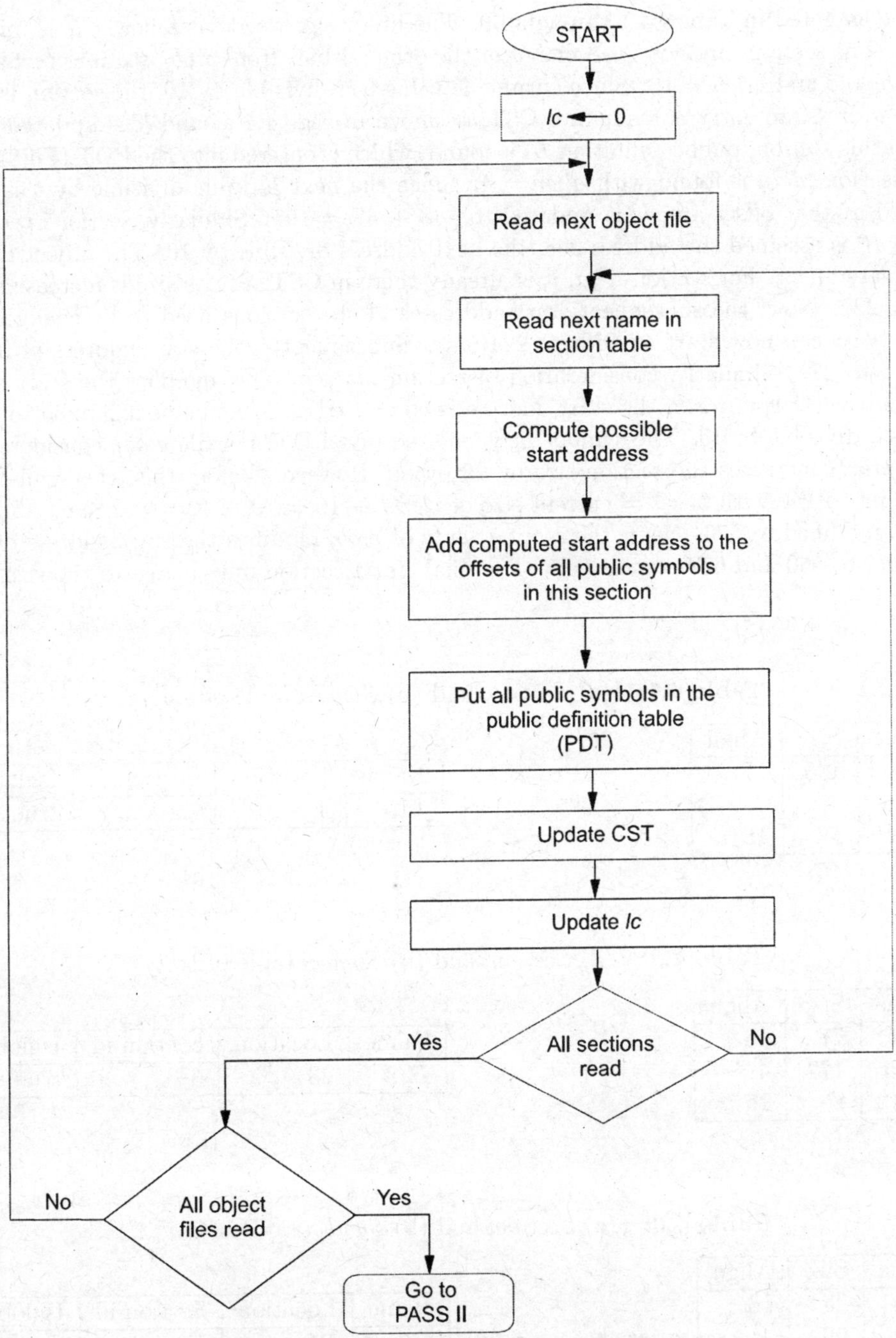

FIGURE 4.3 Pass I of the linker.

EXAMPLE 4.1 Let a set of object files named *a.obj, b.obj,* and *c.obj* be given to the linker to produce the executable file. The *section* and *symbol* tables (showing the *public* declarations only) be as noted in Tables 4.1 through 4.3. The linking proceeds as follows. *lc* is initialized to zero. The sections are now read one after the other. First, from *a.obj*, section *.text* is found with size 145 and *align* = 16. Since current *lc* value 0 is divisible by 16, the section is placed at this address, an entry is made into CST as shown in Fig. 4.4(a) and *lc* is updated to 145. Also, in this section, public definition *L1* is found, which is entered into the PDT (Fig. 4.4(b)). Next, section *.data* is found with *align* = 4. Since the next *lc* value divisible by 4 is 148, it is placed at that offset and *lc* is updated to 148 + 47 = 195. Similarly, section *.text1* with *align* = 16 is assigned the address 208, the next address divisible by 16. The object file *b.obj* is considered next. For section *.text*, it is already there in CST. So, its size is increased to 145 + 77 = 222. Now, the subsequent start addresses of the sections need to be changed. The section *.data* can now start at address 224 only. Subsequently, the start address of *.text1* is modified to 272. Similarly, consideration of section *.data* in *b.obj* modifies the start address of *.text1* to 464. For *.text2*, the start address is computed as 544, the next number of 464 + 79 = 543, divisible by 16. The symbol *L2* is entered into PDT. For file *c.obj*, consideration of section *.text1* increases the section size by 25 bytes. However, before this, the symbol *L3* is entered into PDT with offset = current size of *.text1* + 10 = 79 + 10 = 89. Start address of *.text2* is modified to 576. Next, the section *.data* of *c.obj* modifies the start address of *.text1* and *.text2* to 560 and 672 respectively. The final *.text2* section only increases the size to 155 bytes.

Table 4.1: (a) *Section*, and (b) *Symbol* table of *a.obj*

Name	Size	Align
.text	145	16
.data	47	4
.text1	79	16

(a)

Name	Location	Section-id	Isglobal
L1	4	1	true

(b)

Table 4.2: (a) *Section*, and (b) *Symbol* table of *b.obj*

Name	Size	Align
.text	77	16
.data	179	4
.text2	85	16

(a)

Name	Location	Section-id	Isglobal
L2	23	3	true

(b)

Table 4.3: (a) *Section*, and (b) *Symbol* table of *c.obj*

Name	Size	Align
.text1	25	16
.data	99	4
.text2	70	16

(a)

Name	Location	Section-id	Isglobal
L3	10	1	true

(b)

Section name	Start address	Size	Align
.text	0	~~145~~ 222	16
.data	~~148~~ 224	~~47~~ ~~226~~ 325	4
.text1	~~208~~ ~~272~~ ~~464~~ 560	~~79~~ 104	16
.text2	~~544~~ ~~576~~ 672	~~85~~ 155	16

(a)

Symbol name	Section name	Offset
*L*1	.text	4
*L*2	.text2	23
*L*3	.text1	89

(b)

FIGURE 4.4 (a) Combined section table, and (b) public definition table.

4.1.4 Pass II of Linking

Pass II of linking is responsible for writing the final code into the executable file. The *Combined Section Table (CST)* contains information about the relative positions of sections within this final file to be created. Thus, the main task of this phase is to copy the object files into their corresponding locations. Another very important task to be accomplished in this phase is that of *offset correction* or *relocation*, which we discuss next before going into the algorithm for Pass II.

Relocation. As noted in the assembler design phase, the assembler, while generating object module, assumes the start addresses of individual sections to be zero. All references to variables in a program are translated to their distances from the beginning of the section containing them. However, later on, all the object modules are to be combined into one executable module and all offsets should be taken with respect to the start of the module. Thus, the code corresponding to instructions containing memory references needs to be corrected. This process is called *relocation.* It is useful for,

1. moving around object files during linking, and
2. loading a piece of code at a specified address.

Relocation needs to be carried out both at link-time and at load-time. At link-time, relocation is needed to arrange the object files into the executable module starting at offset zero. At load-time, relocation is needed for arranging shared libraries and the executable module into the address space. For the time being, we concentrate on link-time relocation strategies only. Link-time relocation is performed using *direct editing* that will modify the address sensitive locations within the code during concatenating object modules. There can be two different ways in which the locations requiring relocation can be specified.

Relocation bitmap: Here, for every instruction, the assembler associates a relocation bit. If the instruction does not need any relocation (that is, instructions not involving memory addresses), the bit is set to zero, else the bit is set to one. For cases with relocation bit = 1, Pass II of linking does the necessary modifications to the code.

Relocation table: It is a table consisting of locations requiring corrections and a *Delta* value that should be added to the offset of the symbol to get the address corrected.

Table 4.4 shows the relocation bits for the program of Program 2.1 reproduced in columns 1, 2, and 3 of the table. Column 4 shows the relocation bits. For the same program, Table 4.5 shows the relocation table.

Algorithm for Pass II

In Pass II, the object files are read again per section and the corresponding codes with necessary relocation changes are put into the executable file. For each section that is read, its start address is looked for in the CST produced in Pass I. The code corresponding to this section is next put into the executable module. The CST entries for the section are updated by incrementing the *start address* of the section by the size of the current section read, and the *size* field in CST is decremented by the size of the section. This ensures that a subsequent occurrence of a section with the same name will get concatenated to the end of this section. Moreover, when all sections have been put into the executable module, the *size* field of all entries in CST will become zero. Next, the code written into the file is modified to sort out the relocation problems (if any). For each entry marked as requiring relocation, the start address of the section in which the symbol has been defined is added to the code. This ensures that all offsets are now with respect to the start address of the executable module. The locations referring to the *shared library* functions and/or variables cannot be corrected at this stage, as their addresses are not known. These relocations are to be performed at the time of loading the program into memory for execution. The entries should then point to the actual location of those shared elements at that time of execution. It may be noted that the addresses of those shared library elements can vary from execution to execution of the program, and thus be handled best by the loader in association with the memory management module of the operating system. The linker will produce a list of such locations requiring load-time relocations. Another important information passed by the linker to the loader is the *start address* of the program. The specification of the start address depends upon the underlying language. For example, the language *C* expects a unique function *main*, to be present in the executable module that defines the start address. In our examples in this book, we have used a global symbol *main* which is used by *gcc* linker to pass on the start address information to the loader.

EXAMPLE 4.2 Continuing Example 4.1, the Pass II algorithm first looks into the sections of *a.obj*. For section *.text*, it puts the code into the executable file as shown in Fig. 4.6, updates the *start address* in CST to 145 and *size* to 77. Next, *.data* is put into the file. *Start address* and *size* are updated to 271 and 278 respectively. The section *.text1* is next put into the file at offset 560. *Start address* and *size* for *.text1* in CST are updated to 639 and 25 respectively.

Table 4.4: Program with relocation bits

Line no.	Code	Source line	Relocation bit
1		global main	
2		extern printf	
3			
4		section .data	
5		my_array:	
6	00000000 0A000000140000001E-	dd 10, 20, 30, 100, 200, 56, 45,	0
7	00000009 00000064000000C800-	67, 89, 77	0
8	00000012 0000380000002D0000-		0
9	0000001B 004300000059000000-		0
10	00000024 4D000000		0
11		format:	
12	00000028 25640A00	db '%d', 10, 0	0
13		section .text	
14		main:	
15	00000000 B900000000	MOV ECX, 0	0
16	00000005 A1[00000000]	MOV EAX, [my_array]	1
17		L2:	
18	0000000A 41	INC ECX	0
19	0000000B 81F90A000000	CMP ECX, 10	0
20	00000011 7412	JZ over	0
21			
22	00000013 3B048D[00000000]	CMP EAX, [my_array + ECX*4]	1
23	0000001A 7D07	JGE L1	0
24	0000001C 8B048D[00000000]	MOV EAX, [my_array + ECX*4]	1
25		L1:	
26	00000023 EBE5	JMP L2	
27			
28		over:	
29	00000025 50	PUSH EAX	0
30	00000026 68[28000000]	PUSH dword format	1
31	0000002B E8(00000000)	CALL printf	1
32	00000030 81C408000000	ADD ESP, 8	0
33			
34			
35	00000036 C3	RET	0

For *b.obj*, section *.text* is put at address 145. *Start address* and *size* fields of CST are updated to 222 and 0 respectively. Next, section *.data* of *b.obj* is placed into the object file at offset 271, *start address* and *size* are updated to 450 and 99 respectively. The section *.text2* is put at offset 672. *Start address* and *size* in CST for *.text2* are updated to 757 and 70 respectively. From *c.obj*, section *.text1* is placed at offset 639. *Start address* and *size* are updated to 664 and 0 respectively. The section *.data* from *c.obj* is placed at offset 450. *Start address* and *size* are updated to 549 and 0 respectively. Finally, section *.text2* of *c.obj* is placed at offset 757. The

Table 4.5: Relocation table

Offset	Delta
00000005	.data
00000013	.data
0000001C	.data
00000026	.data
0000002B	External

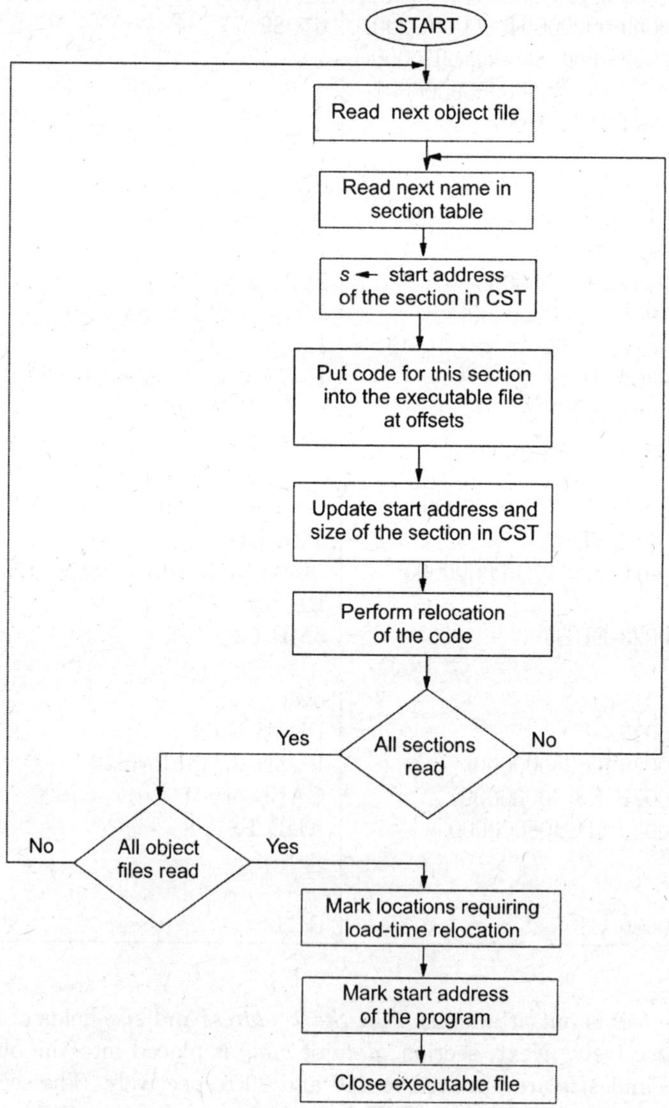

FIGURE 4.5 Algorithm for Pass II of linking.

start address and *size* fields are accordingly updated to 827 and 0 respectively. The layout of the sections in the executable file has been shown in Fig 4.7.

Section name	Start address	Size	Align
.text	~~0~~ ~~145~~ 222	~~222~~ ~~77~~ 0	16
.data	~~224~~ ~~271~~ ~~450~~ 549	~~325~~ ~~278~~ ~~99~~ 0	4
.text1	~~560~~ ~~639~~ 664	~~104~~ ~~25~~ 0	16
.text2	~~672~~ ~~757~~ 827	~~155~~ ~~70~~ 0	16

FIGURE 4.6 Modifications in CST for Example 4.2.

EXAMPLE 4.3 Next we consider another example of Pass II of linking to elaborate the relocation. For this, we have split the program in Program 2.1 into two files *a1.asm* and *a2.asm*. File *a1.asm* contains the data declarations, input and output, while *a2.asm* contains the function *get_max* to determine the maximum element in an array *my_array* defined external in it. The corresponding list files *a1.lst* and *a2.lst* have been shown in Table 4.6, which also shows the code generated side-by-side. The default alignments of 16 for *.text* and 4 for *.data* are assumed. The *Combined Section Table (CST)* after Pass I of linking is as shown in Table 4.7. *Relocation tables* after Pass I of linking is as shown in Table 4.8. It may also be noted that at the end of Pass I of linking, the *Public Definition Table (PDT)* holds information about all public symbols defined in the two object modules. The PDT has been shown in Table 4.9. The Pass II process will put the sections into the final executable module with relocation carried out at offsets 00000007 of *a1.obj* for *format* and at offsets 00000006, 00000016 and 0000001F of *a2.obj* for *my_array*. However, for the symbol *printf* at offset 0000000C of the executable module, the relocation address is not known. Thus it is left for the loader with an indication to be resolved at the time of loading the program into main/virtual memory. The symbol *main* at offset zero is marked as the *start address* of the entire module. The executable module after performing relocations has been shown in Table 4.10. The relocated values have been shown in boldface for clarity.

4.2 LIBRARY LINKING

As we have noted earlier, apart from the symbols defined by the user in different object modules, the program may also contain references to external symbols that are defined in

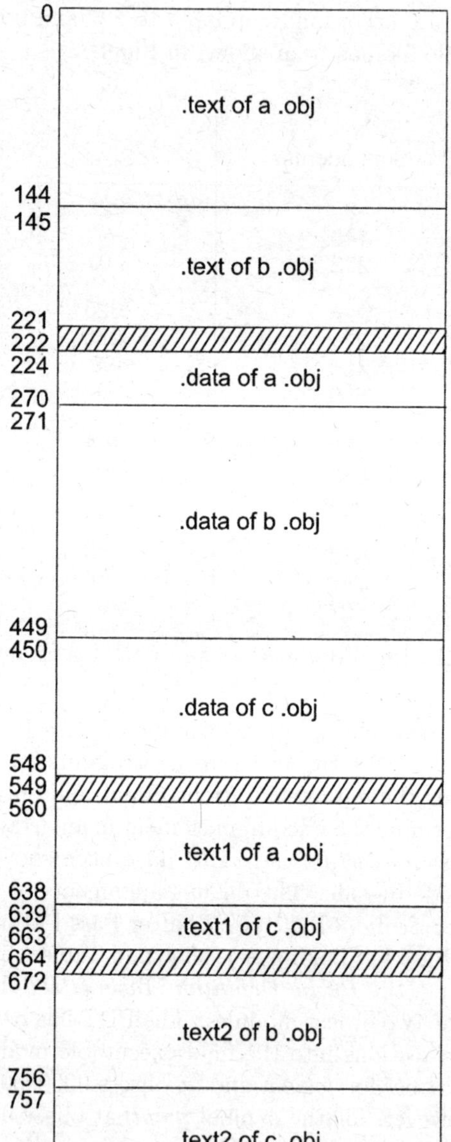

FIGURE 4.7 Layout of the executable file for Example 4.2.

library modules. For example, the mathematical routines are clubbed together into a library, string functions may be kept together into another one. This facilitates the users to refer to a particular library and include it along with other object modules for complete execution of programs. External libraries are usually provided in two forms: *static libraries* and *shared libraries.* In Linux, for example, static libraries have extension ".s" in their file names, whereas

Table 4.6: List files for Example 4.3

a1.lst		*a2.lst*	
	global main, my_array		extern my_array
	extern printf, get_max		global get_max
	section .text		section .text
	main:		get_max:
00000000 E8(00000000)	CALL get_max	00000000 B900000000	MOV ECX, 0
00000005 50	PUSH EAX	00000005 A1[00000000]	MOV EAX, [my_array]
			L2:
00000006 68[28000000]	PUSH dword format	0000000A 41	INC ECX
0000000B E8(00000000)	CALL printf	0000000B 81F90A000000	CMP ECX, 10
00000010 81C408000000	ADD ESP, 8	00000011 7412	JZ over
00000016 C3	RET	00000013 3B048D[00000000]	CMP EAX, [my_array + ECX*4]
	section .data		
	my_array:	0000001A 7D07	JGE L1
00000000 0A000000140000001E-	dd 10, 20, 30, 100, 200	0000001C 8B048D[00000000]	MOV EAX, [my_array + ECX*4]
00000009 00000064000000C800-			L1:
00000012 0000			
00000014 380000002D00000043-	dd 56, 45, 67, 89, 77	00000023 EBE5	JMP L2
0000001D 000000590000004D00-			over:
00000026 0000		00000025 C3	RET
	format:		
00000028 25640A00	db '%d', 10, 0		

Table 4.7: Combined section table for Example 4.3.

Section name	Start address	Size	Align
.text	0	61	16
.data	64	43	4

Table 4.8: Relocation tables for Example 4.3

a1.obj

Offset	Delta	Symbol
00000001	External	*get_max*
00000007	*.data*	*format*
0000000C	External	*printf*

a2.obj

Offset	Delta	Symbol
00000006	External	*my_array*
00000016	External	*my_array*
0000001F	External	*my_array*

Table 4.9: Public definition table for Example 4.3

Symbol name	Section name	Offset
main	*.text*	0
my_array	*.data*	64
get_max	*.text*	23

Table 4.10: Executable module for Example 4.3.

Address	Code	Comments
00000000	E8(**17**000000)	
00000005	50	
00000006	68[**68**000000]	.text of *a1.obj*
0000000B	E8(00000000)	
00000010	81C408000000	
00000016	C3	
00000017	B900000000	
0000001C	A1[**40**000000]	
00000021	41	
00000022	81F90A000000	
00000028	7412	
0000002A	3B048D[**40**000000]	.text of *a2.obj*
00000031	7D07	
00000033	8B048D[**40**000000]	
0000003A	EBE5	
0000003C	C3	
00000040	0A000000140000001E	
00000049	00000064000000C800	
00000052	0000	.data of *a1.obj*
00000054	380000002D00000043	
0000005D	000000590000004D00	
00000066	0000	
00000068	25640A00	

for shared libraries, the extension is ".so". When a program is linked against a static library, for each of the external functions used by the program, the corresponding machine code is copied from the object file containing the library. The extracted code is attached with other modules to create the overall executable module. However, in some linkers, instead of including the particular function, the entire library object module is included in the code. In turn, any library module containing symbols referred to by the first library module are also included. The process continues until a complete set of required library modules have been determined and included in the code.

The term *shared library* is a bit ambiguous, as it covers at least two different concepts. First, it is the sharing of code located on disk by unrelated programs. On the other hand, it can be sharing of code in memory. In this case, the programs execute the same piece of code loaded at the same physical page of the memory, but mapped to the address spaces of the programs. Obviously, the second approach has got a lot of advantages. For example, the applications may now be only a few hundred kilobytes in size and loaded instantly—the majority of the code being in the libraries that has been loaded for other purposes by the operating system. However, the major price paid is that the shared code must be specifically written in a multi-tasking environment, and this has effects on performance. Main memory sharing can be accomplished by using *Position Independent Code (PIC)* as in UNIX, leading to a complex but flexible architecture, or by using normal (that is, non-PIC) code as in Windows and OS/2. These systems make sure, by various tricks such as pre-mapping the address space, reserving slots for the shared library modules. In Windows environment, such modules are called *DLL (Dynamic Link Library)*. It may be noted that Windows DLLs are not shared libraries in the UNIX sense. In most modern operating systems including Windows, shared libraries can be of the same format as the *regular* executables. This provides two main advantages: first, it requires making only one loader for both of them, rather than two. The added complexity of the one loader is considered well worth the cost. Secondly, it allows the executables also to be used as DLLs, if they have a symbol table. Most dynamic library systems link a symbol table with blank addresses into the program at compile/assemble time. All references to code or data in the library pass through this table, the *import directory*. At load time, the table is modified with the location of the library code/data by the linker/loader. The biggest disadvantage of this shared library is that the executables depend on the separately stored libraries in order to function properly. If the library is deleted, moved, or renamed, or if an incompatible version of the DLL is copied to a place that is earlier in the search, the executable could malfunction or even fail to load. This impedes the performance and stability of the operating system also. On Windows, this is commonly known as *DLL hell*.

4.3 POSITION INDEPENDENT CODE (PIC)

Position independent code (PIC) is a form of absolute object code that does not contain any absolute addresses and therefore does not depend on where it is loaded in the process's virtual address space. This is an important property for building shared libraries. Most modern compilers can be asked to generate PIC (for example, *-fpic* option for *gcc*). Position independence is achieved via the following two mechanisms:

1. **IP-relative** addressing is used wherever possible for branches within modules.
2. **Indirect addressing** is used for all accesses to global variables, or for intermodule procedure calls and other branches and literal accesses where *IP-relative* addressing cannot be used.

For example, the following is a coding technique that may be used to implement function-calls in a position independent manner.

```
            ...
            MOV EAX, ESI[format]
            CALL EAX
            ...
format:
            ...
```

Here, if ESI is preloaded with the start address of the module containing this piece of code, the statement CALL EAX will call the function *format* indirectly. In general, a shared library will contain a number of related functions. As noted earlier, the object code for such library module will also contain a symbol table containing all the functions and variables that may be accessed by other modules. Consider a shared library for the *C* language containing the functions *printf, format,* and *atoi.* In the module, let *printf* be defined at offset 0, *format* at offset 1000, and *atoi* at offset 1100. Then the symbol table will look as shown in Table 4.11.

Table 4.11: Symbol table

printf	0
format	1000
atoi	1100

Any program using calls to these functions should first locate the position of the library module either in the main memory or in the virtual memory and use indirect addressing (as shown earlier for the function *format*) to access them. A program named *Program-A* can be like the following.

```
Initialize LIBC_VECTOR
MOV ESI, LIBC_VECTOR
MOV EAX, ESI[printf]
CALL EAX
```

Whereas another program named *Program-B* can use the same library similarly, as shown below.

```
Initialize LIBC_VECTOR
MOV ESI, LIBC_VECTOR
MOV EAX, ESI[atoi]
CALL EAX
```

For *Program-A*, if the virtual address at which the library has been attached is 50000, the *Initialize LIBC_VECTOR* should get this value, so that ESI is adjusted accordingly. On the other hand, for *Program-B*, the virtual address may be 20000. Thus, the initialization should get this value to set ESI. The virtual memory manager may identify that the virtual pages at address 50000 for *Program-A* and at address 20000 for *Program-B* are referring to the same code, and thus decide to load the corresponding pages only once in the main memory with *shared*-bit turned *ON* for the pages. Thus, the processes maintain implicitly some table of addresses for the shared library functions and call the routines via this table. The variables in the shared library can be accessed in a similar manner by maintaining another table, may be named as *Global Offset Table* and using another register to hold the address of this table. All accesses to shared variables thus need two memory references—one to read the offset from the table and the other one to actually access the variable.

To summarize, PIC enjoys the following advantages over the ordinary executables.

- No need to relocate.
- Library is shared on disk.
- Library is shared in primary memory as well. All the page tables of various processes can share the main memory frames for the library.

On the other hand, it has the following drawbacks.

- We sacrifice one register to hold pointer to the indirect table.
- Each method invocation needs two memory accesses.
- We have to use another register to access the variables in the shared library.
- Each access to variables in the shared library requires two memory accesses.

4.4 SHARED LIBRARY LINKING

Shared libraries are compiled and linked independently from the application. However, when used in conjunction with the application, the following problems come up.

- Offset of various routine can now change.
- The linking process of the application cannot take care of the shared libraries, because it has no idea where the shared library is actually located at the time of execution. Moreover, the position may vary from one execution to another.
- Loader has to take care of the situation. PIC provides a nice solution. However, the scheme is improved further by using *stub* routines in the individual processes.

For example, an application program may have a call to a shared library routine *atoi* like,

```
        PUSH 25
        CALL atoi
```

The application is augmented with a dummy (stub) *atoi* function, which, in turn, calls the *real_atoi* function residing in the shared library as follows.

```
atoi:   MOV ESI, LIBC_VECTOR
        MOV EAX, ESI[real_atoi]
        JMP EAX
```

On the other hand, the shared library may be located in another file *Libc.so* containing the actual routines, that is *real_atoi*, etc. Let the file contain three such routines with their offsets as shown in Table 4.12. This table is called *Procedure Linkage Table (PLT)*. As is obvious, for correct execution of the the application, LIBC_VECTOR should contain the start address of the memory at which *Libc.so* has been loaded.

Table 4.12: Symbol table for the library

real_printf	0
real_format	1000
real_atoi	1100

With such a scheme, object code generation for the application and library can continue independently. Linker resolves the undefined entries in the object modules of the application with PLT entries of the shared library. During loading, the value of LIBC_VECTOR is known (since either the library is already present in the memory, or it is loaded at this time). Thus, the *loader* can resolve this reference ensuring a smooth execution of the application.

Versioning. A typical problem arises if several versions of the same library are present in the system simultaneously. Some programs use the older version, while some others use newer ones. Versions are not downward compatible, mainly because due to the addition and deletion of code, the offsets of the routines within the library will vary from one version to another. Ensuring correct execution of all applications in such a situation is really a challenge. The situation is the *DLL Hell* as mentioned earlier.

Among the probable solutions, the following may be tried out.

1. *Rename the shared library every time.* In this case, the system does not provide any support for versioning. The burden is entirely on the programmer. A variant of this puts a copy of the library in each program directory. However, in this case, all forms of sharing are lost!

2. *Integrate numbering scheme in the file name.* For example, *libc.so.5.1.* Here, 5 is the *major revision number* and 1 is the *minor revision number.* Major upgrade increments the major version number. It is better than renaming, however, still rely on basic convention.

4.5 LOADER

Loading is the process of making a program ready for execution by copying the file from secondary storage to the primary or virtual memory. It is often a part of the operating system, and thus not visible to the system user directly. The major objectives of a loader are as follows.

- Bring a binary image into memory.
- Bind relocatable addresses to absolute addresses.

As pointed out earlier, at the end of linking, we are left with a single executable module which needs to be further coupled with the shared libraries that may or may not be already loaded. The task of the loader is now to locate the position of the shared library, correct the appropriate entries in the executable referring to shared library routines and variables, and hence create the binary image that is ready for execution from all angles. Thus, the inputs to the loader are the following.

- One executable
- Zero or more shared libraries

The output of the loader is:

- A usable binary image at an absolute address in the virtual address space. The virtual memory manager takes care of the image now for its correct execution.

The inputs and outputs of a loader have been shown in Fig. 4.8.

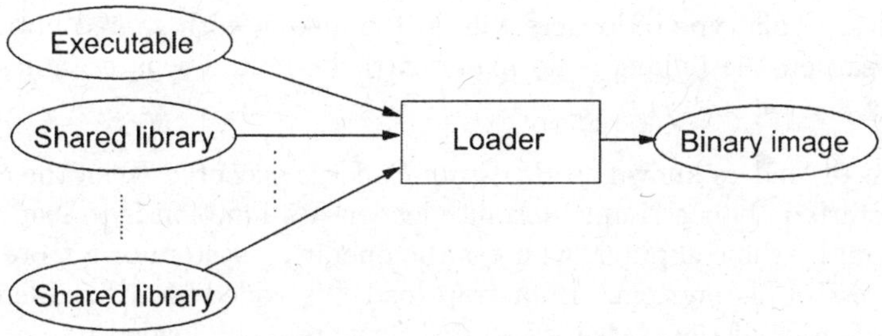

FIGURE 4.8 Input-Output of the loader.

4.5.1 Binary Image

The binary image of a program consists of the following components.

1. *A header.* It indicates the type of the image. An image may be an executable file, some library, etc. Some of the images are to be loaded at some preassigned address, or it may be determined by consulting the memory management routine.

2. *Text of the program.* It consists of the actual piece of code. The code may be in some specific format, like *Intel Hex format*, *elf*, etc. It holds the object files, static libraries, and stub tables for shared libraries.

3. *List of shared libraries.* The shared library routines that are called by the module. The loader needs to resolve the addresses accordingly.

The loader checks the file header to determine how to load the program. A virtual memory area is added for the text of the program. The virtual memory area is backed up by the file containing the code. When a page fault occurs, the virtual memory subsystem goes to the backing store (the file) and maps the missing page. A complete discussion on virtual memory manager to load and manage the executable modules is beyond the scope of this book. Interested readers are requested to refer to some book on *Operating Systems.*

4.5.2 Types of Loaders

There are three main categories of loaders, namely:

1. Absolute loaders
2. Relocating loaders
3. Linking loaders

Absolute loaders. This is the simplistic type of situation in which the assembler generates code and writes instructions in a file together with their load addresses. The loader reads the file and places the code at the absolute address given in the file.

Relocating loaders. Here the assembler produces code and the relocation information. The loader, while loading the program performs relocation as well.

Linking loaders. This type of loaders will do the linking with shared libraries as well. As discussed earlier, the linking is normally carried out in a separate phase to reduce the complexity.

Another class of loaders known as *Bootstrap loader* is executed when the computer is first turned on or restarted. It is a simple absolute loader. Its function is to load the first system program to be run by the computer, which is the operating system or a more complex loader that loads the rest of the system. Bootstrap loader is coded as a fixed-length record and added to the beginning of the system programs that are to be loaded into an empty system. A built-in hardware or a very simple program in ROM reads this record into the memory and transfers control to it. When it is executed, it loads the program which is either the operating system itself or other system programs to be run without the operating system.

4.6 CONCLUSION

In this chapter, we have seen how the object modules created by an assembler or compiler can be combined together using the process of linking. The task often requires relocation to be done to rectify the address references within the module. Techniques to create *position-independent-code* have been detailed that can be used for shared-library development. Loading process has also been discussed. However, the details like how a program be loaded into virtual memory has been skipped, as it is covered rigorously in books on *operating systems.* In the next chapter, we will see another feature used in both assembly- and high-level-language programs to reduce the program size. The technique is called *macro.* Processing of these macros is often done in a separate preprocessing phase known as *macroprocessing.*

EXERCISES

4.1 Explain the responsibilities of the linker and the loader in program development.

4.2 What is the difference between static and shared libraries? Can a system have all its libraries only as static or only as dynamic? Is it advisable?

4.3 What advantage does dynamic linking provide over static linking?

4.4 Explain the linking process for the object file x, y, and z for which the *section tables* are shown in Fig. 4.9. Also, show the layout of the final executable module.

Name	Size	Align
.text	305	16
.data	59	4
.data1	65	4

Section table for x

Name	Size	Align
.text	200	16
.data	175	4
.data2	300	4

Section table for y

Name	Size	Align
.text	75	4
.data	89	4
.data2	76	16

Section table for z

FIGURE 4.9 Section tables for *Exercise 4.4.*

4.5 What is relocation? Explain different ways by which the assembler can pass relocation information to the linker.

4.6 What is position-independent-code? How does it help in solving the relocation problem? Explain.

4.7 How does DLL work in *windows* platform? What is meant by *DLL Hell*?

4.8 Identify the instruction-set features useful to develop PIC.

4.9 How is shared library linking performed using the PIC method?

4.10 Explain the different types of loaders commonly available.

Chapter 5

Macroprocessor

Macros are special code fragments that are defined once in the program and are used repetitively by calling them from various places within the program. It is similar to the *subprogram* in the sense that both can be used to organize the program better by separating out the frequently used fragment into a different block. The main program calls this block of code as and when needed. Both of them can have an associated list of parameters. However, the implementation of macro differs significantly from subprograms. In the case of subprogram, during execution of the program, at each call to the subprogram, control branches to it and returns to the calling point at the end of executing the subprogram. This involves saving a lot of context information (such as values of arguments passed, local variables, CPU registers, return address, etc.) into the stack. The context is to be restored when control returns after executing the subprogram. Macroprocessors work by simple code substitution. Moreover, the substitution takes place at the time of compiling/assemblying the program. Each call to the macro is replaced by the body of the macro directly with the parameters substituted by the arguments passed. Thus, once the expansion has taken place, there is no necessity to do context switching during execution. This saves a lot of time, particularly if the macro is called quite often.

To decide upon whether a code fragment be realized as a subprogram or as a macro, the following points are to be noted.

1. *Size:* The size of the code fragment is an important parameter. In the case of a macro, each call is replaced by the code fragment. Thus, if the size is significantly high, with all these substitutions, the compiled/assembled program may be quite big, which may result in slower execution of the program. On the other hand, a small fragment may better be implemented as macro, since substitution of it will not increase the code size significantly. At the same time, the saving in context switching will result in faster execution of the program.

2. *Number of parameters:* A large number of parameters in a subprogram will necessitate creating all of them in the stack at the time of its invocation. This will require large stack-area and may slow down execution.

3. *Debugging:* Debugging may be easier with a subprogram since the execution may be suspended at the entry to the subprogram. But, in the case of macros, the code

substitution will change the source line numbers and also setting breakpoints at each of the substituted code fragments become cumbersome.

4. *Recursion:* It cannot be implemented with a macro because the recursive calls are to be executed at the run-time and this is not possible at compile-time.

5. *Parameter passing:* Since in the macro expansion, each reference to a parameter within the body is substituted by the argument passed from the corresponding macro call, the only type of parameter passing strategy that can be supported is *call-by-name*. On the other hand, subprograms in most of the programming languages support *call-by-value* and/or *call-by-reference* strategies.

5.1 MACRO IN NASM

The syntax for macro definition in NASM is as follows:

```
%macro <macro-name> <num-of-parameters>
        Body of the macro
%endmacro
```

Thus, the macro definition is bounded by the %macro ... %endmacro directives. The declaration %macro is followed by the name of the macro being defined and an integer specifying the number of parameters. For example, a typical macro definition may look like this:

```
%macro foo 1
        PUSH EBP
        MOV EBP, ESP
        SUB ESP, %1
%endmacro
```

Here we have defined a macro named *foo* and having a single parameter. The parameters can be referred to within the body of the macro as %1, %2, etc. In this case, we have referred to the first (and only) parameter as %1 in "SUB ESP, %1".

A call to the macro follows the syntax,

```
<macro-name> <list-of-arguments>
```

The *list-of-arguments* will contain the arguments separated by commas. The first argument corresponds to the parameter %1, second one to %2, and so on. For example, a macro call may be like,

```
foo 12
```

This will be expanded into a piece of code as follows:

```
PUSH EBP
MOV EBP, ESP
SUB ESP, 12
```

If we need to pass a comma as part of a parameter, we can do so by enclosing the entire parameter in braces. For example, consider the macro *foo1*.

```
%macro foo1 2
    %2: DB %1
%endmacro
```

A call to the macro

```
foo1 'a', letter_a
```

expands as,

```
letter_a: DB 'a'
```

whereas a call like

```
foo1 {13,10}, crlf
```

will expand as,

```
crlf: DB 13,10.
```

5.1.1 Local Labels in Macro Body

A problem occurs if we have defined a label inside the macro body, and the macro is called more than once. In this case, in the expanded version of the code, the label gets multiply defined. This creates duplicate definitions during program compilation/assembly. For example, consider the following macro definition.

```
%macro foo2 2
        CMP %1, %2
        JGE L1
        MOV EAX, 0
        JMP L2
    L1: MOV EAX, 1
    L2:
%endmacro
```

Now, if the main program contains two calls to the macro, such as,

```
foo2 EAX, EBX
/* Do something */
foo2 ECX, EDX
```

the calls when expanded give the following piece of code.

```
CMP EAX, EBX
JGE L1
MOV EAX, 0
JMP L2
```

```
L1:     MOV EAX, 1
L2:
/* Do something */
        CMP ECX, EDX
        JGE L1
        MOV EAX, 0
        JMP L2
L1:     MOV EAX, 1
L2:
```

Clearly, in the expanded file there are two instances of $L1$ and two instances of $L2$. The assembler will definitely produce error messages that these labels have been redefined. However, while writing the macro, our intention was to associate $L1$ and $L2$ with a particular call to the macro. In NASM, this can be accomplished by modifying $L1$ and $L2$ as %%$L1$ and %%$L2$ respectively. Thus, the macro *foo2* is redefined as follows:

```
%macro foo2 2
        CMP %1, %2
        JGE %%L1
        MOV EAX, 0
        JMP %%L2
    %%L1:MOV EAX, 1
    %%L2:
%endmacro
```

This macro can be called as many times as we want, and every time we call it, NASM will internally make up different *real* names to substitute for the labels %%$L1$ and %%$L2$. The names NASM invents are of the form "..@2345.$L1$", where the number 2345 changes with every macro call. As a programmer, we should avoid this type of labels (that is, labels starting with "..@") in our program, as these may interfere with the names used in NASM macro expansion.

5.1.2 Nested Macros

Though not supported fully by NASM, a powerful feature of many macroprocessors including MASM is to handle nested macros. Nesting can come in two different ways.

1. **Macro definition nesting.** New macros may be defined within the body of another macro. For example, in the following, we define macro *foo4* within the body of *foo3*.

```
%macro foo3 2
    MOV EAX, %1
    MOV EBX, %2
    ADD EAX, EBX
    %macro foo4 1
        MOV ECX, %1
        INC ECX
    %endmacro
```

```
    MOV %2, EAX
%endmacro
```

Here, the macro *foo4* is encapsulated within macro *foo3*. Thus, *foo4* is not directly visible to the code outside *foo3*. However, once *foo3* has been called, *foo4* also becomes visible. From that point onwards, *foo4* can also be called directly without calling *foo3* anymore. Thus, the calling sequence,

```
foo3 ECX, data1
    ⋮
foo4 EDX
```

is a valid one. But the sequence,

```
foo4 EDX
    ⋮
foo3 ECX, data1
```

will produce an error as *foo4* at the first place is undefined.

2. **Macro call nesting.** Macro calls may be nested in the sense that from within the body of one macro, there can be a call to a previously defined macro. For example, in the following, we have first defined the macro *foo4* and then in the body of *foo3*, a call has been made to *foo4*.

```
%macro foo4 1
    MOV ECX, %1
    INC ECX
%endmacro
%macro foo3 2
    MOV EAX, %1
    MOV EBX, %2
    ADD EAX, EBX
    foo4 EDX
    MOV %2, EAX
%endmacro
```

5.2 DESIGN OF MACROPROCESSORS

In this section, we will discuss the design of macroprocessors. Since in a program there can be a few macro definitions and some calls to them, it is quite intuitive to follow a two-pass macroprocessor design, in which the first pass takes note of the macro definitions, while the second pass performs the actual expansions. However, in the light of nested macro definitions, a two-pass design of macroprocessor is not a desirable one. This is because of the fact that in such a situation, Pass I will take a note of the outer macro definition but have no idea about the inner one. Later, in the second pass, at the time of expanding a call to the outer macro, it will come across the inner nested macro definition. Since macro definition is to be handled in Pass I, Pass II should now transfer the control back to Pass I for dealing with the definition. Thus effectively, the design of macroprocessor becomes a single pass one. In this section, we will concentrate on the design of single-pass macroprocessors only. However, a two-pass design may be followed if there are no nested macro definitions. A two-pass design will also provide flexibility in putting the macro calls even before the definition of the corresponding macro in the file.

5.2.1 Major Data Structures

The major data structures involved in the design of a macroprocessor are as follows:

- Macro Definition Table (MDT)
- Macro Name Table (MNT)
- Argument List Array (ALA)

1. **Macro Definition Table (MDT):** It holds the macro definitions present in the input source file. As the macroprocessor scans through the source lines, it comes across the definition of newer macros. The body of a newly defined macro is put into MDT. Structurally, an MDT is a one-dimensional array of character strings. Each entry in this array corresponds to a line in the macro. The table helps in the process of expansion, during which the lines are retrieved from the MDT, the parameters (if any) are replaced by the actual arguments passed and are substituted into the source file.

2. **Macro Name Table (MNT):** This table holds one entry for each macro defined in the input source file. Typical entries in this table include:

   (a) *Name* — the name of the macro being defined.

   (b) *Num-of-parameters* — the number of parameters that the macro uses.

   (c) *MDT-start-index* — index of the MDT from which the body of the macro is stored in MDT.

   (d) *MDT-end-index* — index of the MDT up to which the body of the macro occupies in MDT.

The structure of MNT has been shown in Fig. 5.1.

Name	Num-of-parameters	MDT-start-index	MDT-end-index

FIGURE 5.1 Macro name table structure.

3. **Argument List Array (ALA):** This is a table dynamically created upon encountering a macro call to hold the arguments passed. The content of this table is utilized during the expansion process. Structurally, this is a one-dimensional array of strings, each entry corresponding to an argument passed. Once the processing of a call is over, the content of this table is not needed any more, and thus can be deleted or overwritten by the arguments passed in the next macro expansion call.

   A problem arises when nested macros are encountered. For example, consider the following scenario.

```
%macro foo4 1
   ⋮
%endmacro
%macro foo3 2
   ⋮
   foo4 EDX
   ⋮
%endmacro
foo3 EAX, EBX
```

   Here, on seeing the call *foo3 EAX, EBX*, ALA is set up with two entries in it. This ALA is used to expand the body of *foo3*. However, at the call *foo4 EDX*, the ALA gets overwritten. The new ALA has got only entry EDX in it. With this, *foo4* is expanded. At the end of this expansion of *foo4*, we need the previous ALA to expand the remaining part of *foo3* after the call to *foo4*. It suggests that we preserve the previous ALA in a stack so that it can be retrieved later. In this modified scheme, ALA gets created into stack. At a call to a macro, the stack frame is created and pushed into the stack. Upon the end of expansion, the frame is to be popped out. A typical frame structure has been shown in Fig. 5.2. Apart from the original arguments passed, it also holds the value of the *previous frame pointer*. A pointer named *current frame pointer* points to the frame containing ALA for the current macro expansion under progress. Assuming that the stack grows upwards with decreasing address, *previous frame pointer* can be accessed by negative offset from the *current frame pointer*, while the actual arguments can be accessed with positive offsets.

5.2.2 Macroprocessing Technique

After having an idea about the major data structures involved in macroprocessing, next we will look into the exact steps in handling macro definitions and calls. We will assume that the macroprocessor will take as input a source file containing macro definitions and calls. After processing the file, it produces an output file in which all the calls are replaced by the bodies of the corresponding macros, the macro definitions have been filtered out and other parts (not corresponding to macros) have been copied verbatim. The idea has been shown in Fig. 5.3.

We will look into the design of macroprocessors with increasing complexities. First, we will look into a design that does support only simple macro definitions and calls, that is, it neither

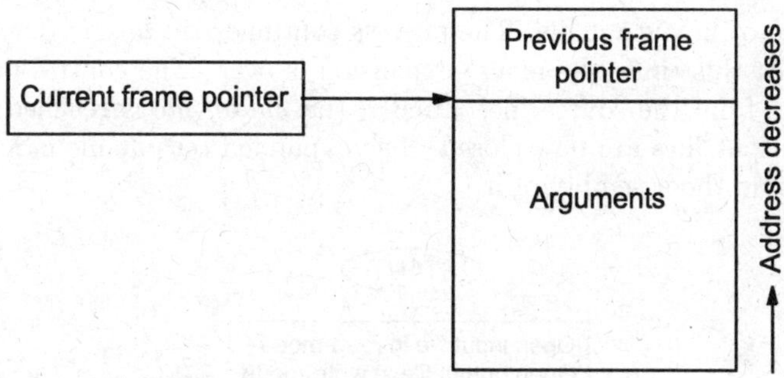

FIGURE 5.2 Argument list array structure.

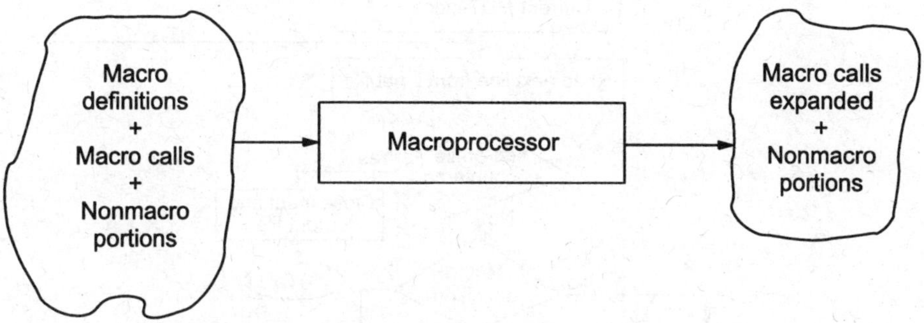

FIGURE 5.3 Input-output of a macroprocessor.

supports nested macro definitions nor nested calls. The second design will be able to handle nested calls, but not nested definitions. While the third one will have the full capability to handle both the nested definitions and calls.

5.2.3 Simple Macroprocessor without Nesting

The control flow for this simple macroprocessor has been shown in Fig. 5.4. To start with, the input file is opened in read-mode, while the output file is opened in write-mode. The variable *current-MDT-index* is set to one. This variable holds the index of the MDT where the next line of the body of a macro definition can be put. The source lines are now read one-by-one. If the line read next is neither a macro definition nor a macro call, it is copied verbatim into the output file. On the other hand, if the line contains a macro definition, entries are made into the MNT for this newly seen macro. The name of the macro and number of parameters are put into the MNT. *MDT-start-index* is set to *current-MDT-index* as this is the place from where the macro body will reside in MDT. Now, the next lines are read from the source file and copied into successive locations in MDT till the *end-of-macro* declaration is seen. At this point *MDT-end-index* in MNT is set to *current-MDT-index - 1.* Processing continues by reading the next input line. If the input line contains a macro call, first the corresponding ALA is created to hold the parameters passed. Since we are not considering the nested macro calls, the ALA can be a simple array instead of a stack frame. Now the system is ready to do the expansion. The variable *lno* is set to the *MDT-start-index* of the macro being called. The successive lines are now read from the MDT, the arguments are replaced by the parameters passed through

ALA and copied into the output file. The process continues till *lno* becomes greater than the *MDT-end-index*. At this time, the macro expansion is over. The control passes back to read the next input line from the source file. Finally, the *end-of-file* is reached for the input file. Both input and output files are now closed. The expanded output file can now be passed on to an assembler to do the assembly of it.

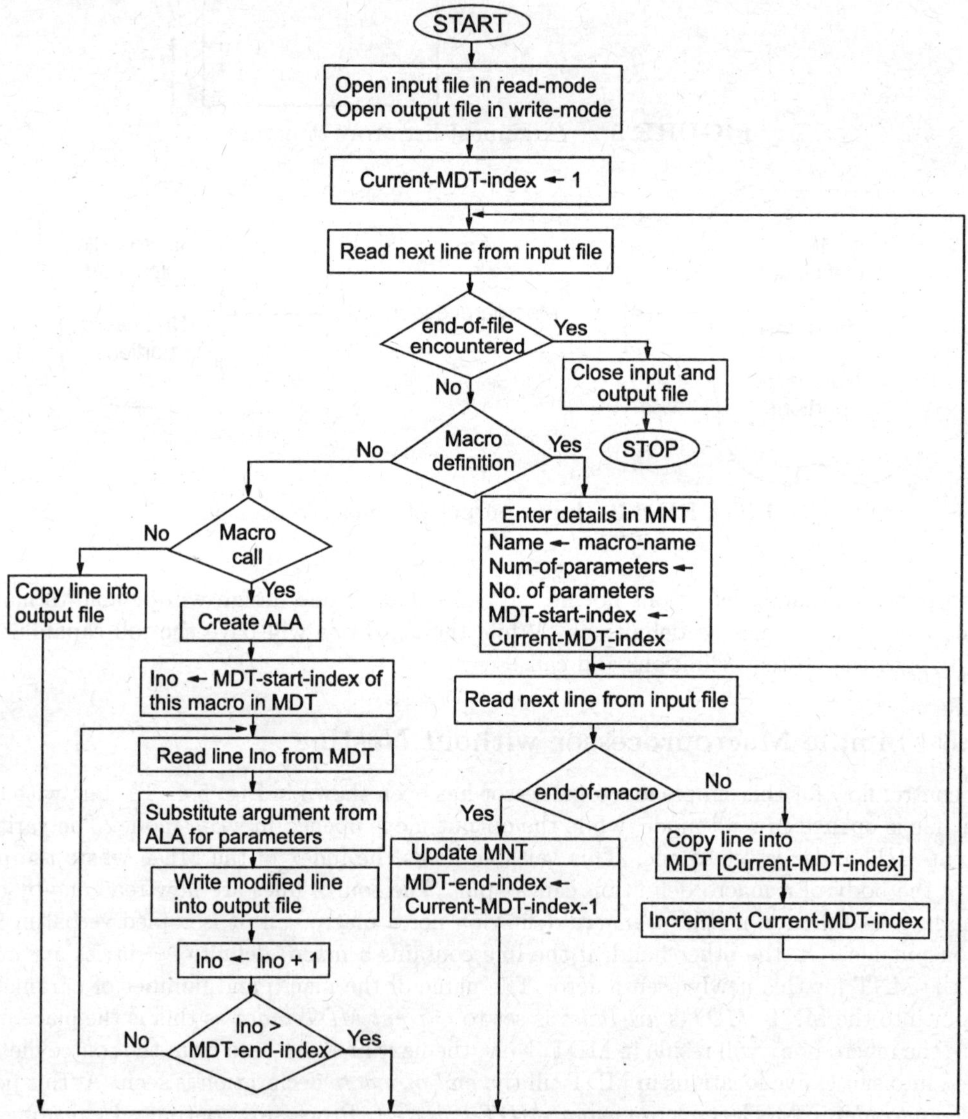

FIGURE 5.4 Design of a simple macroprocessor.

EXAMPLE 5.1 To understand the operation of this simple macroprocessor further, let us consider the following code fragment.

```
1   PUSH EAX
2   %macro foo1 1
3   PUSH EBP
4   MOV EBP, ESP
5   SUB ESP, %1
6   %endmacro
7   MOV EAX, EBX
8   %macro foo2 2
9   %2: db %1
10  %endmacro
11  foo1 ECX
12  MOV EBX, EAX
13  foo2 'a', letter_a
14  ADD EAX, EBX
```

At line 1, it is neither a macro definition, nor a call. Hence, the line is copied as it is to the output file. At line 2, it comes across the definition of macro *foo1*. Appropriate entries are made into MNT. The next few lines (line 3, 4, and 5) are copied to the MDT. At line 6, on getting the end of macro declaration, MNT is updated. The content of MNT and MDT at this position has been shown in Fig. 5.5(a) and (b) respectively. The next line, 7 is copied directly to the output file. At line 8, another macro definition *foo2* is found. The corresponding entries are made into MNT. Line 9 is put into MDT. At line 10, MNT is updated to end the definition of macro *foo2*. The MNT and MDT entries at this point have been shown in Fig. 5.5(c) and (d) respectively. At line 11, a call to the macro *foo1* is encountered. ALA is created accordingly as shown in Fig. 5.5(e). Expansion of *foo1* starts. MNT tells that the macro starts at MDT index 1. Thus, the first line "PUSH EBP" is retrieved. Since there is no argument to be substituted here, the line is put into the output file. The next line is also copied to the output file without any change. The line "SUB ESP, %1" is modified as "SUB ESP, ECX" by consulting the ALA. The modified line is written into the output file. This ends expansion of *foo1*. The control goes back to read from the input file at line no. 12, and it is copied as it is to the output file. At line 13, in response to the call to macro *foo2*, the ALA is created with two entries as shown in Fig. 5.5(f). The lines corresponding to *foo2* are read from MDT. The line "%2: db %1" is modified as "letter_a: db 'a' " and written to the output file. Control returns to line 14 and the line is copied as it is into the output file. The final content of the output file becomes as follows:

```
PUSH EAX
MOV EAX, EBX
PUSH EBP
MOV EBP, ESP
SUB ESP, ECX
MOV EBX, EAX
letter_a: db 'a'
ADD EAX, EBX
```

Name	Num-of parameters	MDT-start-index	MDT-end-index
foo1	1	1	3

(a) MNT after line 6.

PUSH EBP
MOV EBP, ESP
SUB ESP, %1

(b) MDT after line 6.

Name	Num-of parameters	MDT-start-index	MDT-end-index
foo1	1	1	3
foo2	2	4	4

(c) MNT after line 10.

PUSH EBP
MOV EBP, ESP
SUB ESP, %1
%2: db %1

(d) MDT after line 10.

ECX

(e) ALA created at line 11.

'a'
letter_a

(f) ALA created at line 13.

FIGURE 5.5 Various stages in processing Example 5.1.

5.2.4 Macroprocessing with Nested Calls

Now we will consider a more powerful macroprocessor that can handle nested macro calls. However, we do not consider nested definition at this stage. As compared to the simple macroprocessor design in Section 5.2.3, in case of nested macro calls, we can come across another macro call while expanding a previous one. As discussed earlier, for this case we need to create the ALA in a stack, so that the previous ALA can be restored once the expansion of the inner macro is over. Another variable *Nesting_Depth* is necessary to take a decision about whether the next line to be processed be read from the source file or the MDT. At the beginning, *Nesting_Depth* is initialized to zero. As we go into a macro expansion, *Nesting_Depth* is incremented by one. On the other hand, it is decremented as soon as a macro expansion is over. Thus, if *Nesting_Depth* is greater than zero, the next line should be read from the MDT, otherwise it is to be read from the input source file. The design of this improved macroprocessor has been shown in Fig. 5.6.

EXAMPLE 5.2 To understand the process better, let us consider the following piece of code with nested macro calls.

```
PUSH EAX
%macro foo1 1
PUSH EBP
MOV EBP, ESP
SUB ESP, %1
%endmacro
MOV EAX, EBX
```

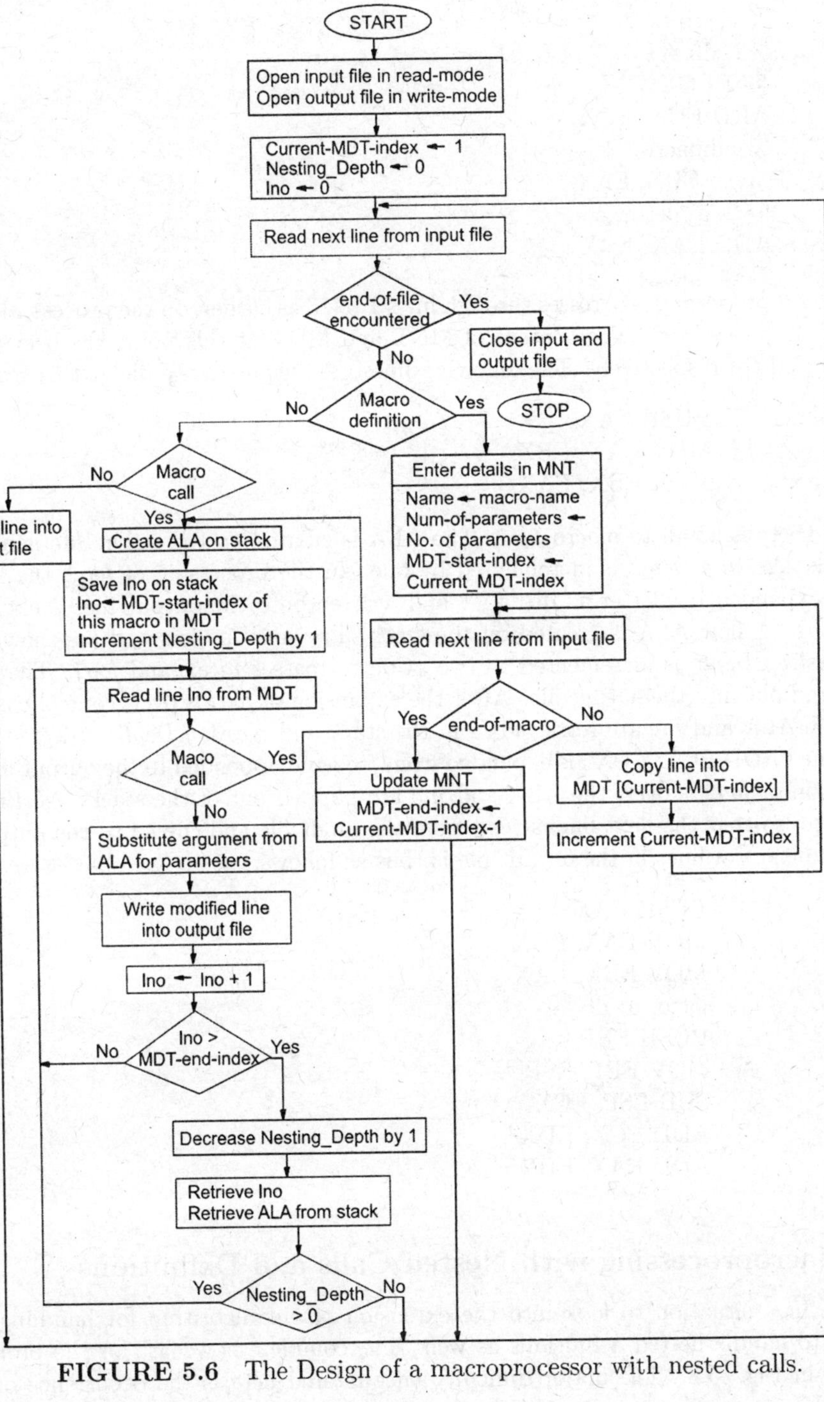

FIGURE 5.6 The Design of a macroprocessor with nested calls.

```
8    %macro foo2 2
9    %2: db %1
10   fool ECX
11   ADD ECX, EDX
12   %endmacro
13   MOV EBX, EAX
14   foo2 'a', letter_a
15   ADD EAX, EBX
```

Here the macroprocessing progresses through lines 1 to 13 as earlier. In the process, the macros *foo1* and *foo2* get defined. The content of MNT and MDT at this point has been shown in Fig. 5.7(a) and (b) respectively. The following lines are output to the file at this stage.

```
PUSH EAX
MOV EAX, EBX
MOV EBX, EAX
```

At line 14, there is a call to macro *foo2*. The ALA is created on the stack. *lno* is also saved in the stack. *Nesting_Depth* is incremented by one. In the processing of *foo2*, the line "%2: db %1" is expanded to "letter_a: db 'a' ", and written onto the output file. Next, there is a call to *foo1*. A new ALA is created on the stack. Previous *lno* is saved (as shown in Fig. 5.7(c)). *Nesting_Depth* is incremented to two. Control passes to expand *foo1*. The lines are expanded and put into the output file. After the expansion of *foo1* is over, control comes back to *foo2*. The ALA and *lno* are retrieved from the stack and *Nesting_Depth* is decremented to one. The line "ADD ECX, EDX" is expanded from *foo2* and appended to the output file. After the expansion of *foo2* is over, the ALA and *lno* are popped out of the stack. *Nesting_Depth* becomes zero, so that the next line is read from the input file and copied to the output. The complete sequence of lines in the output file is thus as follows:

```
PUSH EAX
MOV EAX, EBX
MOV EBX, EAX
letter_a: db 'a'
PUSH EBP
MOV EBP, ESP
SUB ESP, ECX
ADD ECX, EDX
ADD EAX, EBX
```

5.2.5 Macroprocessing with Nested Calls and Definitions

Now we are in a situation to look into the extension of our algorithm for handling nested macro calls to handle nested definitions as well. The complete flowchart for the process has been shown in Fig. 5.8. The major difficulty encountered here is the occurrence of macro definition while expanding a call. If the control is inside a macro expansion, the value of *Nesting_Depth* is greater than zero. This information has been utilized to choose the source to read next line during a macro definition. If the macro definition is part of an expansion call,

Name	Num-of parameters	MDT-start-index	MDT-end-index
foo1	1	1	3
foo2	2	4	6

(a) MNT after line 12.

PUSH EBP
MOV EBP, ESP
SUB ESP, %1
%2: db %1
fool1 ECX
ADD ECX, EDX

(b) MDT after line 12.

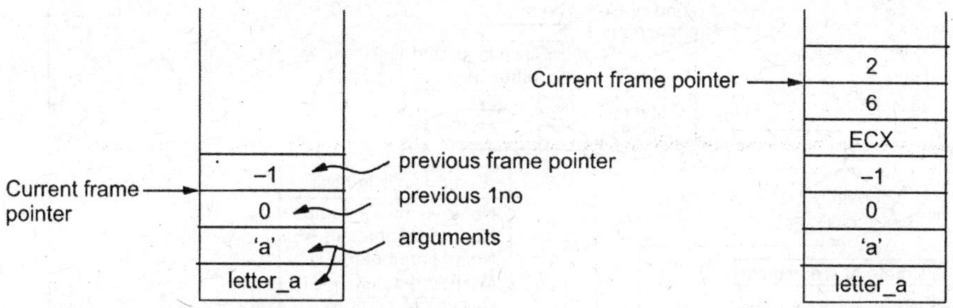

(c) Stack content at call to foo2. (d) Stack content at call to foo1.

FIGURE 5.7 Various stages in processing Example 5.2.

Nesting_Depth is non-zero. In that case, lines are read from MDT instead of input source file. On the other hand, if the value is zero, lines are read from the input file directly. Similarly, at the end of definition of a macro, a check is made (via *Nesting_Depth*) to see the point to which control be transferred. For a non-zero *Nesting_Depth*, control is transferred to the previous macro expansion that was in progress, otherwise, control is transferred to read source-file lines. Finally, during the processing of a macro expansion, check is made to see whether we have come across a macro definition or not. In that case, control is transferred to enter the macro into MNT and MDT.

EXAMPLE 5.3 Let us consider the following piece of code to understand the handling of nested macro definitions.

```
PUSH EAX
%macro fool 1
PUSH EBP
%macro foo2 2
%2: db %1
%endmacro
MOV EBP, ESP
SUB ESP, %1
%endmacro
MOV EAX, EBX
fool ECX
ADD ECX, EDX
foo2 'a', letter_a
ADD EAX, EBX
```

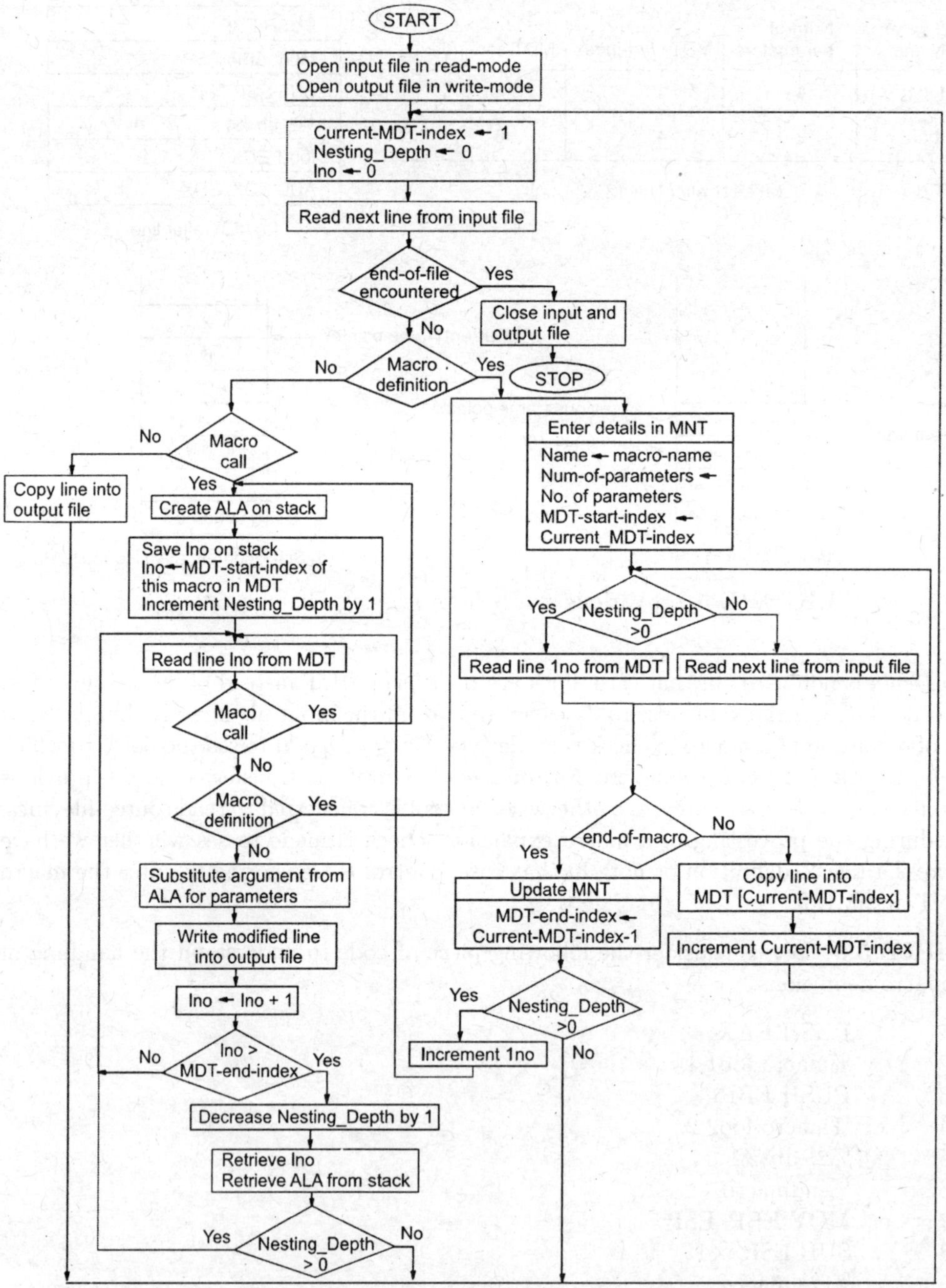

FIGURE 5.8 The design of a macroprocessor with nested definitions and calls.

Here, when we have seen up to line 9, only one macro, namely, *foo1* has been defined. The content of MNT and MDT at this point has been shown in Fig. 5.9(a) and (b) respectively.

Line 10 is copied to the output. At line 11, there is a call to *foo1*. Thus, *Nesting_Depth* is incremented to one. ALA is created on the stack and control passes to expand *foo1*. The line "PUSH EBP" is copied to the output. Next, the definition of *foo2* is encountered. Appropriate entries are made into MNT. The body of *foo2* is put into MDT. The content of MNT and MDT at this point has been shown in Fig. 5.9(c) and (d) respectively. After reaching the end of the definition of *foo2*, control returns to the expansion of *foo1*. The line "MOV EBP, ESP" is copied to the output file. The line "SUB ESP, %1" is substituted as "SUB ESP, ECX" and put into the output file. Expansion of *foo1* is now over. The line "ADD ECX, EDX" is copied to the output. At line 13, a call to *foo2* is encountered and is processed as discussed earlier. It may be noted that before the call to *foo1* at line 11, the macro *foo2* is undefined, as there is no MNT entry for this till then. Thus, for nested macro definition, the inner macro remains undefined till the outer one has been called for the first time. Of course, beyond the first time, the inner macro is always having an entry into MNT, and thus it is defined. The complete expanded code is as shown below:

```
PUSH EAX
MOV EAX, EBX
PUSH EBP
MOV EBP, ESP
SUB ESP, ECX
ADD ECX, EDX
letter_a: db 'a'
ADD EAX, EBX
```

Name	Num-of parameters	MDT-start-index	MDT-end-index
foo1	1	1	6

(a) MNT after line 9.

PUSH EBP
%macro foo2 2
%2: db %1
%endmacro
MOV EBP, ESP
SUB ESP, %1

(b) MDT after line 9.

Name	Num-of parameters	MDT-start-index	MDT-end-index
foo1	1	1	6
foo2	2	7	7

(c) MNT after line 11.

PUSH EBP
%macro foo2 2
%2: db %1
%endmacro
MOV EBP, ESP
SUB ESP, %1
%2: db %1

(d) MDT after line 11.

FIGURE 5.9 Various stages in processing Example 5.3.

5.3 CONCLUSION

In this chapter, we have seen the design of a macroprocessor to handle macros defined in an assembly language program. The major data structures have been reviewed. A detailed discussion has been carried out to design macroprocessors with increasing complexity. In the next chapter, we will look into the design of another very useful system program—the *compiler*.

EXERCISES

5.1 What is a macro? How does it differ from a subprogram?

5.2 For a small code fragment to be used repetitively in the program, how is it decided whether to implement it using subprogram or using macro?

5.3 Write a macro to compare between two numbers and determine the maximum. Use it for the following:

(a) Determine maximum of 10 numbers.

(b) Sort 10 numbers.

5.4 How are local labels handled in macroprocessing?

5.5 Enumerate the major data structures for macroprocessors.

5.6 Why macroprocessors with nested definitions are generally single-pass?

5.7 Explain the operation of the macroprocessor over the example in *Exercise 5.3*.

5.8 For the example macro shown below, explain the operation of the macroprocessor.

```
PUSH EAX
%macro foo1 3
PUSH EBP
%macro foo2 4
%2: db %1
%3: db %1
%4: db %1
%endmacro
MOV EBP, ESP
SUB ESP, %1
ADD ESP, %2
MOV EDX, %3
%endmacro
MOV EAX, EBX
foo1 ECX, EAX, ECX
ADD ECX, EDX
foo2 'a', letter_a, letter_b, letter_c
ADD EAX, EBX
```

5.9 For the example macro shown below, explain the operation of the macroprocessor.

```
PUSH EAX
%macro foo1 1
PUSH EBP
%macro foo2 2
foo1 EBX
%2: db %1
%endmacro
MOV EBP, ESP
SUB ESP, %1
%endmacro
MOV EAX, EBX
foo1 ECX
ADD ECX, EDX
foo2 'a', letter_a
ADD EAX, EBX
```

Chapter 6

Compiler

Compilers are tools to convert high-level language programs to machine language. It may directly convert the program to machine language or generate the assembly language code, which is further converted to machine language using an *assembler.* Complexity of the design of the compiler depends on various factors, including the programming language constructs, target machine architecture, level of optimization, etc. To handle the complex process of compiler designing, it is divided into a number of submodules/phases. A diagram showing the flow of control through the phases has been given in Fig. 6.1. Essentially, it consists of the stages, namely, *lexical analysis, syntax analysis, semantic analysis, intermediate code generation, target code generation,* and *code optimization.* In this chapter, we will be discussing each of them.

6.1 LEXICAL ANALYSIS

The lexical analyzer acts as an interface between the input source program to be compiled and the later stages of the compiler. The input program can be considered to be a sequence of characters. Lexical analyzer converts this character stream into a stream of valid words of the language, better known as *tokens.* The parser looks into the sequence of tokens and identifies the language constructs occurring in the input program. However, the parser and the lexical analyzer work hand-in-hand, in the sense that whenever the parser needs further tokens to proceed, it requests the lexical analyzer. The lexical analyzer, in turn, scans the remaining input stream and returns the next token occurring there. The idea is explained in Fig. 6.2. Apart from that, the lexical analyzer also participates in the creation and maintenance of *Symbol Table.* This is because, lexical analyzer is the first module to identify the occurrence of a symbol. If the symbol is getting defined for the first time, it needs to be installed into the symbol table. Lexical analyzer is mostly used for doing this. Some of the other fields of the symbol table (like, *type, size,* etc.) are generally filled up by the parser. For later occurrences of the symbol, the symbol table is searched to extract the relevant information about it. The lexical analyzer is also responsible for removing the cosmetics from the program—like extra white spaces, comments, etc.

Definitions. Next we introduce a few definitions to make our further discussion clear. To

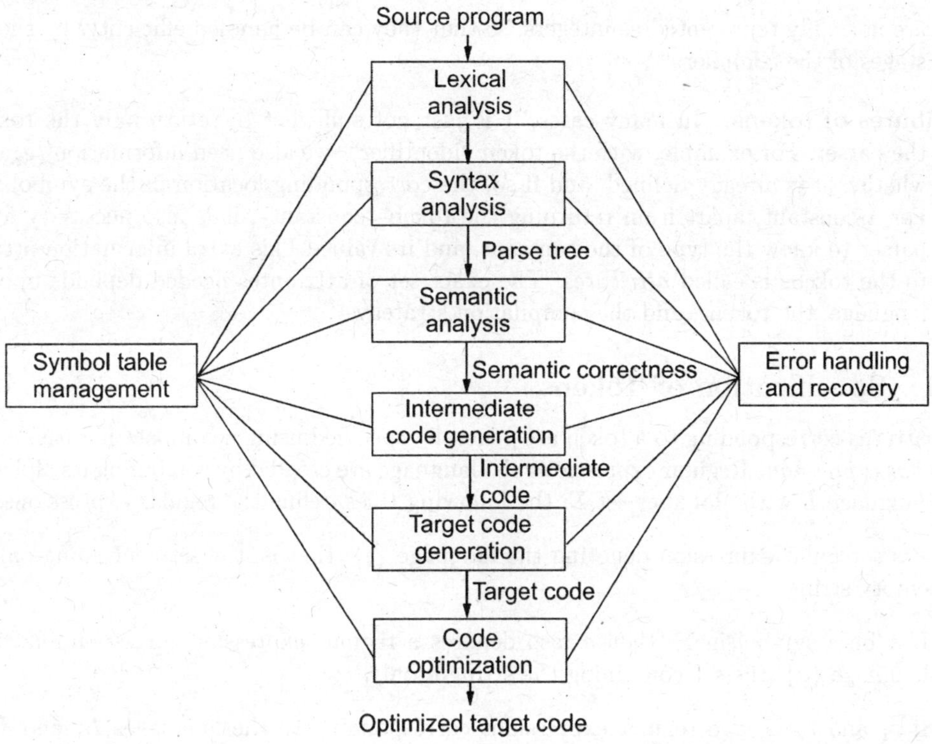

FIGURE 6.1 Phases of a compiler.

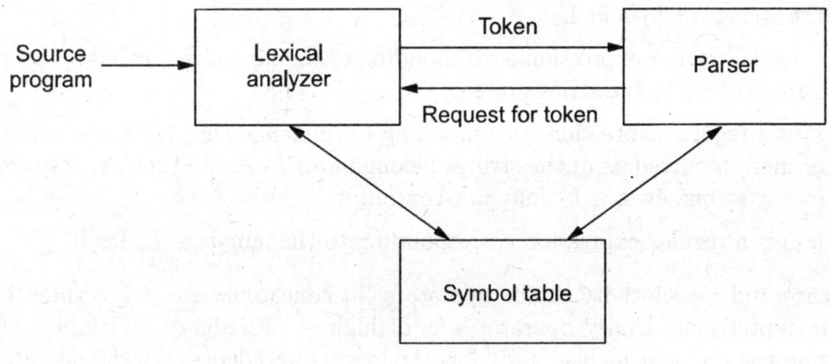

FIGURE 6.2 Role of the lexical analyzer.

start with, let us think of the definition of possible identifiers that can occur in some programming language. Suppose, in the language, identifiers are defined to be a sequence of characters consisting of letters 'a' to 'z', digits '0' to '9', and the underscore character '_'. Then, a few possible identifiers are "abc", "a_b1", etc. — each of these occurring in a program is called a *lexeme*. The definition of the identifier is called a *pattern*. For each of these lexemes, the lexical analyzer returns the token "identifier". The tokens are normally represented as integers, so that they can be handled efficiently by the later stages of the compiler.

Attributes of tokens. In many cases, it is just not sufficient to return only the token to the parser. For example, with the token "identifier", we also need information regarding whether it is already defined, and if so, the corresponding location in the symbol table. For a constant, apart from returning the token "constant", it is also necessary for the parser to know the type of the constant, and its value. This extra information attached to the tokens is called *attributes.* The exact set of attributes needed depends upon the language, the tokens, and the compilation strategy.

6.1.1 Specification of Tokens

The patterns corresponding to a token are generally specified using a compact notation known as *regular expression.* Regular expressions of a language are created by combining its alphabets. For a language L with alphabet set Σ, the following rules define the regular expressions:

1. ϵ is a regular expression denoting the language $\{\epsilon\}$, that is, the set containing only the empty string.

2. If a be a symbol in Σ, then a also denotes a regular expression corresponding to the language $\{a\}$, the set containing the string a only.

3. If r_1 and r_2 be two regular expressions corresponding to the languages L_1 and L_2 respectively then,

   (a) $r_1|r_2$ is a regular expression corresponding to the language $L_1 \cup L_2$, containing all the strings of L_1 and L_2.

   (b) r_1r_2 is a regular expression corresponding to the language created by concatenating strings of L_2 to the strings of L_1.

   (c) r_1^* is a regular expression corresponding to the language L_1^*, that is, containing zero or more occurrences of the strings belonging to L_1. Note that, L_1^* also contains the empty string, even if L_1 may not contain it.

   (d) (r_1) is a regular expression corresponding to the language L_1 itself.

Precedence and associativity of the operators '|', concatenation and '$*$' may be used to simplify the expression. Unary operator $*$ is of highest precedence and is left associative. Concatenation has the next highest and | has the lowest precedence. All the operators are left associative.

EXAMPLE 6.1 For $\Sigma = \{0,1\}$, let us consider the following regular expressions:

1. $(0|1)^*$ denotes all binary strings including the empty string.

2. $(0|1)(0|1)^*$ denotes all the nonempty binary strings.

3. $0(0|1)^*0$ denotes all binary strings of length at least two, both starting and ending with 0's.

4. $((\epsilon|0)1^*)^*$ denotes all binary strings.

5. $(0|1)^*0(0|1)(0|1)$ denotes all binary strings with at least three characters, in which the third-last character is always zero.

6. $0^*10^*10^*10^*$ denotes all binary strings possessing exactly three 1's.

Most of the programming languages define variables as *letter (letter | digit | '_')**, that is, any variable name is a sequence of *letters*, *digits* and the underscore character ('_') with the restriction that it must start with a letter. The set of signed integers may be specified as

$$(+|-|\epsilon)\ \textit{digit}\ (\textit{digit})^*$$

Here, the portion '$+|-|\epsilon$' represents the fact that an integer may have an explicit sign (+ or −), or the sign may be absent (ϵ), in which case, it is assumed to be a positive number. The later part *digit (digit)** corresponds to the one or more digits that the number contains. The set of floating point numbers similarly be specified as,

$$(+|-|\epsilon)\ \textit{digit}\ (\textit{digit})^*\ (\cdot\ \textit{digit}\ (\textit{digit})^*|\epsilon)((\mathrm{E}\ (+|-|\epsilon)\ \textit{digit}\ (\textit{digit})^*)\ |\epsilon)$$

6.1.2 Token Recognition

In the previous section, we have seen how to specify tokens of a language using the compact notation called *regular expression.* In this section, we describe how to construct recognizers that can identify the tokens occurring in an input stream. These recognizers are most widely known as *Finite Automata.* As the name suggests, it is a machine with a finite number of states in which the machine can remain. There is a distinctive *Start state,* in which the machine starts. Between the states, there are transitions labelled by alphabets of the language. If the machine is at state S_i, and there is a transition labelled $a_k \in \Sigma$ (the alphabet set) to the state S_j, then the machine can perform that transition provided that the current input symbol is a_k. Starting from the *Start state*, depending upon the input stream, the machine finally reaches some state after exhausting all input symbols. There are two types of such final states. The set of final states reachable for valid input streams (tokens) are called *acceptor states* or simply *final states.* On the other hand, states reached by input streams not corresponding to any of the tokens are called *failure states* or *reject states.* For example, consider the finite automata shown in Fig. 6.3. It corresponds to the regular expression *ab*. Here, state-0 is the start state, 3 is a final state, and 4 is a reject state. *Start* state is identified by an incoming edge without any predecessor. *Final* states are double-circled. A *reject* state contains a self-loop labelled by all possible input symbols. Input streams are assumed to be terminated by \$. It is easy to see that only for the input *ab*\$, the machine reaches the accepting state 3. For any other input, it reaches the reject state 4. For the sake of brevity, the reject states are normally not shown. In that case, if the machine is in state s_i and there does not exist any possible transition from s_i on the next input symbol, the input is rejected. Transitions on \$ are also not shown. Thus the simplified machine is as shown in Fig. 6.4.

There are two types of finite automata – *Nondeterministic finite automata (NFA)* and *Deterministic Finite Automata (DFA).* The basic difference between the two lies in the presence of non-determinism in the transitions of NFA, which is made deterministic in DFA. In the discussion that follows, we detail the NFA and DFA constructions.

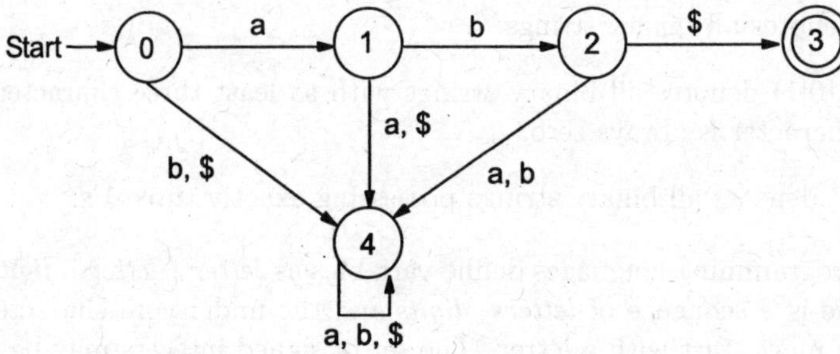

FIGURE 6.3 Finite automata for *ab*.

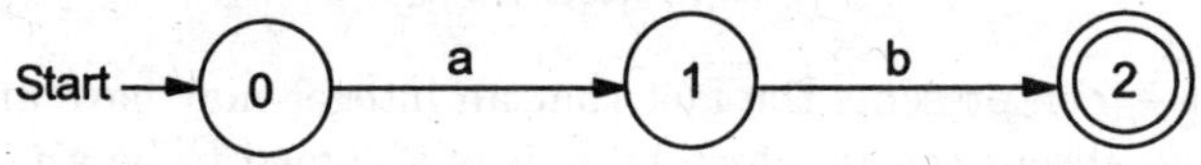

FIGURE 6.4 Simplified finite automata for *ab*.

Nondeterministic Finite Automata (NFA). The basic feature of a nondeterministic finite automata is its ability to have more than one possible transitions from a state on the same input symbol. For example, from state s_i, there may be transitions to two distinct states s_j and s_k labelled by the same input symbol a_m. The actual transition occurring is to be chosen nondeterministically by the machine. Another nondeterminism lies with the transitions labelled by ϵ, known as ϵ-transitions. If there is an ϵ-transition from state s_i to state s_j, then the machine can do such a transition without consuming any further inputs. An input stream is said to be accepted (that is, recognized) by the automata if there exists at least one path (deterministic/nondeterministic) from the start state of the machine to one of its final states whose transitions are governed by the input stream.

EXAMPLE 6.2 The following are a few examples of NFA.

1. For the regular expression 0(0|1)*0, the NFA is shown in Fig. 6.5. Here, from state 1, there are two transitions labelled 0—one to the state 1 itself, and the other to state 2.

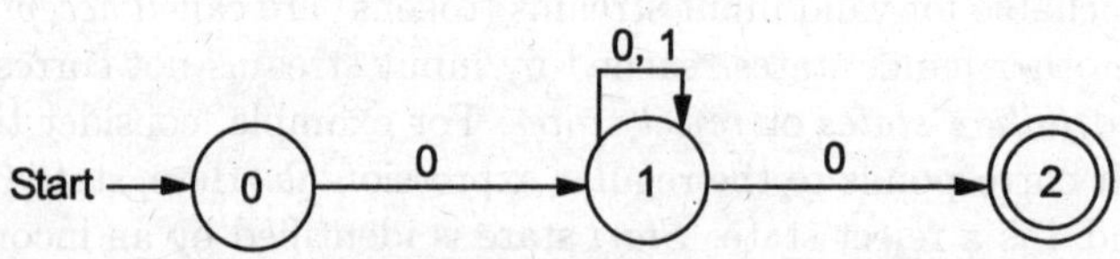

FIGURE 6.5 NFA for 0(0|1)*0.

2. For the regular expression 01|10, the NFA is shown in Fig. 6.6. Here from state 0, there are two ϵ-transitions to the states 1 and 4 respectively.

Deterministic Finite Automata (DFA). As compared to an NFA, in a DFA the transitions are deterministic. Thus, there cannot be more than one transition emanating from the same state labelled by the same input symbol. Secondly, there cannot be any ϵ-transitions.

EXAMPLE 6.3 The following are a few examples of DFA.

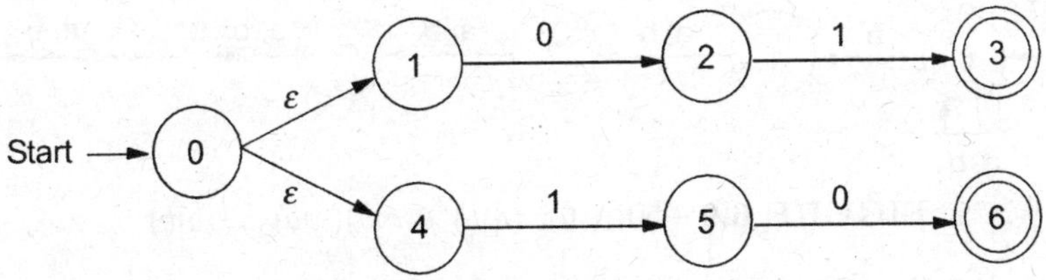

FIGURE 6.6 NFA for 01|10.

EXAMPLE 6.3 The following are a few examples of DFA.

1. For the regular expression 0(0|1)*0, the DFA is shown in Fig. 6.7. As it can be seen, for any state, no two transitions have been labelled the same.

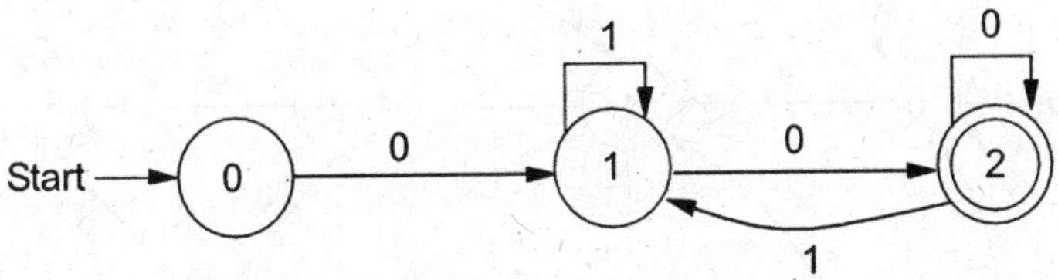

FIGURE 6.7 DFA for 0(0|1)*0.

2. For the regular expression 01|10, the DFA is shown in Fig. 6.8.

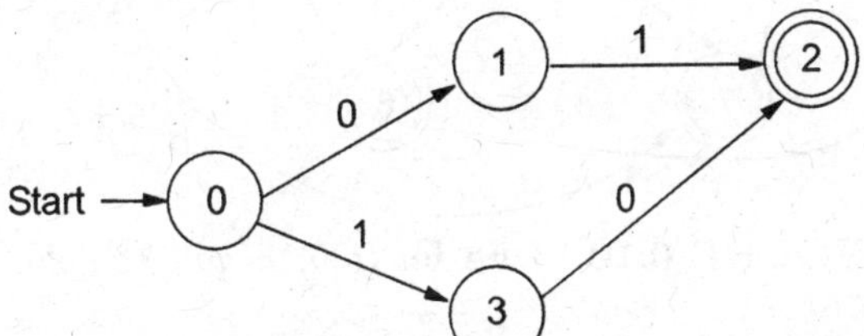

FIGURE 6.8 DFA for 01|10.

We will see shortly that for every NFA, we can construct an equivalent DFA. Thus, the availability of nondeterminism does not make NFA more powerful as compared to a DFA. However, what matters are the sizes (number of states) of these machines. As it should be understood, the absence of nondeterminism may require a good penalty to be paid by DFA in terms of number of states. Each and every nondeterministic alternative of an NFA gets converted into an explicit path from start state to a final state in the corresponding DFA. This often results into an explosion in the number of states for a DFA. For example, consider the regular expression $(a|b)^*a(a|b)(a|b)\ldots(a|b)$, where there are $(n-1)$ such $(a|b)$ at the end. This represents strings over the alphabet set $\Sigma = \{a, b\}$, in which the n-th character from the end is always a. The NFA for this regular expression is shown in Fig. 6.9. It has $(n+1)$ states, with a nondeterminism in state 0, from which it can either make a transition to state 1, or remain in state 0, for the same input a.

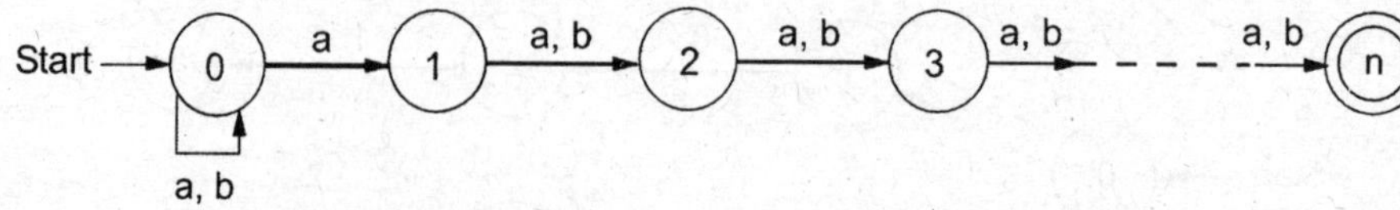

FIGURE 6.9 NFA for $(a|b)^*a(a|b)(a|b)\ldots(a|b)$.

On the other hand, if we try to construct a DFA for this, we have to consider all possible strings over $\{a, b\}$ in which the n-th character from the end is a, and the remaining $(n-1)$ characters after it are a's or b's. Thus, for $n = 3$, we have to consider the cases $(a|b)^*a(aa|ab|ba|bb)$. A DFA for this is shown in Fig. 6.10. Here we essentially construct a machine that keeps track

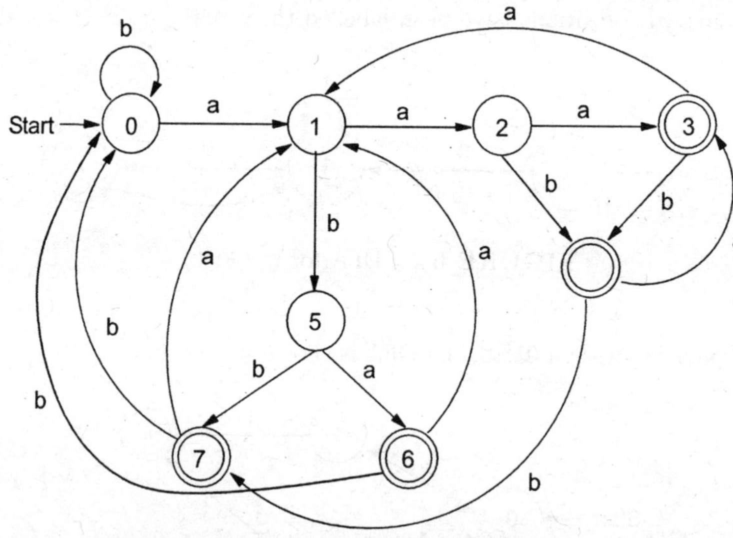

FIGURE 6.10 DFA for $(a|b)^*a(aa|ab|ba|bb)$.

of last three symbols seen. If these symbols are *aaa*, *aab*, *aba*, or *abb*, it declares *accept*, else *failure*. To remember three symbols, we need to have eight distinct states remembering them. Thus, for n such symbols, we will need at least 2^n states in the DFA.

However, in the ordinary programming languages, we do not encounter many such tokens for which the DFA has got exponential number of states as compared to the corresponding NFA. Moreover, DFA does not have any nondeterminism in its operation, which means that to test whether an input stream forms a valid token or not, we just have to follow the transitions that are possible from the start state, guided by the input symbols. The algorithm to test whether an input stream is acceptable by a DFA or not, is depicted next.

Algorithm DFA-test
Input: A DFA with start state S_0
An input stream
Output: "yes" if accepted, "no" otherwise
Begin
$S = S_0$

```
        S = S_1
    end while
    If S is a final state and c = end-of-input then
        return "yes"
    else return "no"
End
```

EXAMPLE 6.4 For the DFA shown in Fig. 6.7, given the input stream "0110", the Algorithm DFA-test makes transitions of states $0 \to 1 \to 1 \to 2$, and returns "yes". Whereas for the input stream "011", it traverses $0 \to 1 \to 1$. Since 1 is not a final state, the stream is rejected and the algorithm returns "no".

The existence of nondeterminism makes the task of testing whether an input stream is acceptable by an NFA difficult. Because, in this case, we need to try out all possible alternatives that may occur in nondeterministic transitions of states. For example, if for an input symbol a there are two transitions from state S to S_1 and S_2 respectively, both the alternatives need to be explored before declaring the input as rejected. The presence of ϵ-transitions also creates problems, as in that case also we may have multiple choices of transitions from a state. Hence, in order to have a lexical analyzer with the ability to detect the tokens fast, DFA is often used. However, in many cases it is easier to design the NFA than the corresponding DFA. We need to have a tool that can convert an NFA into a DFA. In the following, we discuss a technique for this conversion.

NFA to DFA. To construct the DFA equivalent to a given NFA, we note that a set of states in an NFA correspond to a state in the DFA. All these states of the NFA are reachable from at least another state of the same set using ϵ-transition only (that is, without consuming any further input). Also from this set of states, based on some input symbol, we can reach another set of states. In the DFA we take these sets as unique states. To start with, we define two sets:

Definition 6.1 ϵ-closure(s): *ϵ-closure of a state s in an NFA is defined to be the set of states (including s) that are reachable from s using ϵ-transitions only.*

Definition 6.2 ϵ-closure(S): *ϵ-closure of a set of states S of an NFA is defined to be the set of states reachable from any state in S using ϵ-transitions only.*

The ϵ-closure of a set of states S can thus be computed by the following algorithm:

```
ε-closure(S) = S
Set all states of ε-closure(S) to be unmarked
While there are unmarked states in ε-closure(S) do
    Let s be such a state
    Mark s
    For all state s' having an ε-transition from s to it do
        If s' not in ε-closure(S) then
            ε-closure(S) = ε-closure(S) ∪ {s'}
            Set s' unmarked
```

For all state s' having an ϵ-transition from s to it do
  If s' not in ϵ-closure(S) then
    ϵ-closure(S) = ϵ-closure(S) $\cup \{s'\}$
    Set s' unmarked

Next, we look into the algorithm to convert an NFA to the corresponding DFA.

Algorithm NFA-to-DFA
Input: An NFA with set of states S, start state s_0, set of final states F
Output: Corresponding DFA with start state d_0, set of states S_D, set of final states F_D
Begin
  $d_0 = \epsilon$-closure(s_0)
  $S_D = \{d_0\}$
  If d_0 contains a state from F then $F_D = \{d_0\}$ else $F_D = \phi$
  Set d_0 unmarked
  For each unmarked state d in S_D do
    For each input symbol a do
      Let T be the set of states in S (of NFA) having transitions on a from any state of the NFA corresponding to the DFA state d
      $d' = \epsilon$-closure(T)
      If d' is already present in S_D, add the transition $d \rightarrow d'$ labelled by a
      else
        $S_D = S_D \cup \{d'\}$
        Add transition from d to d' labelled a
        Set d' unmarked
        If d' contains a state of F then $F_D = F_D \cup \{d'\}$
End

EXAMPLE 6.5 Consider the NFA shown in Fig. 6.11 corresponding to the regular expression $a(a|b)^*ab$. We will construct the corresponding DFA using the algorithm *NFA-to-DFA*. To start with, the initial state of the DFA is constructed as,

$d_0 = \epsilon$-closure(1) = $\{1\}$

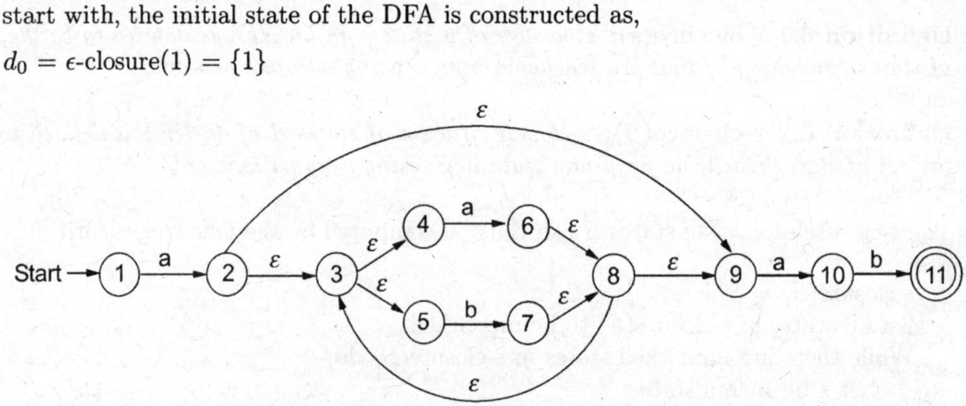

FIGURE 6.11 NFA for $a(a|b)^*ab$.

This is the only state in D now. From d_0 we consider the transitions on a. The new state constructed is,

$d' = \epsilon\text{-closure}(\{2\}) = \{2,3,4,5,8,9\}$

In this way, we can construct the new states and transitions in the DFA as shown in the Table 6.1. The DFA is shown in Fig. 6.12.

Table 6.1: DFA state construction.

DFA state	Set of NFA states	Transition on		Is *final*
		a	b	
1	{1}	2	—	no
2	{2,3,4,5,9}	3	4	no
3	{3,4,5,6,8,9,10}	3	5	no
4	{3,4,5,7,8,9}	3	4	no
5	{3,4,5,7,8,9,11}	3	4	yes

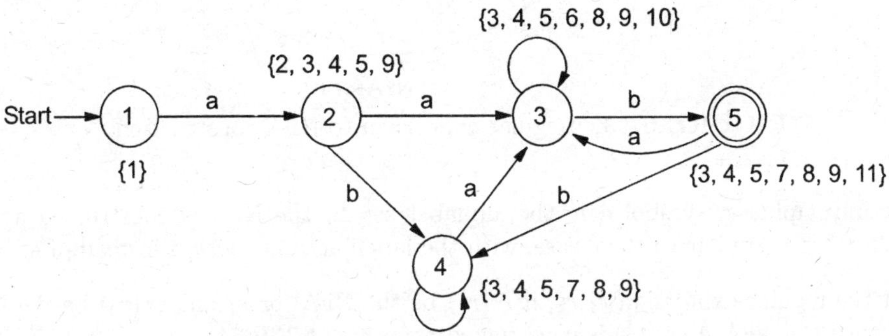

FIGURE 6.12 DFA for $a(a|b)^*ab$.

Since state 5 of the DFA contains the final state of the NFA (state 11), it is the only *final* state of the DFA. It may be verified that the DFA accepts the same set of strings $a(a|b)^*ab$ as the original NFA.

6.1.3 Regular Expression to NFA

In this section, we present the technique to construct an NFA that can be used as a recognizer for the tokens corresponding to a regular expression. The NFA thus obtained can then be converted into a DFA using the approach depicted in the previous section. The conversion of a regular expression to an NFA essentially follows breaking down the regular expression into simplest subexpressions, constructing the corresponding NFAs, and then combining these small NFAs, guided by the operators of the regular expression. This construction is known as *Thompson's construction.* The set of rules for this construction are as follows. The rules are also shown in Fig. 6.13.

1. For ϵ, the NFA is as shown in Fig. 6.13(a), consisting of two states—start state and final state. The transition is labelled by ϵ.

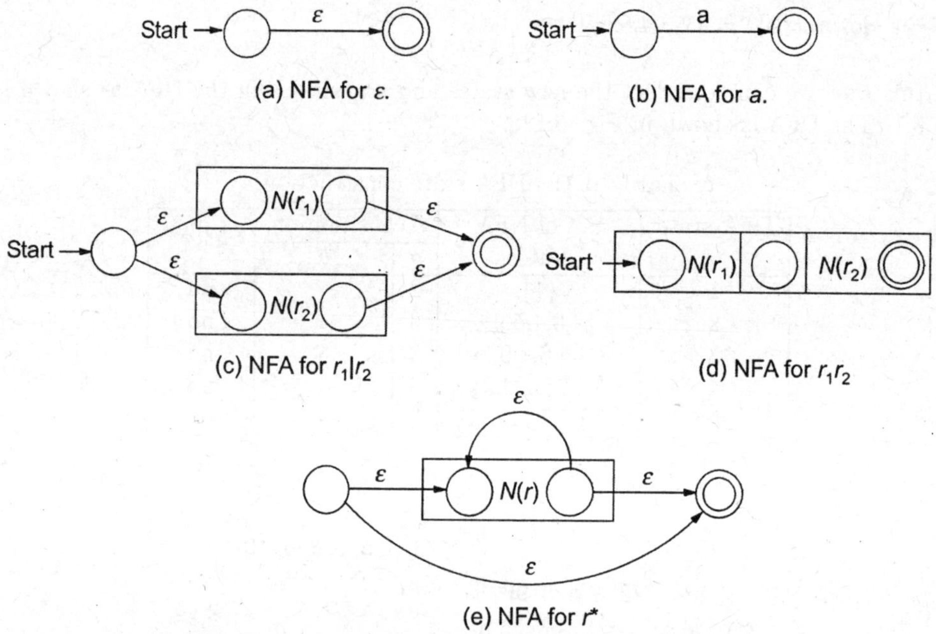

FIGURE 6.13 Regular expression to NFA construction.

2. For any alphabet symbol a in the alphabet set Σ, the NFA is constructed as in Fig. 6.13(b). It is similar to the ϵ-case, with the labelling done with a instead of ϵ.

3. For the regular expression $r_1|r_2$, if $N(r_1)$ be the NFA for r_1 and $N(r_2)$ be the NFA for r_2, then the NFA $N(r_1|r_2)$ is constructed as in Fig. 6.13(c).

   In this case, a new start state and final state are added. ϵ-transitions are introduced from the new start state to the start states of $N(r_1)$ and $N(r_2)$. Similarly, ϵ-transitions are added from the final states of $N(r_1)$ and $N(r_2)$ to the newly created final state. The final states of $N(r_1)$ and $N(r_2)$ cease to be final states any more.

4. For the regular expression r_1r_2, the NFA $N(r_1r_2)$ is constructed by merging the NFAs $N(r_1)$ and $N(r_2)$. The final state of $N(r_1)$ is merged with the start state of $N(r_2)$. It is shown in Fig. 6.13(d). The transitions emanating from the start state of $N(r_2)$ now originates at the final state of $N(r_1)$. The start state of $N(r_1)$ becomes the start state of the new NFA and the final state of $N(r_2)$ is the final state of the new NFA. The final state of $N(r_1)$ ceases to be the final state any more.

5. For the regular expression r^*, the NFA $N(r^*)$ is constructed from the NFA $N(r)$ of r as follows:

   First a new start state and a new final state are introduced. Then, ϵ-transitions are added from the new start state to the start state of $N(r)$, from the final state of $N(r)$ to the new final state, from the final state of $N(r)$ back to the start state of $N(r)$, and from the new start state to the new final state. The addition of ϵ-transition from new start state to new final state corresponds to the zero-occurrence of r, whereas the ϵ-transition from the final to initial state of $N(r)$ corresponds to the repeated occurrence of r. The situation has been shown in Fig. 6.13(e).

6. If $N(r)$ be the NFA for a regular expression r, it is also the NFA for the parenthesized expression (r).

EXAMPLE 6.6 Let us consider the construction of the NFA for the regular expression $a(a|b)^*ab$. Here the subexpressions are:

1. a
2. b
3. $a|b$
4. $(a|b)^*$
5. $a(a|b)^*$
6. ab
7. $a(a|b)^*ab$

The corresponding NFAs are shown in Fig. 6.14. First, the basic NFAs are constructed, which are then combined using the rules discussed earlier.

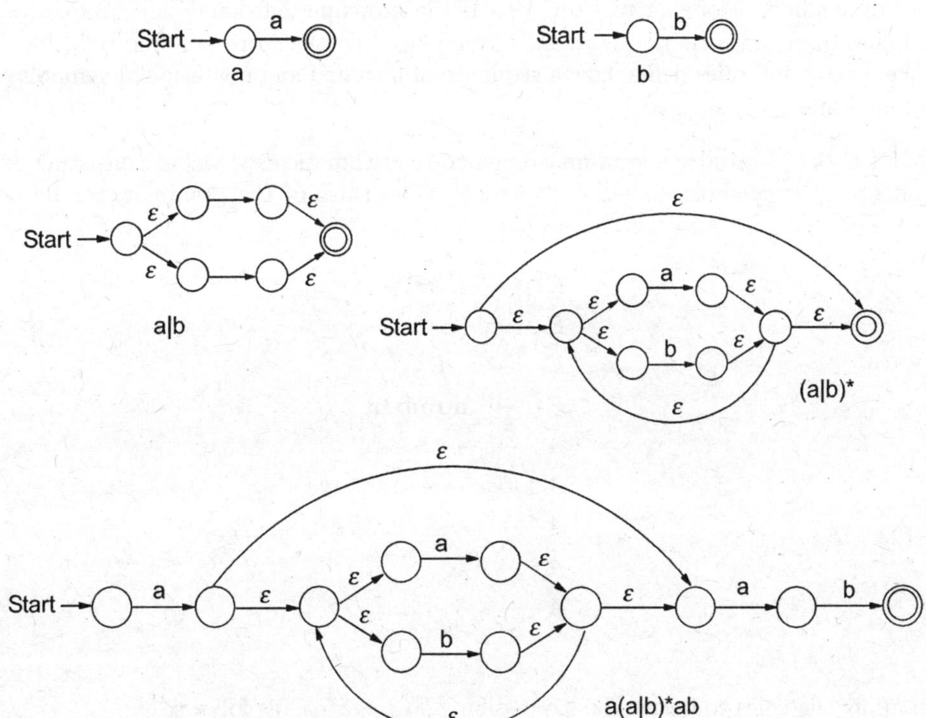

FIGURE 6.14 NFA construction for a regular expression.

6.2 SYNTAX ANALYSIS

Syntax analysis or parsing is the most important phase of a compiler. This extracts the syntactic units within the input stream. As noted earlier, syntax analyzer works hand-in-hand with the previous lexical analysis phase. The lexical analyzer determines the tokens occurring next in the input stream, and returns the same to the parser when asked for. The syntax analyzer considers the sequence of tokens for possible valid constructs of the programming language. Based upon the complexity of the parsing strategies, there exist a number of parsing algorithms which are broadly classified as *top-down* and *bottom-up* strategies. A *top-down* parser attempts to derive the input program starting with a special *start symbol*, whereas a *bottom-up* parser reduces a valid input program to the *start symbol*. We will be discussing some representative parsers from each of these categories. However, before that, we need to understand a few definitions and concepts like *grammar of a language, derivation* etc.

6.2.1 Grammar

A grammar G is defined as a 4-tuple $< V_N, V_T, P, S >$, where V_N is a set of nonterminal symbols used to write the grammar, V_T is the set of terminals (that is, the set of words of the language), P is a set of production rules, and $S \in V_N$ is a special nonterminal called the *start symbol* of the grammar. The strings of the language are derived from S by applying the production rules from the set P. The rules are applied on intermediary strings consisting of sequence of symbols belonging to $V_N \cup V_T$. If the matching left-hand side of a certain rule can be found to occur in the string, it may be replaced by the corresponding right-hand side. Thus, the production rules define how a sequence of terminal and nonterminal symbols can be replaced by some other sequence.

EXAMPLE 6.7 Consider a grammar to generate arithmetic expressions consisting of numbers and operator symbols $+$, $-$, $*$, $/$, and $\uparrow$. The rules of the grammar can be written as,

$$\begin{aligned}
E &\rightarrow EAE \\
E &\rightarrow (E) \\
E &\rightarrow -E \\
E &\rightarrow \textbf{number} \\
A &\rightarrow + \\
A &\rightarrow - \\
A &\rightarrow * \\
A &\rightarrow / \\
A &\rightarrow \uparrow
\end{aligned}$$

We can apply the rules to derive the expression "2*(3 + 5*4)" as follows:

$$E \rightarrow EAE \rightarrow EA(E) \rightarrow EA(EAE) \rightarrow EA(EAEAE) \rightarrow EA(EAEA4) \rightarrow EA(EAE * 4) \rightarrow EA(EA5 * 4) \rightarrow EA(E + 5 * 4) \rightarrow EA(3 + 5 * 4) \rightarrow E * (3 + 5 * 4) \rightarrow 2 * (3 + 5 * 4)$$

In this grammar E and A are nonterminals, whereas the rest of the symbols, that is, $(,), -,$ **number**, $+, -, *, /, \uparrow$ are terminals.

There exist several classes of languages based on the production rules. A detailed discussion can be found in books on *Formal Languages*. Most of the programming language constructs belong to the class of *Context Free Languages*. The grammar of a context free language consists of production rules in which the left-hand side contains only a single nonterminal and no terminals. The name "context free" originates from the fact that since the left-hand side has a single nonterminal, there is no context dependency for applying the rule in the derivation process.

Notational Conventions. In order to make the discussion clear and concise, we will use a few notational conventions throughout the chapter. The notations used are as follows:

1. The following will be taken as terminals:
   - Lower case letters occurring near the beginning of alphabet, such as a, b, c.
   - All operator symbols
   - Punctuation symbols including parentheses
   - The digits
   - Boldface strings such as **id, number, while**, etc.
2. The following will represent nonterminals:
   - Upper case letters occurring near the beginning of alphabet, such as A, B, C.
   - The letter S to represent start symbol
   - Lower case names like *expr, stmt* are also used to represent nonterminals
3. Upper case letters in the later part of the alphabet, such as X, Y, Z represent grammar symbols (may be terminal or nonterminal).
4. Lower case letters late in the alphabet represent strings of terminals.
5. Lower case Greek letters like α, β, etc. represent strings of grammar symbols.
6. A set of productions with the same left-hand side, like $A \rightarrow \alpha_1$, $A \rightarrow \alpha_2$, ..., $A \rightarrow \alpha_k$ is usually written as $A \rightarrow \alpha_1|\alpha_2|\ldots|\alpha_k$.
7. If no start symbol is mentioned, the nonterminal appearing in the left-hand side of the first production rule is taken as the start symbol.

Derivation. The sequence of intermediary strings generated to expand the start symbol of the grammar to a desired string of terminals is called a *derivation.* Each step of derivation modifies an intermediary string to a new one by replacing a substring of it, that matches with the left-hand side of a production rule by the string on the right-hand side of the rule. The derivation can also be represented in the form of a tree, called *parse tree.* For example, the derivation of "2*(3 + 5*4)" in Example 6.7 can be represented as a parse tree as shown in Fig. 6.15.

Leftmost and Rightmost Derivations. The derivation in which always the leftmost nonterminal is replaced at each step is called *leftmost derivation.* Similarly, the derivation in which the rightmost nonterminal is replaced at each step is called *rightmost derivation.* In a leftmost derivation, the intermediate strings are called *left sentential forms.* It

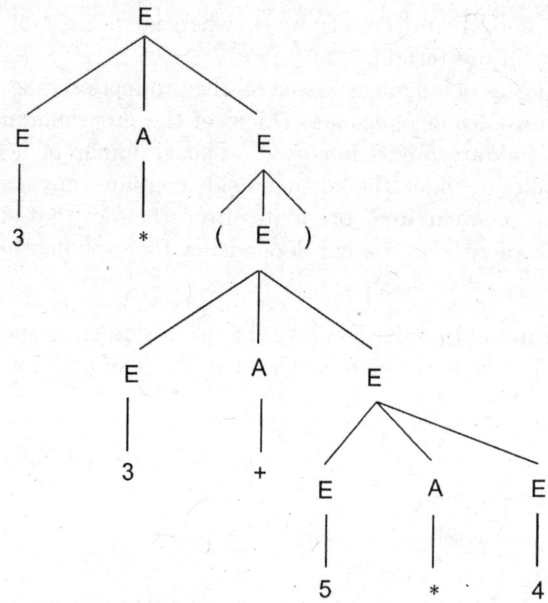

FIGURE 6.15 Parse tree for "2*(3 + 5*4)".

consists of a sequence of grammar symbols (both terminals and nonterminals). On the other hand, the intermediary strings of a rightmost derivation are called *right sentential forms.* The rightmost derivation is also called the *canonical representation.*

Ambiguity. A grammar is said to be ambiguous if there exists more than one parse tree for the same sentence. An ambiguous grammar can have more than one leftmost and rightmost derivations. For example, consider the grammar,

$$S \rightarrow aSbS \mid bSaS \mid \epsilon$$

For the string "*abab*", we have two different parse trees as shown in Fig. 6.16.

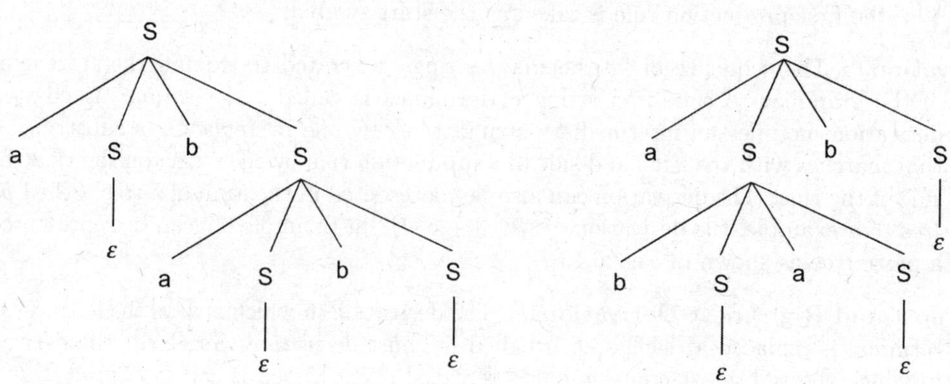

FIGURE 6.16 Two parse trees for "*abab*".

A classical example of an ambiguous grammar is that of *if-then-else* construct of many programming languages. Most of the languages have both *if-then* and *if-then-else* versions of the statement. The grammar rules for it are as follows:

stmt → **if** *condition* **then** *stmt* **else** *stmt*
  | **if** *condition* **then** *stmt*

Now, consider the following code segment,

if $a > b$ then
  if $c > d$ then $x = y$
  else $x = z$

We can have two different parse trees as shown in Fig. 6.17. The first figure shows the situation in which the *else* is taken with the outer *if*-statement. In the second case, the *else* is taken with the inner *if*. Thus, the outer one is an *if-then* statement and the inner one is *if-then-else* statement. Most of the programming languages accept second one as the correct syntax, that is, associate *else* with the innermost *if*.

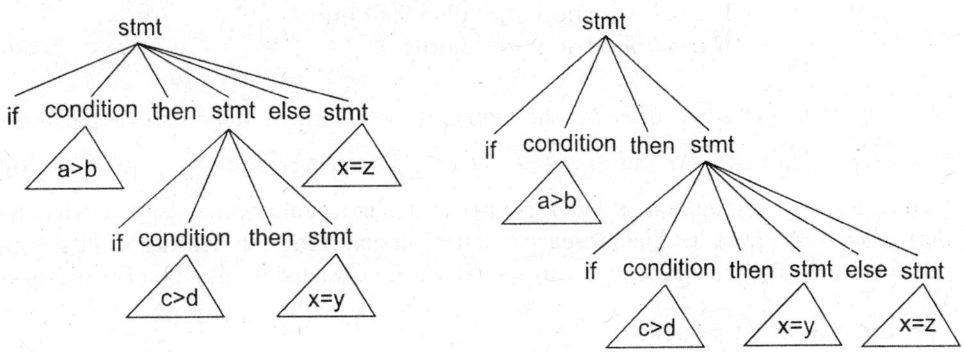

FIGURE 6.17 Two parse trees for *if-then-else* statement.

Eliminating Ambiguity. Ambiguities may be eliminated by rewriting the grammar. For example, the *if-then-else* grammar may be rewritten as follows.

stmt → *matched_stmt* | *unmatched_stmt*
matched_stmt → **if** *condition* **then** *matched_stmt* **else** *matched_stmt*
  | **other_stmt**
unmatched_stmt → **if** *condition* **then** *stmt*
  | **if** *condition* **then** *matched_stmt* **else** *unmatched_stmt*

Here **other_stmt** represents all other statements apart from **if**. The only parse tree possible now is shown in Fig. 6.18.

Another technique to resolve ambiguity may be to modify the language a bit. Many languages require that an *if* should have a matching *endif*. Thus the grammar is modified as,

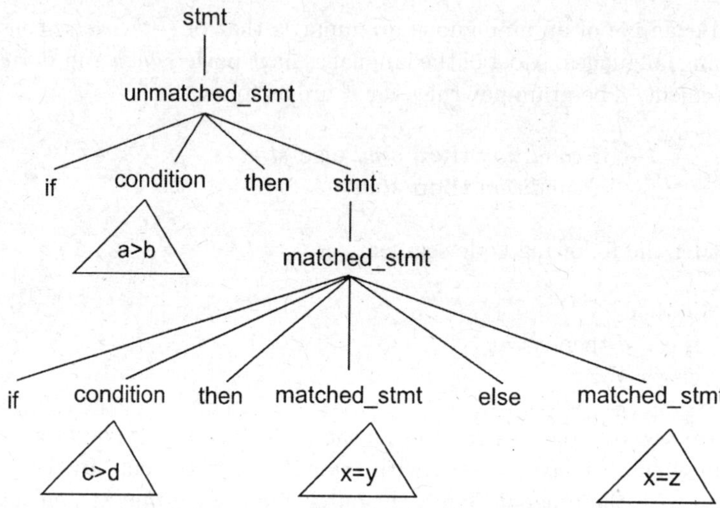

FIGURE 6.18 Parse tree for *if-then-else*.

$$\begin{array}{lll} stmt & \rightarrow & \textbf{if } condition \textbf{ then } stmt \textbf{ else } stmt \textbf{ endif} \\ & | & \textbf{if } condition \textbf{ then } stmt \textbf{ endif} \end{array}$$

Here due to the presence of *endif*, the ambiguity is not there, only a single parse tree is possible.

Left Recursion. A grammar is *left recursive* if it has a nonterminal (say A) that has a derivation of $A\alpha$ from it. The presence of left recursion creates difficulties while designing the corresponding parsers (as we will see later). Left recursion may be of two types:

- Immediate left recursion
- General left recursion

An immediate left recursion happens with a nonterminal A having production rule of the form $A \rightarrow A\alpha \mid \beta$. The immediate left recursion can be eliminated by modifying the grammar introducing a new nonterminal symbol, say A'. The grammar rule $A \rightarrow A\alpha \mid \beta$ is modified as,

$$\begin{array}{lll} A & \rightarrow & \beta A' \\ A' & \rightarrow & \alpha A' \mid \epsilon \end{array}$$

Thus, the rule $A \rightarrow A\alpha_1 \mid A\alpha_2 \mid \ldots \mid A\alpha_m \mid \beta_1 \mid \beta_2 \mid \ldots \mid \beta_n$ can be modified as,

$$\begin{array}{lll} A & \rightarrow & \beta_1 A' \mid \beta_2 A' \mid \ldots \mid \beta_n A' \\ A' & \rightarrow & \alpha_1 A' \mid \alpha_2 A' \mid \ldots \mid \alpha_m A' \mid \epsilon \end{array}$$

EXAMPLE 6.8 Consider the following left-recursive grammar for arithmetic expressions,

$$E \rightarrow E + T \mid T$$
$$T \rightarrow T * F \mid F$$
$$F \rightarrow (E) \mid \mathbf{id}$$

Elimination of immediate left recursion from the rules modifies the grammar as,

$$E \rightarrow TE'$$
$$E' \rightarrow +TE' \mid \epsilon$$
$$T \rightarrow FT'$$
$$T' \rightarrow *FT' \mid \epsilon$$
$$F \rightarrow (E) \mid \mathbf{id}$$

However, even if there may be no immediate left recursion, a number of production rules may act together to give a general left recursion. For example, consider the grammar,

$$S \rightarrow Aa$$
$$A \rightarrow Sb \mid c$$

Here S is left recursive, because $S \rightarrow Aa \rightarrow Sba$. This form of general left recursion can be eliminated with the following algorithm. The algorithm is guaranteed to work if the grammar has no cycles (that is, it is not possible to derive a nonterminal, say A, starting from itself) and no ϵ productions.

Algorithm eliminate_left_recursion

1. Arrange nonterminals in some order, say $A_1, A_2, \ldots, A_m$.
2. For $i = 1$ to m do
   For $j = 1$ to $i - 1$ do
      For each set of productions $A_i \rightarrow A_j\gamma$ and $A_j \rightarrow \delta_1 \mid \delta_2 \mid \ldots \mid \delta_k$
         Replace $A_i \rightarrow A_j\gamma$ by $A_i \rightarrow \delta_1\gamma \mid \delta_2\gamma \mid \ldots \mid \delta_k\gamma$
3. Eliminate immediate left recursion from all productions.

For example, for the grammar,

$$S \rightarrow Aa$$
$$A \rightarrow Sb \mid c$$

let the order of nonterminals be S, A. For $i = 1$, the rule $S \rightarrow Aa$ is through, since there is no immediate left recursion, For $i = 2$, $A \rightarrow Sb \mid c$ is modified as, $A \rightarrow Aab \mid c$, which has immediate left recursion, and hence eliminated by modifying the rule as,

$$A \rightarrow cA'$$
$$A' \rightarrow abA' \mid \epsilon$$

6.2.2 LL(k) Parsing – Topdown Predictive Parsing

LL(k) parsing is a table-driven top-down parsing strategy. The parser scans over the input stream using a prefix of tokens to identify which production applies. The languages accepted by these parsers are called $LL(k)$, where k is the length of the prefix. "LL" stands for *left-to-right* scanning of the input stream and *left-most* derivation respectively. The term *left-most* derivation implies that at each step the leftmost nonterminal is replaced by a string of terminals and non-terminals as guided by the grammar rules. For the remainder of the section, we will consider the case of $k = 1$.

The construction of an LL(1) parser for a grammar (V_N, V_T, P, S) requires first computing the following properties:

$$\begin{aligned}
\text{First}(A) &= \{U | U \in V_T \text{ and } A \text{ can derive a string starting with } U\} \\
\text{Follow}(A) &= \{U | U \in V_T \text{ and } S \text{ can derive a string like } \alpha A U \beta\} \\
\text{First}(\alpha) &= \{U | U \in V_T \text{ and } \alpha \text{ can derive a string like } U\beta \}
\end{aligned}$$

Intuitively, First(A) is the set of terminals that can start a string that is derivable from A, Follow(A) is the set of terminals that can follow an occurrence of A, and First(α) is the set of terminals that can start a string that is derivable from α. To compute these sets for a grammar, we need to define another property:

$$\text{nullable}(A) = \begin{cases} \text{true} & \text{if } A \text{ can derive } \epsilon \text{ in zero or more steps} \\ \text{false} & \text{otherwise} \end{cases}$$

We say that a nonterminal A is *nullable* if *nullable(A)* = *true*. A terminal symbol is never nullable. Then the algorithm for computing First and Follow sets for a grammar is as follows:

```
forall A ∈ V_N do
    First(A) = φ;
    Follow(A) = φ;
forall U ∈ V_T do
    First(U) = {U};
do
    foreach A → X_1 ...... X_n ∈ P do
        foreach i ∈ [1...n] do
            if X_1, ... X_{i-1} are all nullable then
                First(A) = First(A) ∪ First(X_i)
            if X_{i+1}, ... X_n are all nullable then
                Follow(X_i) = Follow(X_i) ∪ Follow(A)
            foreach j ∈ [i + 1, ..., n] do
                if X_{i+1}, ..., X_{j-1} are all nullable then
                    Follow(X_i) = Follow(X_i) ∪ Follow(X_j)
        if all the X_i's are nullable then nullable(A) = true
until First, Follow and nullable sets do not change
```

Note that to simplify the presentation, we extend the notion of First and Follow sets to terminal symbols (we can avoid doing so by adding extra conditional statements to the algorithm). We extend the notion of First sets to include ϵ and define them for strings as follows:

$$\begin{aligned}
\text{First}(\epsilon) &= \{\epsilon\} \\
\text{First}(X\ \ \alpha) &= \begin{cases} X & \text{if } X \in T \\ \text{First}(X) & \text{if nullable}(X) = \text{false} \\ \text{First}(X) \cup \text{First}(\alpha) & \text{if nullable}(X) = \text{true} \end{cases}
\end{aligned}$$

A grammar is an LL(1) grammar if all productions conform to the following LL(1) conditions:

1. For each production $A \rightarrow \sigma_1 \mid \sigma_2 \mid \ldots \mid \sigma_n$, $\text{First}(\sigma_i) \cap \text{First}(\sigma_j) = \phi, \forall i \neq j$
2. If non-terminal X can derive an empty string, then $\text{First}(X) \cap \text{Follow}(X) = \phi$

The first condition means we always know which alternative to choose. The second alternative means we always know whether something optional is there or not.

EXAMPLE 6.9 The grammar $S \rightarrow A \mid B$, $A \rightarrow cA{+}b \mid a$, $B \rightarrow cB{+}a \mid b$ is not LL(1) since $\text{First}(A) \cap \text{First}(B) = \{c\}$.

Once we have computed the First and Follow sets, we can construct an LL(1) parse table M that maps pairs of nonterminals and terminals to productions using the following algorithm:

```
foreach A → α ∈ P do
    if ε ∈ First(α) then
        foreach U ∈ Follow(A) do
            Add A → α to M[A,U]
    foreach U ∈ First(α) do
        Add A → α to M[A,U]
```

If the resulting table has at most one production per (A, U) pair, then the grammar is LL(1). For example, consider the grammar,

$$
\begin{aligned}
E &\rightarrow ME' \\
E' &\rightarrow \epsilon \\
E' &\rightarrow +ME' \\
M &\rightarrow AM' \\
M' &\rightarrow \epsilon \\
M' &\rightarrow *AM' \\
A &\rightarrow \textbf{num} \\
A &\rightarrow (E)
\end{aligned}
$$

The *nullable, first,* and *follow* sets are given in the following table:

Symbol	nullable	First	Follow
E	false	{**num**, (}	{), \$}
E'	true	{+}	{), \$}
M	false	{**num**, (}	{), +, \$}
M'	true	{*}	{), +, \$}
A	false	{**num**, (}	{), +, *, \$}

Note that we have included the special "end-of-input" symbol (\$) in the Follow set. The parsing table for the grammar is,

	num	+	*	(	)	\$
E	$E \rightarrow ME'$			$E \rightarrow ME'$		
E'		$E' \rightarrow +ME'$			$E' \rightarrow \epsilon$	$E' \rightarrow \epsilon$
M	$M \rightarrow AM'$			$M \rightarrow AM'$		
M'		$M' \rightarrow \epsilon$	$M' \rightarrow *AM'$		$M' \rightarrow \epsilon$	$M' \rightarrow \epsilon$
A	$A \rightarrow$ **num**			$A \rightarrow (E)$		

The table-driven parser for LL(1) grammars works using a parsing table (as constructed above) and an auxiliary stack of grammar symbols. The table-driven parser works as follows:

```
while stack is not empty do
    Let X be the top symbol on the stack
    Let U be the next input symbol
    if X ∈ T then
        if X = U then
            pop X off the stack and advance the input
        else
            parsing error
    elsif M[X,U] = A → Y1 ... Yn then
        pop X and push Yn, ..., Y1 onto the stack
    else
        parsing error
```

Here is a trace of running this algorithm on the string "1 + 2*3" using the above parsing table:

Stack	Input	Action
E	1+2*3$	parse $E \to ME'$
$E'M$	1+2*3$	parse $M \to AM'$
$E'M'A$	1+2*3$	parse $A \to$ **num**
$E'M'$**num**	1+2*3$	advance input
$E'M'$	+2*3$	parse $M' \to \epsilon$
E'	+2*3$	parse $E' \to +ME'$
$E'M+$	+2*3$	advance input
$E'M$	2*3$	parse $M \to AM'$
$E'M'A$	2*3$	parse $A \to$ **num**
$E'M'$**num**	2*3$	advance input
$E'M'$	*3$	parse $M' \to *AM'$
$E'M'A*$	*3$	advance input
$E'M'A$	3$	parse $A \to$ **num**
$E'M'$**num**	3$	advance input
$E'M'$	$	parse $M' \to \epsilon$
E'	$	parse $E' \to \epsilon$
	$	done

EXAMPLE 6.10 Consider the following grammar for **if-then-else** statement.

$$S \rightarrow \textbf{if expr then } S\ S' \mid \textbf{assignment}$$
$$S' \rightarrow \textbf{else } S \mid \epsilon$$

To simplify the grammar, we have assumed **expr** to be a terminal modelling an expression, and **assignment** another terminal modelling the assignment statement. The parsing table is shown in Table 6.2. The entry $M[S'$, **else**] is multiply defined. This is because the Follow(S') = {**else**, \$}. First(**else** S) = {**else**}, forcing the entry $S' \to$ **else** S to $M[S'$, **else**]. Now, for

Table 6.2: An example LL parsing table.

	if	expr	then	assignment	else	$
S	$S \rightarrow$ **if expr then** $S\ S'$			$S \rightarrow$ **assignment**		
S'				$S' \rightarrow \epsilon$	$S' \rightarrow \epsilon$ $S' \rightarrow$ **else** S	

the rule $S' \rightarrow \epsilon$, First(ϵ) = $\{\epsilon\}$, and **else** is in Follow(S'), thus, $S' \rightarrow \epsilon$ is added to $M[S'$, **else**]. The situation is justified since the dangling else problem occurs after getting the token **else** — the options are either to expand through the else branch, or consider the statement seen so far as an **if-then** statement.

6.2.3 LR Parsing–Bottomup Approach

One of the best methods for syntactic recognition of programming languages is LR parsing. An LR parser uses the *shift-reduce* technique discussed later. L stands for left-to-right scanning, and R for a rightmost derivation in reverse.

When we speak about LR parsing, we are actually speaking of LR(1) parsing, that is, LR parsing with one symbol lookahead. In general, we can have LR(k) parsing, with k symbols of lookahead.

Some of the advantages of LR parsing are as follows:

1. An LR parser can recognize virtually all programming language constructs written with context-free grammars.

2. It is the most general nonbacktracking technique known.

3. It can be implemented in a very efficient manner.

4. The languages it can recognize is a proper superset of that for predictive parsers.

5. It can detect syntax errors quickly.

The primary disadvantage to LR parsers is that it is far too much work to manually create LR parsing tables. However, tools exist to automatically generate an LR parser from a given grammar. These are called LR parser generators, such as *yacc, bison.* These parser generators are not only useful in creating the parser, but in finding errors in the grammar also.

There are actually three different methods to perform LR parsing.

1. *SLR* parsing stands for simple LR. It is easy to implement, but is less powerful in that it recognizes less.

2. *Canonical LR* is the most general and powerful, but tedious and costly to implement. For the same grammar, the canonical LR parser has got much more number of states as compared to the simple LR parser.

3. *LALR* stands for lookahead LR. It is a mix of SLR and canonical LR, but can be implemented efficiently. It contains the same number of states as the simple LR parser for the same grammar.

Most parser generators generate LALR parsers, since they are the trade-off between power and efficiency.

LR Parsing algorithm. An LR parser has nearly the same form as a nonrecursive predictive parser, except the parsing table consists of two parts: *action* and *goto*. The algorithm used is much the same as the shift-reduce method.

The stack for an LR parser consists of *grammar symbols* and *states*. The states summarize what is below that state on the stack and pairing the state on top of the stack with the next input symbol indexes into the parsing table to determine the next action.

An LR parsing configuration has the following form:

$$(s_0 X_1 s_1 \ldots X_m s_m, a_i a_{i+1} \ldots a_n \$)$$

where s_j is a state, X_k is a grammar symbol and a_l is an input symbol. The configuration is just a pair with the current stack and the current unused input.

The LR parsing table, as mentioned, is split into the *action* and *goto* sections. The *goto* section actually implements a finite automaton that recognizes the viable prefixes of the grammar. The *action* portion is indexed by *action*$[s_m,a_i]$ to perform the following actions:

1. **shift** pushes the next input symbol and next state (s) onto the stack to enter the configuration

$$(s_0 X_1 \ldots X_m s_m a_i s, a_{i+1} \ldots a_n \$)$$

2. **reduce** matches the handle to some production $A \to \beta$. It then pops $r = 2 * |\beta|$ elements off the stack and pushes A and $s = goto[s_{m-r}, A]$. The configuration ends up as

$$(s_0 X_1 \ldots X_{m-r} s_{m-r} A s, a_{i+1} \ldots a_n \$)$$

3. **accept** means the parser is finished.

4. **error** causes the parser to call an error handling routine of some sort, as it has found an illegal configuration.

Algorithm LR Parsing
Input: LR parsing table and input string w
Output: true, if parse is successful

```
Begin
    Push initial state
    repeat forever
        Let s = top of stack, a = next input symbol
        if action[s,a] = shift s' then
            Push a and s'
            Advance input pointer to the next input symbol
        else if action[s,a] = reduce A → β then
            Pop 2|β| symbols
            s' = top of stack
```

Push A and goto[s', A]
else if action[s,a] = accept then return true
else error

End

Obviously, the table is an essential part of LR parsing. But how does one go about making the tables? It is, in fact, a rather mechanical process. However, it is a daunting task if one does not use automated tools for the purpose. In the following we will look into the table construction for SLR only, since it is the simplest and can be constructed by hand, others require automated tools for their construction.

One important fact to keep in mind when constructing LR parsing tables is that the state on the top of the stack provides a wealth of information to the parser. Essentially, an LR parser is keeping track of viable prefixes for the handles. It uses an automaton to recognize these prefixes. The *goto* portion of the table simulates this automaton, but it does not need to scan the stack on every input symbol to figure out what state it is in. Instead, it is kept on the top of the stack.

Items. The first concept in LR table construction is that of an *item*. An item is a production rule with a position indicator (dot) at some point on the right-hand side. If $A \to XYZ$ is a production, the possible items of this production are:

$$\begin{aligned} A &\to \cdot XYZ \\ A &\to X \cdot YZ \\ A &\to XY \cdot Z \\ A &\to XYZ\cdot \end{aligned}$$

Items are also known as *LR(0)* items, since they assume no lookahead. Intuitively, an item denotes how much of a production we have seen so far during the parsing.

SLR Parsing Tables. What we want to do when creating a SLR parsing table is to make a finite automaton that accepts the viable prefixes of the grammar. In order to do this, we use sets of items as our states and grammar symbols to define the transition function. For this, we will step through the process of creating a *canonical LR(0)* collection, that is, collections of items. To do this, we *augment* the grammar and use two functions: *closure* and *goto*.

Definition 6.3 Augmented grammar: *An augmented grammar simply has a new "dummy" start symbol, whose only production is the start symbol of the grammar in question. If G is our grammar with start symbol S, then the augmented grammar $G' = (V_T, V_N \cup \{S'\}, S', F \cup \{S' \to S\})$.*

Definition 6.4 Closure operation: *Let I be a set of items. closure(I) is defined by the following rules:*

1. *All elements of I are in closure(I).*
2. *If $A \to \alpha \cdot B\beta \in$ closure(I) and $B \to \gamma$ is a production, then add $B \to \cdot\gamma$ to closure(I). Continue until no new items are added to closure(I).*

Definition 6.5 Goto operation: *The goto operation is a function goto(I,X) where I is a set of items and X is a grammar symbol. It is defined as the closure of the set of all items* $[A \rightarrow \alpha X \cdot \beta]$ *such that* $[A \rightarrow \alpha \cdot X\beta] \in I$.

We can think of the goto operation as consuming the next input in the production. If we look at the dot as the position of the automata, we want to take the closure of all the items in I that would be advanced on the input X.

Creating the Sets of Items

Algorithm Set of Items for SLR parsing table
Input: Augmented grammar G'
Output: Set of items $I_0, \ldots, I_n$

```
Begin
    C ← {closure({S' → ·S})}
    repeat
        foreach X ∈ V_N ∪ V_T
            foreach I_k ∈ C with goto(I,X) ≠ φ
            if goto(I,X) ∉ C then
                C ← C∪ goto(I,X)
    until no more items can be added to C
End.
```

The sets of items I_k are in fact the results of the *goto* function. The initial set I_0 is the closure of $S' \rightarrow \cdot S$. The next sets are a result of running *goto*(I_0,X) for each symbol X in the grammar. Each set of items created represents a state in the finite automata to recognize the viable prefixes of the grammar. This is because *goto* is defined on a grammar symbol. What it says is that all items in the set I_k can be advanced on input X to the set created by the *goto* call.

Creating the SLR Parsing Table. The following are the steps to create the SLR parsing table.

1. Construct the collection of sets of LR(0) items.
2. State i is constructed from I_i. We determine the actions in the table as follows:
   (a) If $[A \rightarrow \alpha \cdot a\beta] \in I_i$ and *goto*(I_i,a) $= I_j$ with $a \in V_T$ then action[i,a] = shift j.
   (b) If $[A \rightarrow \alpha\cdot] \in I_i$ then action[i, a] = reduce $A \rightarrow \alpha$ for all $a \in$ Follow(A)with $A \neq S'$.
   (c) If $[S' \rightarrow S\cdot] \in I_i$ then action[i,\$] = accept.

   If any entry is multiply defined, the grammar is ambiguous and not SLR(1). We can then quit.
3. If *goto*(I_i, A) $= I_j$ then goto[i, A] $= j$.
4. All entries not defined are marked "errors".
5. The initial state is the set of items containing $[S' \rightarrow \cdot S]$

EXAMPLE 6.11 Let us consider the following augmented grammar for constructing the SLR parsing table:

$$\begin{aligned} S' &\rightarrow S \\ S &\rightarrow aABe \\ A &\rightarrow Abc \\ A &\rightarrow b \\ B &\rightarrow d \end{aligned}$$

The sets of items for the augmented grammar computed using the process outlined above are:

$$\begin{aligned} I_0 &= \{[S' \rightarrow \cdot S], [S \rightarrow \cdot aABe]\} \\ I_1 &= \{[S' \rightarrow S \cdot]\} \\ I_2 &= \{[S \rightarrow a \cdot ABe], [A \rightarrow \cdot Abc], [A \rightarrow \cdot b]\} \\ I_3 &= \{[S \rightarrow aA \cdot Be], [A \rightarrow A \cdot bc], [B \rightarrow \cdot d]\} \\ I_4 &= \{[A \rightarrow b \cdot]\} \\ I_5 &= \{[S \rightarrow aAB \cdot e]\} \\ I_6 &= \{[A \rightarrow Ab \cdot c]\} \\ I_7 &= \{[B \rightarrow d \cdot]\} \\ I_8 &= \{[S \rightarrow aABe \cdot]\} \\ I_9 &= \{[A \rightarrow Abc \cdot]\} \end{aligned}$$

The *goto* function for this grammar is:

$$\begin{aligned} goto(I_0, S) &= I_1 \\ goto(I_0, a) &= I_2 \\ goto(I_2, A) &= I_3 \\ goto(I_2, b) &= I_4 \\ goto(I_3, B) &= I_5 \\ goto(I_3, b) &= I_6 \\ goto(I_3, d) &= I_7 \\ goto(I_5, e) &= I_8 \\ goto(I_6, c) &= I_9 \end{aligned}$$

We can use a graph to describe both the canonical item sets and the *goto* function. The graph corresponding to this grammar is shown in Fig. 6.19.

The Follow sets for the grammar are as follows:

$$\begin{aligned} \text{Follow}(S) &= \{\$\} \\ \text{Follow}(A) &= \{b, d\} \\ \text{Follow}(B) &= \{e\} \end{aligned}$$

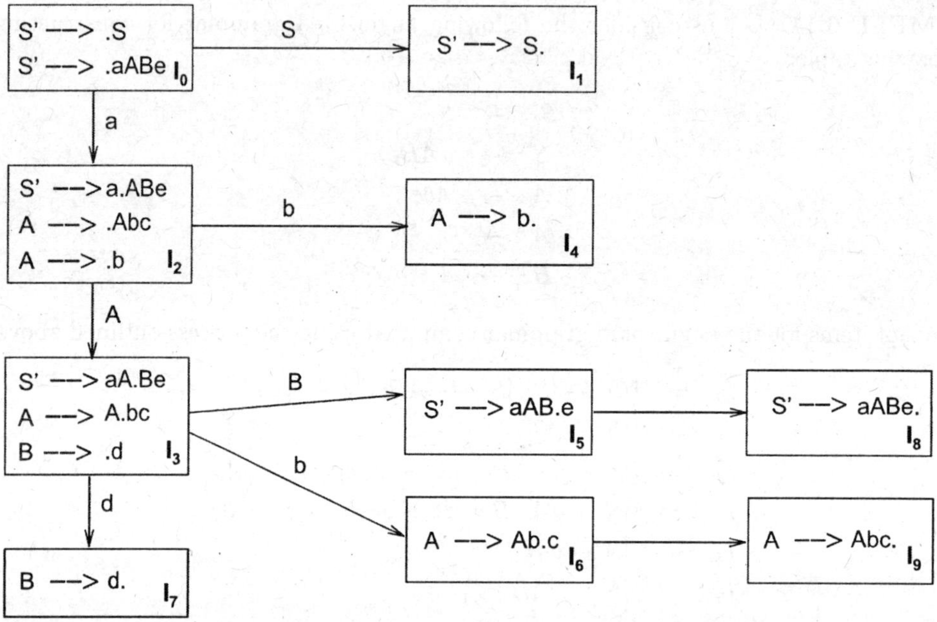

FIGURE 6.19 A graph representing canonical LR(0) items.

The resulting SLR parsing table is shown in Table 6.3. Now consider the string "*abbcbcde*". The operation of the LR parsing algorithm on this string has been shown in Table 6.4.

Table 6.3: Parsing table for Example 6.11

	a	b	c	d	e	\$	S	A	B
I_0	s2						1		
I_1						accept			
I_2		s4						3	
I_3		s6		s7					5
I_4		r4		r4					
I_5					s8				
I_6			s9						
I_7					r5				
I_8						r2			
I_9		r3		r3					

6.2.4 Handling Ambiguity in LR Parsers

The existence of ambiguity in the grammar creates LR parsing tables with conflicting entries. However, the ambiguous grammars are often smaller in size, since they generally have lesser number of nonterminals. Thus, the size of the parsing table is reduced, and hence, the parsing routine runs faster, resulting in faster compilation. The conflicts in the table are often resolved

Table 6.4: SLR operation of Example 6.11

Stack	Input	Action
0	$abbcbcde\$$	shift
$0a2$	$bbcbcde\$$	shift
$0a2b4$	$bcbcde\$$	reduce $A \to b$
$0a2A3$	$bcbcde\$$	shift
$0a2A3b6$	$cbcde\$$	shift
$0a2A3b6c9$	$bcde\$$	reduce $A \to Abc$
$0a2A3$	$bcde\$$	shift
$0a2A3b6$	$cde\$$	shift
$0a2A3b6c9$	$de\$$	reduce $A \to Abc$
$0a2A3$	$de\$$	shift
$0a2A3d7$	$e\$$	reduce $B \to d$
$0a2A3B5$	$e\$$	shift
$0a2A3B5e8$	$\$$	reduce $A \to aABe$
$0A1$	$\$$	accept

by adopting certain rules—known as *disambiguating rules*, which perhaps cannot be specified by the grammar without introducing further nonterminals. For example, consider the following augmented grammar for expressions,

$$
\begin{aligned}
E' &\to E \\
E &\to E+E \mid E-E \mid E*E \mid E/E \mid -E \mid (E) \mid id
\end{aligned}
$$

The LR(0) sets of items created are as follows:

I_0 : $\{[E' \to \cdot E], [E \to \cdot E+E], [E \to \cdot E-E], [E \to \cdot E*E], [E \to \cdot E/E], [E \to \cdot -E],$
$[E \to \cdot(E)], [E \to \cdot id]\},$

I_1 : $\{[E' \to E\cdot], [E \to E \cdot +E], [E \to E \cdot -E], [E \to E \cdot *E], [E \to E \cdot /E]\},$

I_2 : $\{[E \to - \cdot E], [E \to \cdot E+E], [E \to \cdot E-E], [E \to \cdot E*E], [E \to \cdot E/E], [E \to \cdot -E],$
$[E \to \cdot(E)], [E \to \cdot id]\},$

I_3 : $\{[E \to (\cdot E)], [E \to \cdot E+E], [E \to \cdot E-E], [E \to \cdot E*E], [E \to \cdot E/E], [E \to \cdot -E],$
$[E \to \cdot(E)], [E \to \cdot id]\},$

I_4 : $\{[E \to id]\},$

I_5 : $\{[E \to E+\cdot E], [E \to \cdot E+E], [E \to \cdot E-E], [E \to \cdot E*E], [E \to \cdot E/E], [E \to \cdot -E],$
$[E \to \cdot(E)], [E \to \cdot id]\},$

I_6 : $\{[E \to E-\cdot E], [E \to \cdot E+E], [E \to \cdot E-E], [E \to \cdot E*E], [E \to \cdot E/E], [E \to \cdot -E],$
$[E \to \cdot(E)], [E \to \cdot id]\},$

I_7 : $\{[E \to E*\cdot E], [E \to \cdot E+E], [E \to \cdot E-E], [E \to \cdot E*E], [E \to \cdot E/E], [E \to \cdot -E],$
$[E \to \cdot(E)], [E \to \cdot id]\},$

I_8 : $\{[E \to E/\cdot E], [E \to \cdot E+E], [E \to \cdot E-E], [E \to \cdot E*E], [E \to \cdot E/E], [E \to \cdot -E],$
$[E \to \cdot(E)], [E \to \cdot id]\},$

Table 6.5: SLR parsing table with duplicate entries

State	Action								Goto
	+	−	∗	/	(	)	*id*	$	*E*
0		s2			s3		s4		1
1	s5	s6	s7	s8				acc	
2		s2			s3		s4		9
3		s2			s3		s4		10
4	r8	r8	r8	r8		r8		r8	
5		s2			s3		s4		11
6		s2			s3		s4		12
7		s2			s3		s4		13
8		s2			s3		s4		14
9	r6/s5	r6/s6	r6/s7	r6/s8		r6		r6	
10	s5	s6	s7	s8		s15			
11	r2/s5	r2/s6	r2/s7	r2/s8		r2		r2	
12	r3/s5	r3/s6	r3/s7	r3/s8		r3		r3	
13	r4/s5	r4/s6	r4/s7	r4/s8		r4		r4	
14	r5/s5	r5/s6	r5/s7	r5/s8		r5		r5	
15	r7	r7	r7	r7		r7		r7	

$$
\begin{aligned}
I_9 &: \{[E \to -E\cdot], [E \to E \cdot +E], [E \to E \cdot -E], [E \to E \cdot *E], [E \to E \cdot /E]\},\\
I_{10} &: \{[E \to (E\cdot)], [E \to E \cdot +E], [E \to E \cdot -E], [E \to E \cdot *E], [E \to E \cdot /E]\},\\
I_{11} &: \{[E \to E + E\cdot], [E \to E \cdot +E], [E \to E \cdot -E], [E \to E \cdot *E], [E \to E \cdot /E]\},\\
I_{12} &: \{[E \to E - E\cdot], [E \to E \cdot +E], [E \to E \cdot -E], [E \to E \cdot *E], [E \to E \cdot /E]\},\\
I_{13} &: \{[E \to E * E\cdot], [E \to E \cdot +E], [E \to E \cdot -E], [E \to E \cdot *E], [E \to E \cdot /E]\},\\
I_{14} &: \{[E \to E/E\cdot], [E \to E \cdot +E], [E \to E \cdot -E], [E \to E \cdot *E], [E \to E \cdot /E]\},\\
I_{15} &: \{[E \to (E)\cdot]\}
\end{aligned}
$$

The Follow of E is $\{+, -, *, /,), \$\}$. The corresponding SLR parsing table has been shown in Table 6.5. There are several entries with *shift-reduce* conflicts. For example, from state I_9 on input '+', it suggests either to reduce by $E \to -E$ or shift. Since '−' here is the unary one, the correct action is to *reduce*. Thus, all conflicts of state I_9 are to be resolved as *reduce*. From state I_{11}, on '+', it says either to shift, or reduce by $E \to E + E$. The correct action is *reduce* since '+' is *left associative*. Similarly, for '−' also, the entry is to *reduce*. However, for '∗' and '/', since their precedences are more than '+', the correct action is to shift. In this way, all other conflicts can be resolved by noting the associativity and precedence in the following descending order. Here, all operators have been assumed to be left associative.

unary −,
∗, /,
+, −

The parsing table, after removing the ambiguities, is shown in Table 6.6.

Table 6.6: SLR parsing table after resolving duplicate entries

State	Action								Goto
	+	−	*	/	(	)	*id*	$	*E*
0		s2			s3		s4		1
1	s5	s6	s7	s8				acc	
2		s2			s3		s4		9
3		s2			s3		s4		10
4	r8	r8	r8	r8		r8		r8	
5		s2			s3		s4		11
6		s2			s3		s4		12
7		s2			s3		s4		13
8		s2			s3		s4		14
9	r6	r6	r6	r6		r6		r6	
10	s5	s6	s7	s8		s15			
11	r2	r2	s7	s8		r2		r2	
12	r3	r3	s7	s8		r3		r3	
13	r4	r4	r4	r4		r4		r4	
14	r5	r5	r5	r5		r5		r5	
15	r7	r7	r7	r7		r7		r7	

6.2.5 Error Recovery in LR Parser

As noted earlier, the undefined entries in the LR parsing table mean *error.* The parser detects an error while consulting the table for a particular state and input symbol combination, for which the table entry has been left blank. However, each such error situation can be arrived at from some particular sequences of moves by the parser, thus proper error messages can be flashed to the user. Moreover, the error handling routines can be made to modify the parser stack by popping out some entries, or pushing some desirable entries into the stack to make the parser arrive at a descent state from which it can proceed further. This is known as *error recovery.* Error recovery is necessary to enable the parser to detect multiple syntax errors and flashing them to the user for correction. We shall illustrate the idea with the help of a small expression grammar. Consider the grammar,

$$\begin{aligned} E' &\rightarrow E \\ E &\rightarrow E + E \mid E * E \mid id \end{aligned}$$

The LR(0) sets of items are as follows:

$$\begin{aligned}
I_0 &: \{[E' \rightarrow \cdot E], [E \rightarrow \cdot E + E], [E \rightarrow \cdot E * E], [E \rightarrow \cdot id]\}, \\
I_1 &: \{[E' \rightarrow E \cdot], [E \rightarrow E \cdot + E], [E \rightarrow E \cdot * E]\}, \\
I_2 &: \{[E \rightarrow id \cdot]\}, \\
I_3 &: \{[E \rightarrow E + \cdot E], [E \rightarrow \cdot E + E], [E \rightarrow \cdot E * E], [E \rightarrow \cdot id]\}, \\
I_4 &: \{[E \rightarrow E * \cdot E], [E \rightarrow \cdot E + E], [E \rightarrow \cdot E * E], [E \rightarrow \cdot id]\}, \\
I_5 &: \{[E \rightarrow E + E \cdot], [E \rightarrow E \cdot + E], [E \rightarrow E \cdot * E]\},
\end{aligned}$$

$$I_6 \ : \ \{[E \rightarrow E * E\cdot], [E \rightarrow E \cdot +E], [E \rightarrow E \cdot *E]\}$$

The Follow set of E is $\{+, *, \$\}$. The SLR parsing table for the grammar is shown in Table 6.7. The error entries have been marked as $e1$ and $e2$, corresponding to the two error routines to be called in various situations. The routine $e1$ has been called from states 0,3, and 4 on seeing an operator, or end of string, while an *id* was expected. Thus, the routine may push an *id* and state 2 onto the stack and proceed. On the other hand, routine $e2$ has been called from states 1, 2, 5, and 6 upon getting an *id*, while expecting an operator. The error handler will push a '+' and state 3 onto the stack and proceed.

Table 6.7: SLR parsing table with error entries

State	Action				Goto
	id	+	*	$	*E*
0	s2	e1	e1	e1	1
1	e2	s3	s4	acc	
2	e2	r3	r3	r3	
3	s2	e1	e1	e1	5
4	s2	e1	e1	e1	6
5	e2	r1	s4	r1	
6	e2	r2	r2	r2	

Consider the input string "$id + *\$$". The parser proceeds as shown in Table 6.8. Thus, the

Table 6.8 Error recovery

Stack	Input	Error message and action
0	$id + *\$$	shift
$0id2$	$+ * \$$	reduce by $E \rightarrow id$
$0E1$	$+ * \$$	shift
$0E1 + 3$	$*\$$	"*id* expected", pushed *id* and 2 to stack
$0E1 + 3id2$	$*\$$	reduce by $E \rightarrow id$
$0E1 + 3E5$	$*\$$	shift
$0E1 + 3E5 * 4$	$\$$	"*id* expected", pushed *id* and 2 to stack
$0E1 + 3E5 * 4id2$	$\$$	reduce by $E \rightarrow id$
$0E1 + 3E5 * 4E6$	$\$$	reduce by $E \rightarrow E * E$
$0E1 + 3E5$	$\$$	reduce by $E \rightarrow E + E$
$0E1$	$\$$	accept

parsing proceeds to the end recovering from syntax errors, flashing proper error messages and modifying the stack to recover from the error.

6.3 INTERMEDIATE CODE GENERATION

When a compiler compiles a program in high-level language, it produces the machine code targeted to some processor. However, many a time, the compilers are designed to produce an intermediary output which represents the input program in some hypothetical language or data structure. Such representations are known as *intermediate code* to signify that they are representations between the source language and the target machine language programs. Such intermediate codes offer a host of advantages as compared to direct code generations.

1. Intermediate code is closer to the target machine than the source language, and hence easier to generate code from.
2. Unlike machine languages, intermediate code is (more or less) machine independent. This makes it easier to retarget the compiler to various different target processors.
3. It allows a variety of optimizations to be performed in a machine-independent fashion.
4. Typically, intermediate code generation can be implemented via *syntax-directed translation* (that is, along with the parser as it is doing various reductions), and thus can be folded into parsing by augmenting the parser.

Among the intermediate representation techniques, *three-address code* is the widely used one. The statements in three-address code are such that the source language statements can be efficiently represented. Keeping this in view, the intermediate languages normally have the following type of statements:

1. *Assignment:* The three type of assignment statements needed are,

   $x = y$ op z, op being a binary operator
   $x =$ op y, op being a unary operator
   $x = y$

   It should be noted that for all operators in the source language, there should be a counterpart in the intermediate language. Any other translation may lead to unoptimized code.

2. *Jumps:* Both unconditional and conditional jumps are needed. Unconditional jump is like,

   goto L, L being a label

   The conditional jump has the form,

   if x relop y goto L

3. *Indexed assignment:*

   $x = y[i]$
   $x[i] = y$

   Only one-dimensional arrays need to be supported. Arrays of higher dimensions can be converted to one-dimensional arrays.

4. *Address and pointer assignments:* Languages like Pascal and C allow pointer assignments. The three-address codes representing these languages also need statements handling pointers. The following are the type of statements needed:

   $x = \&y$, address of y assigned to x
   $x = *y$, content of location pointed to by y is assigned to x
   $x = y$, simple pointer assignment, where x and y are pointer variables

5. *Procedure call/Return:* A call to the procedure $P(x_1, x_2, \ldots, x_n)$ with the parameters $x_1, x_2, \ldots, x_n$ is converted as

   param x_1
   param x_2
   ⋮
   param x_n
   call P, n

   A procedure is implemented using the following statements (over and above the other three-address statements):

   enter f, setup and initialization
   leave f, cleanup actions (if any)
   return
   return x
   retrieve x, save returned value in x

6. *Miscellaneous:* There may be some other statements needed depending upon the source language. However, one such statement to define the jump target is,

   label L

6.3.1 Three-Address Code Generation

Three-address code for a source language program can be generated efficiently by associating some attributes to the terminals and nonterminals of the grammar and computing the values of these attributes as parsing proceeds. The set of attributes to be associated depends upon the source language constructs. To start with, we will consider the grammar for assigning an expression to an identifier as per the following grammar:

$$S \rightarrow id := E$$
$$E \rightarrow E + E \mid E * E \mid -E \mid (E) \mid id$$

With the nonterminal E, two attributes *E.place* and *E.code* are assigned. *E.place* is the name that will hold the value of E and *E.code* is a sequence of 3-address statements corresponding to the evaluation of E. For S, we have only one attribute *S.code*, that is a sequence of 3-address statements. For the terminal symbol *id*, the attribute *id.place* contains the name of the variable to be assigned. To write the semantic rules, we use two more functions. The function *newtemp()* without any argument returns a unique new temporary variable, while the function *gen* accepts a string and produces it as a three-address quadruple. The operator '||' corresponds to the concatenation and is used to join two 3-address code segments. The semantic actions are shown in Table 6.9.

Table 6.9: Three-address code generation for assignment statements

Grammar Rule	Semantic Actions
$S \to id := E$	$S.code := E.code \|\|$ gen(id.place ':=' $E.place$)
$E \to E_1 + E_2$	$E.place :=$ newtemp();
	$E.code := E_1.code \|\| E_2.code \|\|$ gen($E.place$ ':=' $E_1.place$ '+' $E_2.place$)
$E \to E_1 * E_2$	$E.place :=$ newtemp();
	$E.code := E_1.code \|\| E_2.code \|\|$ gen($E.place$ ':=' $E_1.place$ '*' $E_2.place$)
$E \to -E_1$	$E.place :=$ newtemp();
	$E.code := E_1.code \|\|$ gen($E.place$ ':=' 'uminus' $E_1.place$)
$E \to (E_1)$	$E.place := E_1.place$;
	$E.code := E_1.code$
$E \to id$	$E.place := id.place$;
	$E.code :=$ ' '

EXAMPLE 6.12 Consider the statement:

$$x := (y + z) * (-w + v)$$

The annotated parse tree for the statement is shown in Fig. 6.20. The reduction sequence for a bottom-up parser is marked with the encircled numbers in the figure. The actions at various stages of reductions encircled in the figure are as shown in Table 6.10.

6.3.2 Translation of Boolean Expressions

In most of the programming languages, Boolean expressions are used in the conditional statements to express the condition. The expression evaluates to either *true* or *false*, and accordingly, program control jumps to one statement or the other. Thus, with a Boolean expression B, we can associate two attributes:

1. $B.true$: defining the place control should reach if B is true

2. $B.false$: defining the place control should reach if B is false

Let the grammar for Boolean expressions be,

$$B \to B \text{ or } B \mid B \text{ and } B \mid \text{not } B \mid (B) \mid \text{id relop id} \mid true \mid false$$

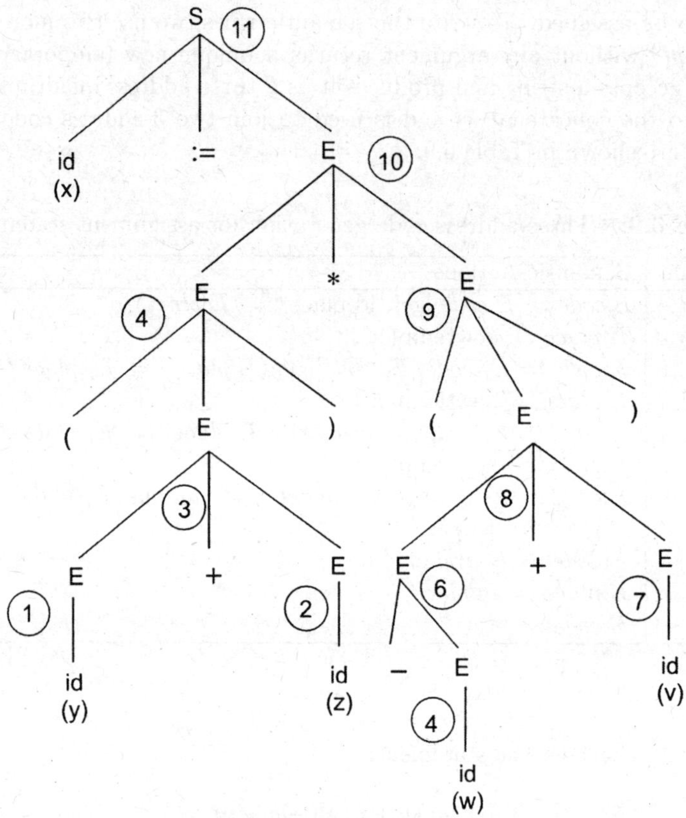

FIGURE 6.20 Parse tree.

A three-address code generation scheme for $B \rightarrow B_1$ or B_2 can be like this,

$$
\begin{array}{l}
\{\ B_1.\text{true} = B.\text{true} \\
\quad B_1.\text{false} = \text{newlabel()} \\
\quad B_2.\text{true} = B.\text{true} \\
\quad B_2.\text{false} = B.\text{false} \\
\quad B.\text{code} = B_1.\text{code} \parallel \text{gen}(B_1.\text{false} \text{ ':'}) \parallel B_2.\text{code} \\
\}
\end{array}
$$

Here we assume that the true and false transfer points for the entire expression B are known beforehand. If B_1 is true, the entire expression B is true. We need not evaluate B_2. This shortening of evaluation for Boolean expression is also known as *short-circuit evaluation.* Thus, if B_1 is true, the control can be transferred to the point corresponding to B.true. However, if B_1 is false, B_2 needs to be evaluated. Thus, B_1.false is assigned a new label (generated by a call to the function *newlabel()*) marking the beginning of evaluation of B_2. The full set of rules for translation are shown next.

Table 6.10: Code generation

Reduction No.	Action
1	$E.place = y$
2	$E.place = z$
3	$E.place = t_1$ $E.code = \{t_1 := y + z\}$
4	$E.place = t_1$ $E.code = \{t_1 := y + z\}$
5	$E.place = w$
6	$E.place = t_2$ $E.code = \{t_2 := uminus\ \ w\}$
7	$E.place = v$
8	$E.place = t_3$ $E.code = \{t_2 := uminus\ \ w, t_3 := t_2 + v\}$
9	$E.place = t_3$ $E.code = \{t_2 := uminus\ \ w, t_3 := t_2 + v\}$
10	$E.place = t_4$ $E.code = \{t_1 := y + z, t_2 := uminus\ \ w, t_3 := t_2 + v, t_4 := t_1 * t_3\}$
11	$S.code = \{t_1 := y + z, t_2 := uminus\ \ w, t_3 := t_2 + v, t_4 := t_1 * t_3, x := t_4\}$

1. $B \rightarrow B_1$ or B_2

   { B_1.true = B.true
   B_1.false = newlabel()
   B_2.true = B.true
   B_2.false = B.false
   B.code = B_1.code || gen(B_1.false ':') || B_2.code
   }

2. $B \rightarrow B_1$ and B_2

   { B_1.true = newlabel()
   B_1.false = B.false
   B_2.true = B.true
   B_2.false = B.false
   B.code = B_1.code || gen(B_1.true ':') || B_2.code
   }

3. $B \rightarrow$ not B_1

   { B_1.true = B.false
   B_1.false = B.true
   B.code = B_1.code
   }

4. $B \to (B_1)$

$$\{\ B_1.\text{true} = B.\text{true}$$
$$B_1.\text{false} = B.\text{false}$$
$$B.\text{code} = B_1.\text{code}$$
$$\}$$

5. $B \to id_1 \text{ relop } id_2$

{
  B.code = gen('if' id_1.place relop id_2.place 'goto' $B.true$) || gen('goto' $B.false$)
}

6. $B \to true$

{
  B.code = gen('goto' $B.true$);
}

7. $B \to false$

{
  B.code = gen('goto' $B.false$);
}

However, this style of translation makes the scheme inherently a two-pass procedure, where in the first pass we compute all the jump targets (that is, $B.true$ and $B.false$, for all Boolean expressions appearing within conditional statements) and the actual code generation occurring in the second pass. The process can be clubbed into a single phase by modifying the grammar a little bit, along with the introduction of a few more attributes for B and a few new procedures. The new attributes of B are as follows:

1. *B.truelist*: containing the list of locations within the generated three-address code for B, at which B is definitely true. All these points should transfer the control to *B.true*, once defined.

2. $B.falselist$: similar to *B.truelist*, however it contains all the locations where B is definitely false, and should be filled up with the value $B.false$, once defined.

The generated three-address code is visualized as an array of quadruples. The following functions are defined to carry out various tasks during code generation.

1. *Createlist(i)*: creates a new list with a single entry i – an index into the array of quadruples.

2. *mergelist*($list_1$, $list_2$): returns a new list containing $list_1$ followed by $list_2$.

3. *backpatch(list, target)*: inserts target as the target label into each quadruple pointed to by the entries in *list*.

To ease the code generation process, we introduce a dummy nonterminal M with an attribute $M.quad$, which can hold the address of a quadruple. The modified grammar is,

$$B \rightarrow B \text{ or } MB \mid B \text{ and } MB \mid \text{not } B \mid (B) \mid \text{id relop id} \mid true \mid false$$

$$M \rightarrow \epsilon$$

The rule $M \rightarrow \epsilon$ has got only one action during reduction:

$$\{M.quad = nextquad()\}$$

where function *nextquad()* returns the address of the next quadruple to be generated. To understand its role in the code generation process, let us consider the rule,

$$B \rightarrow B_1 \text{ or } MB_2$$

Since before the reduction for B_2 starts, reduction of $M \rightarrow \epsilon$ has already taken place, $M.quad$ points to the address for the first quadruple of B_2. Thus, the semantic actions for this rule can be written as,

{ backpatch($B_1.falselist$, $M.quad$)
$B.truelist$ = mergelist($B_1.truelist, B_2.truelist$)
$B.falselist = B_2.falselist$
}

Since if B_1 is false, we have to evaluate B_2, $B_1.falselist$ has been filled up with the address of the starting quadruple of B_2. The full truelist for B is obtained by merging the truelists of B_1 and B_2. The falselist of B is same as the falselist of B_2. The complete set of rules is shown next.

1. $B \rightarrow B_1$ or MB_2

{ backpatch($B_1.falselist$, $M.quad$)
$B.truelist$ = mergelist($B_1.truelist, B_2.truelist$)
$B.falselist = B_2.falselist$
}

2. $B \rightarrow B_1$ and MB_2

{ backpatch($B_1.truelist$, $M.quad$)
$B.truelist = B_2.truelist$
$B.falselist$ = mergelist($B_1.falselist, B_2.falselist$)
}

3. $B \rightarrow$ not B_1

{ $B.truelist = B_1.falselist$
$B.falselist = B_1.truelist$
}

4. $B \to (B_1)$

$$\{\ B.truelist = B_1.truelist$$
$$B.falselist = B_1.falselist\ \}$$

5. $B \to true$

$\{\ B.truelist = makelist(nextquad)$
emit('goto ...')
$\}$

6. $B \to false$

$\{\ B.falselist = makelist(nextquad)$
emit('goto ...')
$\}$

7. $M \to \epsilon$

$$\{M.quad = nextquad\}$$

8. $B \to id\ relop\ id$

$\{\ B.truelist = makelist(nextquad)$
$B.falselist = makelist(nextquad + 1)$
emit('if' id relop id 'goto ...')
emit('goto ...')
$\}$

EXAMPLE 6.13 Consider the Boolean expression

$$x > y \text{ or } z > k \text{ and not } r < s$$

The corresponding parse tree has been shown in Fig. 6.21. Assuming that code generation starts from quadruple number 1 (that is, *nextquad* is initialized to 1), actions at various reductions are as follows:

Red. 1: $B.truelist = \{1\}$
$B.falselist = \{2\}$

The following lines of codes are generated:

1: if $x > y$ goto ...
2: goto ...

Red. 2: $M.quad = 3$

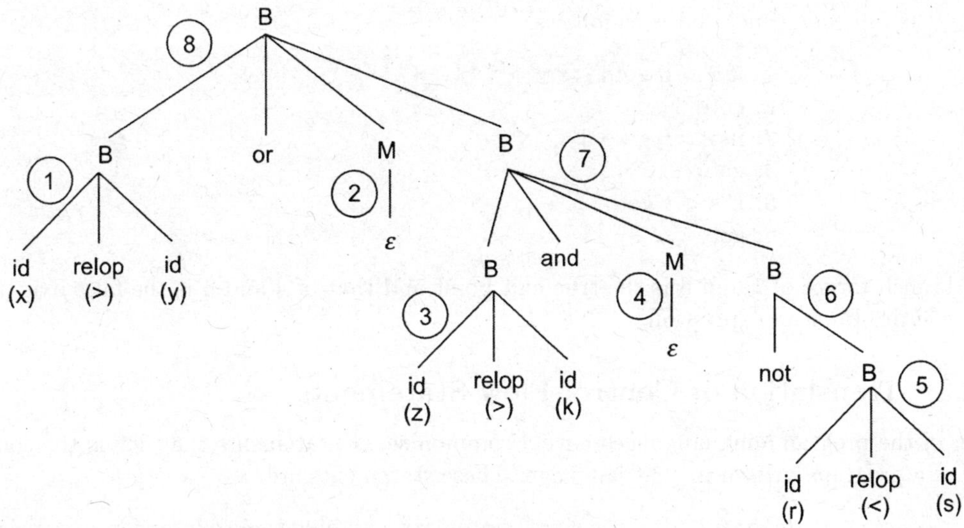

FIGURE 6.21 Parse tree for Boolean expression.

Red. 3: $B.truelist = \{3\}$
$B.falselist = \{4\}$

Codes generated are as follows:

3: if $z > k$ goto ...
4: goto ...

Red. 4: $M.quad = 5$

Red. 5: $B.truelist = \{5\}$
$B.falselist = \{6\}$

Codes generated are as follows:

5: if $r < s$ goto ...
6: goto ...

Red. 6: $B.truelist = \{6\}$
$B.falselist = \{5\}$

Red. 7: This backpatches the list {3} with 5. Thus, quadruple 3 is modified as:

3: if $z > k$ goto 5

Red. 8: Backpatches the list {2} with 3. Thus, quadruple 2 is modified as:

2: goto 3

$B.truelist = \{1, 6\}$
$B.falselist = \{4, 5\}$

Thus, the full code generated is as follows:

1: if $x > y$ goto ...
2: goto 3
3: if $z > k$ goto 5
4: goto ...
5: if $r < s$ goto ...
6: goto ...

The branch target of 1 and 6 is the true exit point and that of 4 and 5 is the false exit point of the entire Boolean expression.

6.3.3 Translation of Control Flow Statements

Most of the programming languages have a common set of statements that define the control flow of a program written in that language. These statements are:

1. *Assignment statement:* It has a single statement assigning some expression to a variable. After executing this statement, control flows to the immediate next statement in the sequence.
2. *if-then-else statement:* It has a condition associated with it. Control flows either to the *then-part* or to the *else-part.*
3. *while-do loop:* The control remains within the loop until a specified condition becomes false.
4. *Block of statements:* A group of statements put within a *begin-end* block marker.

The grammar for these statements is given by,

$$
\begin{aligned}
S &\rightarrow \text{if } B \text{ then } S \\
&\mid \text{if } B \text{ then } S \text{ else } S \\
&\mid \text{while } B \text{ do } S \\
&\mid \text{begin } L \text{ end} \\
&\mid A \text{ /* for assignment */} \\
L &\rightarrow L\ S \\
&\mid S
\end{aligned}
$$

To aid in the code generation process, the grammar is slightly modified by introducing two new marker nonterminals M and N. The modified grammar is as follows:

$$
\begin{aligned}
S &\rightarrow \text{if } B \text{ then } M\ S \\
&\mid \text{if } B \text{ then } M\ S\ N \text{ else } M\ S \\
&\mid \text{while } M\ B \text{ do } M\ S \\
&\mid \text{begin } L \text{ end} \\
&\mid A \text{ /* for assignment */}
\end{aligned}
$$

$$
\begin{aligned}
L &\rightarrow L\ M\ S \\
&\mid S \\
M &\rightarrow \epsilon \\
N &\rightarrow \epsilon
\end{aligned}
$$

Apart from the set of attributes for B (as in Boolean expressions), a few more attributes are defined as follows:

S.nextlist: is a list of quadruples containing jumps to the quadruple following S.

L.nextlist: same as S.nextlist, excepting the fact that L stands for a group of statements.

The nonterminal N has been introduced to enable us to generate a jump after the *then* part of *if-the-else* statement. The attribute N.nextlist holds the quadruple number for this statement. The entire set of actions are as follows:

1. $S \rightarrow$ if B then M S_1

   { backpatch(B.truelist, M.quad)
   S.nextlist := mergelist(B.falselist, S_1.nextlist) }

2. $S \rightarrow$ if B then $M_1 S_1 N$ else $M_2 S_2$

   { backpatch(B.truelist, M_1.quad)
   backpatch(B.falselist, M_2.quad)
   S.nextlist := mergelist(S_1.nextlist, mergelist(N.nextlist, S_2.nextlist)) }

3. $S \rightarrow$ while $M_1 B$ do $M_2 S_1$

   { backpatch(S_1.nextlist, M_1.quad)
   backpatch(E.truelist, M_2.quad)
   S.nextlist := E.falselist
   emit('goto' M_1.quad) }

4. $S \rightarrow$ begin L end

   { S.nextlist := L.nextlist }

5. $S \rightarrow A$

   { S.nextlist := nil }

6. $L \rightarrow L_1$ M S

   { backpatch(L_1.nextlist, M.quad)
   L.nextlist := S.nextlist }

7. $L \to S$

$$\{\ L.\text{nextlist} := S.\text{nextlist}\ \}$$

8. $M \to \epsilon$

$$\{\ M.\text{quad} := \text{nextquad}()\ \}$$

9. $N \to \epsilon$

{ N.nextlist := nextquad()
emit('goto ...') }

EXAMPLE 6.14 Consider the following piece of code:

```
begin
  while a > b do
  begin
    x = y + z
    a = a - b
  end
  x = y - z
end
```

The parse tree for the code segment has been shown in Fig. 6.22. The activities at various stages of reduction are as shown in Table 6.11.

The final code generated is as follows:

1: if $a > b$ goto 3
2: goto 8
3: $t_1 = y + z$
4: $x = t_1$
5: $t_2 = a - b$
6: $a = t_2$
7: goto 1
8: $t_3 = y - z$
9: $x = t_3$

6.4 TARGET CODE GENERATION

The final phase of the compiler is the *target code generation.* The intermediate code generator produces an intermediary code from which a simple template substitution could give the target code. However, due to the heterogeneous structures of target machines, generating an efficient code is always a challenge. The major responsibility of this phase is to ensure the generation of a correct code. Secondly, the code generated should be optimal in terms of space and time required for the execution of it. There are several factors affecting the code generation process. Some of them are discussed below. It may be noted that the peculiarity of the target code requirement can also affect the process significantly.

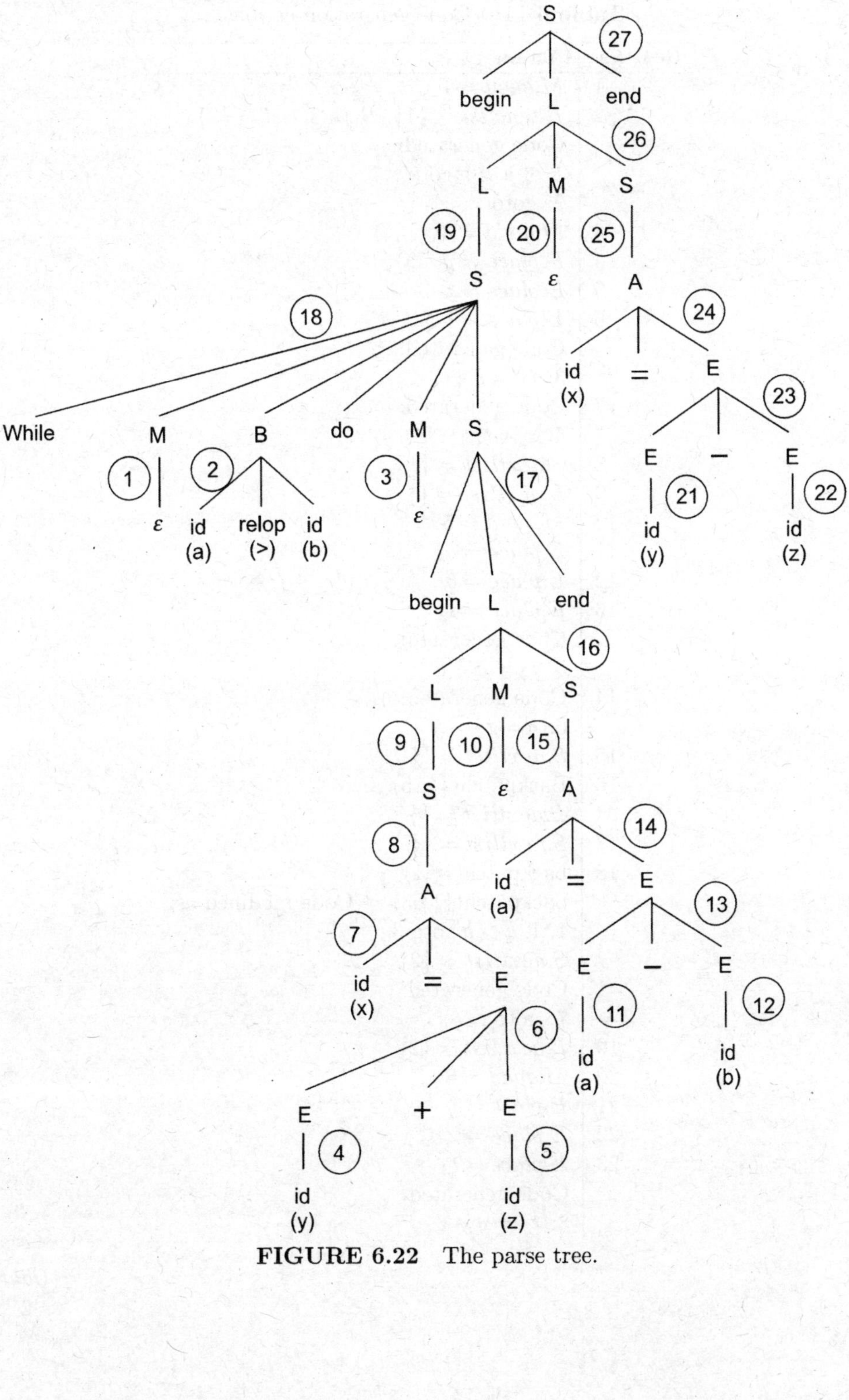

FIGURE 6.22 The parse tree.

Table 6.11: Code generation actions

Red. no.	Action
1	$M.quad = 1$
2	$B.truelist = \{1\}$, $B.falselist = \{2\}$ Code generated: 1: if $a > b$ goto ... 2: goto ...
3	$M.quad = 3$
4	$E.place = y$
5	$E.place = z$
6	$E.place = t_1$ Code generated: 3: $t_1 = y + z$
7	Code generated: 4: $x = t_1$
8	$S.nextlist = \{\}$
9	$L.nextlist = \{\}$
10	$M.quad = 5$
11	$E.place = a$
12	$E.place = b$
13	$E.place = t_2$ Code generated: 5: $t_2 = a - b$
14	Code generated: 6: $a = t_2$
15	$S.nextlist = \{\}$
16	Backpatch({}, 5) $L.nextlist = \{\}$
17	$S.nextlist = \{\}$
18	backpatch({},1) backpatch({1},3) ⇒ Code modified as: 1: if $a > b$ goto 3 $S.nextlist = \{2\}$ Code generated: 7: goto ...
19	$L.nextlist = \{2\}$
20	$M.quad = 8$
21	$E.place = y$
22	$E.place = z$
23	$E.place = t_3$ Code generated: 8: $t_3 = y - z$

(Contd.)

Table 6.11: (*Contd.*)

Red. no.	Action
24	Code generated: 9: $x = t_3$
25	*S.nextlist* = {}
26	Backpatch ({2},8) ⇒ Code modified as: 2: goto 8 *L.nextlist* = {}
27	*S.nextlist* = {}

1. *The input:* As noted earlier, the input comes in the form of an intermediate code. The proximity of the intermediate language to the target language controls the complexity of code generation. If for all operators, datatypes, and addressing modes in the intermediate language, there exist straightforward mappings to the target language, the code generation is simple template substitution, otherwise for each of the non-supported features a good amount of translation effort may be needed.

2. *Target code structure:* The structure of the target code controls the complexity of code generation. The final code may be an ***absolute code*** in which all the addresses are fixed, *relocatable*—allowing runtime relocation, or *assembly language code*—requiring assembler to generate the executable version. *Absolute code generation* may be easy because of the fixed location of program variables and code. *Relocatable code* may or may not be supported by the underlying hardware. For example, many processors support *based addressing, relative addressing*, etc. to aid in the relocation process. If relocation is not supported directly, the compiler must insert code to ensure smooth relocation. *Assembly language code* can be generated to be converted to executable version by an assembler. Features of the assembler may be utilized to make the code generation simpler. Code may also be generated targeted to virtual machine environment like *Java*. Thus, the challenges of code generation may be depicted to a great extent by the target architecture and language.

3. *Instruction selection:* Instruction selection plays a very critical role. This is because the target machine normally has a large variety of instructions, and for performing a particular operation of the intermediate language, there may be several alternative approaches possible. This is particularly true for *Complex Instruction Set Computers (CISC)*. Whereas, the *Reduced Instruction Set Computers (RISC)* offer comparatively fewer alternatives to the compiler designer. Though it is restrictive in some sense, the code generation algorithm can exercise the options in a better fashion when the number of alternatives is less.

4. *Register allocation:* Assigning variables to CPU registers is a difficult task because of the fact that the allocation problem is *NP*-complete. We will see later some heuristic approaches based on *graph colouring* to solve the problem. The issue is further complicated by the underlying hardware differentiating registers as *data* or *address* register. For operations involving some data operand, it should be kept in one of the data registers, while for address operands (like pointers), the address registers should be used. Some

operations need the source and destination operands to be kept in special pair of registers. All these architecture-specific issues make the register allocation for target code generation a non-trivial task.

5. *Evaluation order:* Finding a good evaluation order may affect the target code performance. Some order may require fewer registers, some may ensure higher degree of accurracy for floating point operations. Determining the best order is again an *NP*-complete problem.

6.4.1 Code Generation for Trees

Sethi & Ullman proposed an algorithm to generate target code for a tree using least number of registers. The algorithm can be divided into two phases.

1. *Labeling phase* that assigns a number to each tree node, indicating how many registers are needed to evaluate the subtree rooted at this node.
2. *Code generation phase* that performs the actual code generation.

To understand the process, we will take up an example. Let us consider the expression $(A - B) + ((C + D) + (E * F))$. The parse tree for it is shown in Fig. 6.23. Let the machine

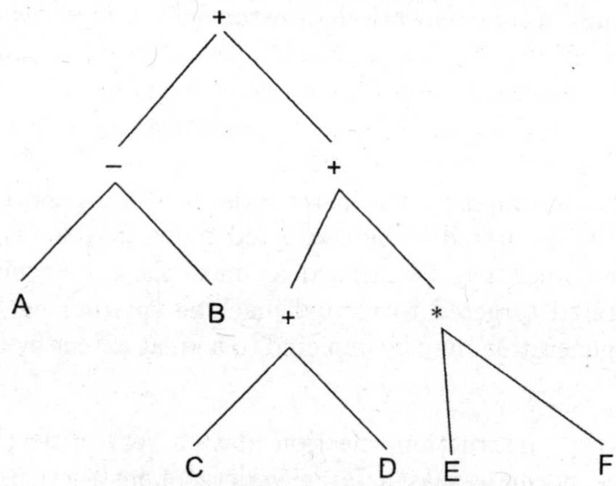

FIGURE 6.23 A tree DAG.

instructions be of the form:

$$op\ R_i,\ T$$

where *op* is an operation (LOAD, ADD, SUB, MULT etc.), R_i is a register, and T can be a memory reference or a register. For a tree node T, let l and r be the number of registers required to evaluate its left and right subtrees respectively. The following cases may occur:

Case 1: $l > r$

In this case we can evaluate the left subtree first, store it into one of the registers, say R_k. Now, we can evaluate the right subtree using the same registers excepting R_k. This is always possible, since $l > r$.

Case 2: $r > l$

This is similar to case 1, excepting the fact that now the right subtree should be evaluated first.

Case 3: $l = r$

In this case we need an extra register R_{l+1} to remember the result of the left subtree.

Case 4: T is a leaf node

If T is a tree leaf, then the number of registers to evaluate T is either 1 or 0, depending upon whether T is a left or a right subtree of its parent. (Because, the parent node "*op* R_i, T" can handle T directly from memory, but R_i must be in a register.) Thus, for a left subtree, the label is 1, whereas for a right subtree, the label is 0.

Thus, the numbering algorithm starts from the tree leaves and assigns 1 or 0 as in Case 4. Then, for each node with the children labelled l and r, if $l = r$, the node is labelled as $l + 1$, else the node is labelled as *max(l,r)*. The labels for the example are shown in Fig. 6.24.

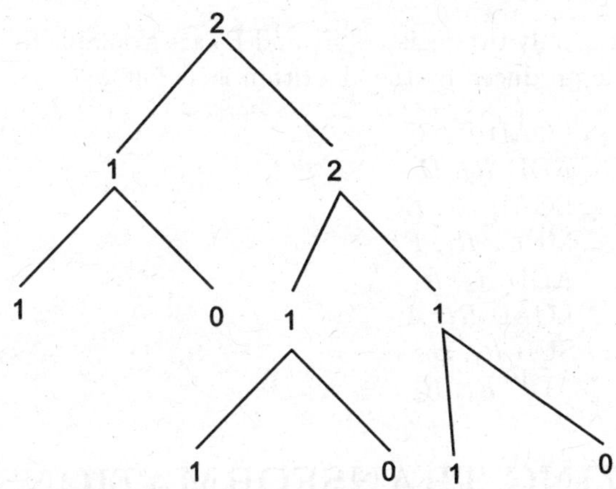

FIGURE 6.24 The labelled tree.

Next, we elaborate on the code generation phase. We use a stack of available registers, which initially contains all the registers in some order. The recursive code generation algorithm is as follows:

Algorithm Generate
Input: The tree rooted at T
Output: Target code for T

```
{
    if T is a leaf node and label(T) = 1 then
        output("load top(), T")
    if T is an internal node with children left and right then {
        if label(right) = 0 then {Generate(left); output("op top(), right")}
        else if (label(left) ≥ label(right)) then {
            Generate(left)
```

```
            R = pop()
            Generate(right)
            output("op R, top()")
            push(R)
        }
        else        /* label(l) < label(r) */
        {
            swap the top two elements of the stack
            Generate(right)
            R = pop()
            Generate(left)
            output("op top(), R")
            push(R)
            swap the top two elements of the stack
        }
    }
}
```

For example, assuming only two registers R_1 and R_2 are available to evaluate the expression in our example, the code produced by the algorithm is as follows:

```
LOAD R2, C
ADD R2, D
LOAD R1, E
MULT R1, F
ADD R2, R1
LOAD R1, A
SUB R1, B
ADD R1, R2
```

6.5 OPTIMIZING TRANSFORMATIONS

In this section, we elaborate various techniques for optimization which may be applied on the code to transform it, probably leading to better implementations. The approaches may be tried out for both local and global optimizations with the scope as found earlier. The major such transformations are:

1. Compile-time evaluation
2. Common sub-expression elimination
3. Variable propagation
4. Code movement optimization
5. Strength reduction
6. Dead code elimination
7. Loop optimization

In the following, we discuss each of these transformations:

6.5.1 Compile-time Evaluation

Compile-time evaluation deals with modifying the code, such that the expressions whose values can be precomputed at the compilation time and used (perhaps repeatedly) in the execution of the program are identified. Then the computations of such expressions are moved to compile-time, rather than during execution. There are two possible avenues through which it can be carried out, namely, *folding* and *constant propagation.*

Folding. Folding corresponds to the evaluation of an expression with constant operands at compilation time. In effect, the expression is replaced by a single value (hence the term *folding*).

EXAMPLE 6.15 Consider the expression to compute the area of a circle that needs the value of the constant π, which is approximated by the expression 22/7. The programmers often write the corresponding code as,

$$area = (22.0/7.0) * r * *2$$

Here, the evaluation of 22.0/7.0 can be performed during compilation to the machine accuracy, and used in the execution.

Typical applications of folding occur in address calculation for array references, where the products of many constants are *folded* into single constant value.

Constant propagation. Constant propagation corresponds to replacing a variable by the constant which has been assigned to it earlier. Though constant propagation alone does not lead to any optimization, it may help in other optimizations. For example, the constant propagation may help in folding an expression.

EXAMPLE 6.16 Consider the following piece of code:

$a = 3.1$

...

$x = a * 2.5$

The constant propagation can propagate the value 3.1 of a assigned at the first statement to the right-hand side of the statement $x = a * 2.5$ to modify it to the statement $x = 3.1 * 2.5$, which may now be folded and evaluated at compile-time.

However, the constant propagation is only possible if there are no intervening statements that may modify the value of the variable directly or indirectly. A direct modification is through an assignment statement whose left-hand side has the variable under consideration. Indirect assignments may result from usage of pointers, function calls, with the variable as a modifiable parameter. Moreover, if the intervening code between the assignment of the variable and its usage is not linear (that is, it contains branchings), a variable should be assigned the same constant value along all paths reaching its use.

EXAMPLE 6.17 Consider the program flow graph shown in Fig. 6.25. Here, constant propagation and folding is possible for $x + 17$ of block 9; however, it is not possible for $a + 7$ of block 10 because of the presence of another assignment $a = b$ at block 4.

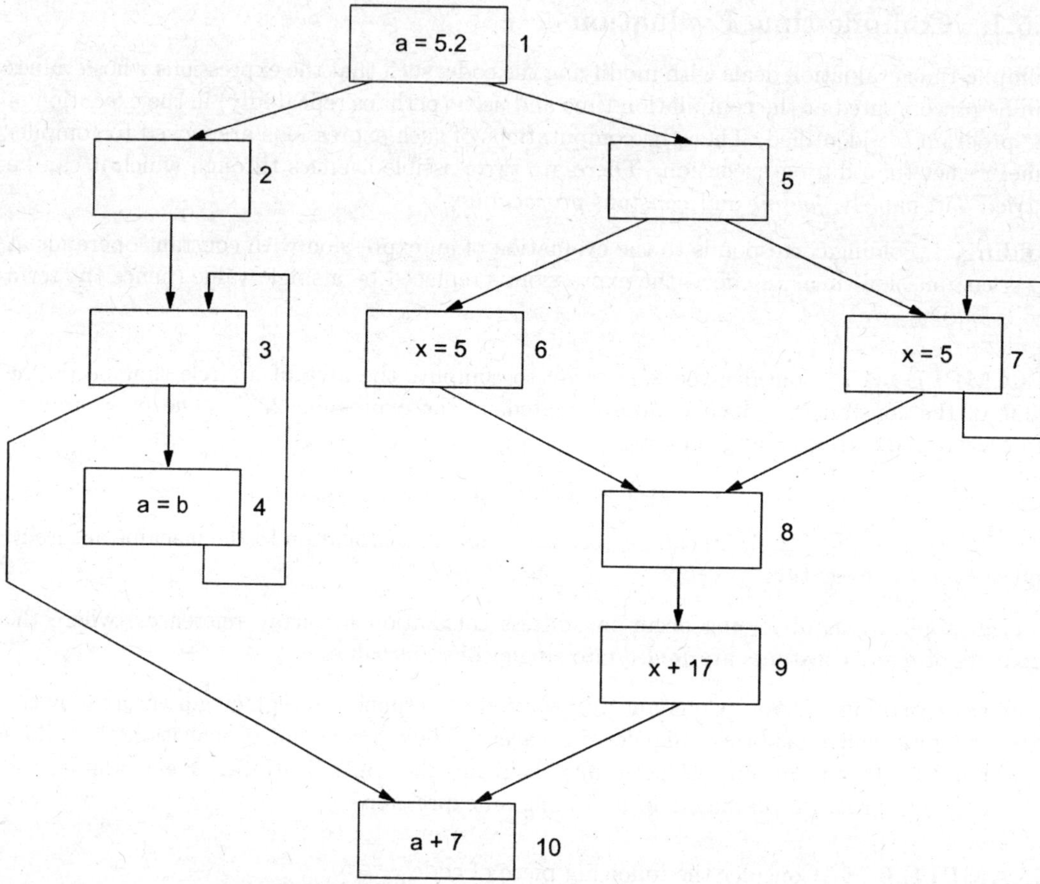

FIGURE 6.25 Constant propagation.

6.5.2 Common Sub-expression Elimination

A major source of optimization is the identification of common sub-expressions that are present in various expressions within the program. Once identified, the common sub-expression may be evaluated just once into a new temporary variable (if needed), and replace all occurrences of the sub-expression by the variable. For example, the code,

$$a = b * c$$
$$\ldots$$
$$x = b * c + 5$$

has the sub-expression $b * c$ common between the two statements, and thus can be reduced to single computation as follows:

$$temp = b * c$$
$$a = temp$$
$$\ldots$$
$$x = temp + 5$$

Identification of common sub-expressions is not a very simple task as explained in the following example. Typically, the search is made only for *lexically equivalent* expressions (that is, the expressions consisting of the same identifiers and operators, and appearing in the same order). The expressions must also evaluate to *identical* values during any course of execution of the program. This ensures the preservation of *semantic equivalence* between the original and transformed code.

EXAMPLE 6.18 Consider the program flow graph shown in Fig. 6.26. The following observations can be made.

1. $a * b$ of block 10 is a common sub-expression.
2. $x + y$ of block 8 is not a common sub-expression to $x + y$ in block 5. This is because in an execution sequence that passes the control from block 5 to block 8 via block 6, the value of x is modified. Thus, the two expressions will not evaluate to identical values.
3. $c*b$ in block 4 is also a common sub-expression to $a*b$ in blocks 1 and 10. The assignment $c = a$ in block 2 ensures this. However, it is very difficult to catch such situations. Here we have a *nonlexical equivalence* between the expressions.

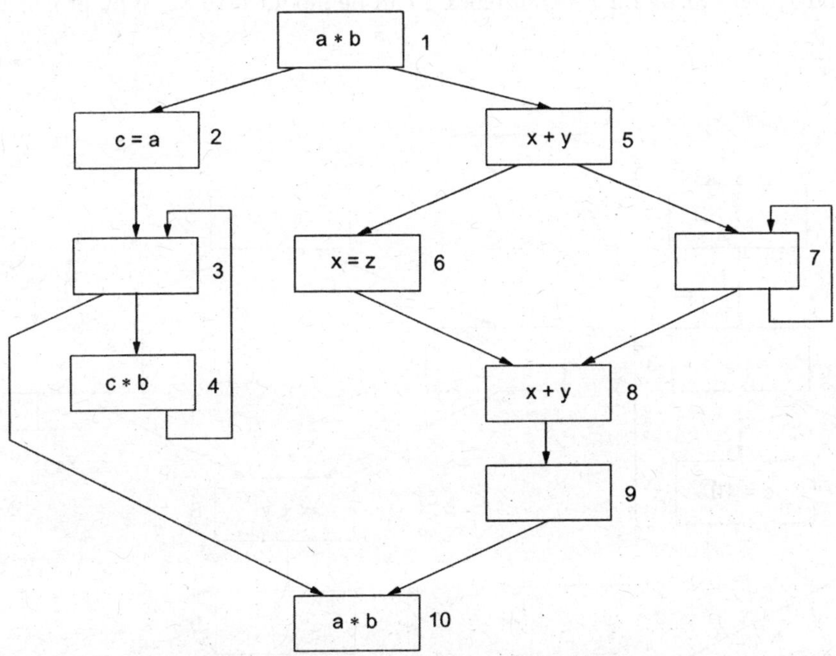

FIGURE 6.26 Common sub-expression.

6.5.3 Variable Propagation

Similar to constant propagation, variable propagation suggests replacing a variable by another, holding identical value. For example, consider the following piece of code.

$$c = d$$
$$\ldots$$
$$\ldots$$
$$z = c + e$$
$$x = d + e - 10.5$$

Here the first statement ensures that the values of c and d are the same. In the subsequent code, if none of them are modified, the statement $z = c + e$ can be modified to $z = d + e$ by propagating the variable d to it. This creates the possibility of identifying $d + e$ as a common sub-expression in the last two statements, and possibly evaluated only once.

Variable propagation should be carried out with the restriction that along all paths reaching to its use, a variable should be assigned the value of the same right-hand side variable, and neither variable should be modified following such assignment. The following example illustrates the case further.

EXAMPLE 6.19 Consider the flow-graph shown in Fig. 6.27. Here, the variable a in block 10 cannot be replaced by c following the assignment $a = c$ in block 1. This is because, block 4 modifies the value of c, and thus the modified expression in block 10 will not be equivalent to the original expression. However, assuming that neither x nor z has been modified in the blocks 6 and 7, the expression $x + y$ in block 8 can be modified to $z + y$ by propagation of z.

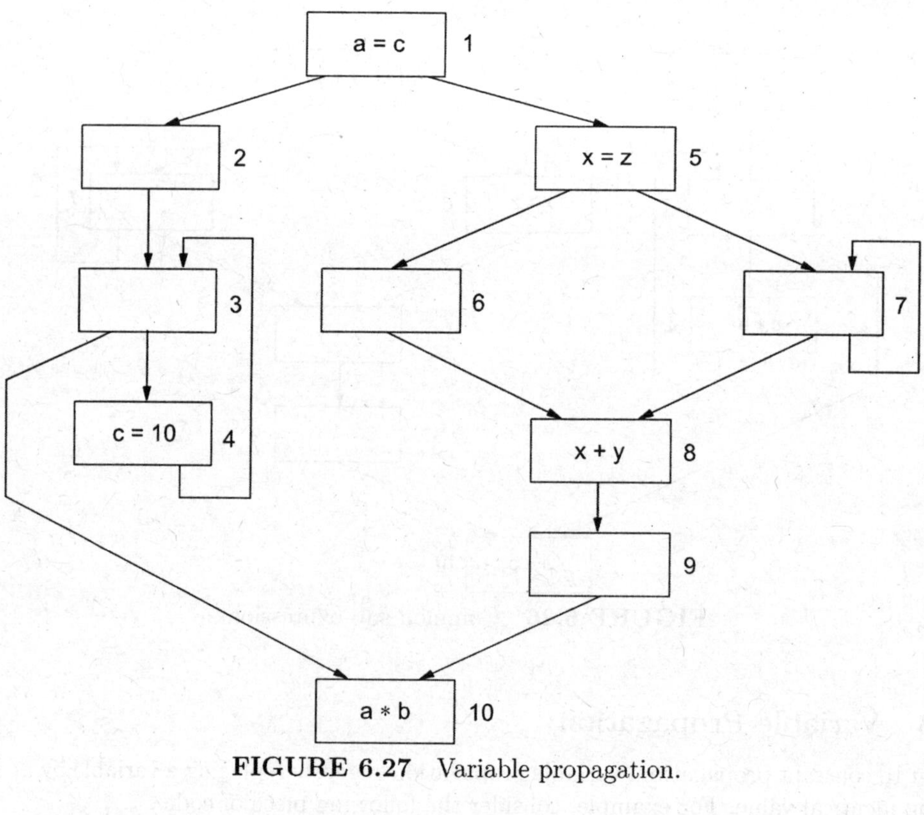

FIGURE 6.27 Variable propagation.

6.5.4 Code Movement Optimization

Code movement refers to moving the code from one part of the program to another, ensuring that the resulting program is equivalent to the original one. Code movement is performed so as to:

- **Reduce the size of the program,** also known as *code space reduction*, and
- **Reduce the execution frequency of the code subjected to movement** – *Execution frequency reduction.*

1. **Code space reduction:** It is similar to common sub-expression elimination. However, here the objective is not to reduce the execution frequency of the common sub-expression, rather it reduces the code size by generating the code for common sub-expression only once. This is often performed by a technique called *code hoisting* that brings the code nearer to the start point. For example, consider the following piece of code.

$$\begin{array}{l} \text{if } a < b \text{ then} \\ \quad z = x**2 \\ \quad \ldots \\ \text{else} \\ \quad y = x**2 + 19 \end{array}$$

   Here the code to compute $x**2$ is repeated in both the *then* and *else*-part of the program. It can be modified to compute $x**2$ only once before the *if*-statement. Thus, though the execution frequency for the sub-expression is not modified, the code is generated for once only.

$$\begin{array}{l} temp = x**2 \\ \text{if } a < b \text{ then} \\ \quad z = temp \\ \quad \ldots \\ \text{else} \\ \quad y = temp + 19 \end{array}$$

2. **Execution frequency reduction:** These techniques identify the common codes to be evaluated at various places in the program and try to move them to the place, so as to reduce the frequency of their execution. There are two avenues of doing such transformations.

   (a) *Code hoisting:* As noted earlier, code hoisting refers to promoting the code to some earlier part of the program. It can be used to reduce execution frequency of expressions if the expression is *partially available.* That is, it is available along at least one path reaching the evaluation of the expression.

EXAMPLE 6.20 Consider the code segment,

$$\begin{array}{l} \text{if } a < b \text{ then} \\ \quad z = x * 2 \\ \quad \ldots \\ \text{else} \\ \quad y = 19 \\ g = x * 2 \end{array}$$

In this case, during execution of the code segment, the expression $x * 2$ is evaluated twice for the condition $a < b$. The computation of $x * 2$ can be hoisted to the *else*-part also to make the evaluation of the expression always one.

$$\begin{array}{l} \text{if } a < b \text{ then} \\ \quad temp = x * 2 \\ \quad z = temp \\ \quad \ldots \\ \text{else} \\ \quad y = 19 \\ \quad temp = x * 2 \\ g = temp \end{array}$$

Safety of code movement. Movement of an expression e from a block b_i to another block b_j is said to be *safe* if it does not introduce a new occurrence of e along any path in the program. *Unsafe* code movement may change the meaning of the program altogether. It may lead to surprising execution conditions (for example, overflow).

EXAMPLE 6.21 Consider the code segment,

$$\begin{array}{l} \ldots \\ \text{if } a < b \text{ then} \\ \quad z = x * 2 \\ \text{else} \\ \quad y = 19 \end{array}$$

The following is an unsafe hoisting of the code as the expression $x*2$ gets introduced into the *else* part also:

$$\begin{array}{l} \quad temp = x * 2 \\ \text{if } a < b \text{ then} \\ \quad z = temp \\ \text{else} \\ \quad y = 19 \end{array}$$

Unsafe movement of the code should be avoided.

(b) *Loop optimization:* This involves identifying the statements within the body of the loop, whose value do not depend on the iteration. Such computations can be taken out of the loop to reduce their frequency of execution. We will discuss about it in detail while handling techniques for *loop optimization.*

6.5.5 Strength Reduction

Strength reduction corresponds to the replacement of an operator requiring higher execution time by an equivalent operator requiring much lesser processor time. For example, it may be possible to replace '*' by '+'. Multiplication/division by the powers of 2 can be modified to be left/right shift of integer data.

EXAMPLE 6.22 Consider the code segment,

```
for i = 1 to 10 do
    ...
    x = i * 5
    ...
end
```

The code segment can be modified as follows to use addition instead of multiplication.

```
temp = 5
for i = 1 to 10 do
    ...
    x = temp
    ...
    temp = temp + 5
end
```

A typical case of strength reduction occurs in address calculation for array references. For example, the code segment,

```
for i = 1 to 50 do
    a[i] = ...
end
```

If each element of the array requires 4 bytes, then the address of $a[i]$ is equal to ((address of $a[0]$) $+i * 4$). Now, strength reduction can be applied as shown in the previous example to optimize the code.

Strength reduction is typically applied to integer expressions involving an *induction variable* (defined later during loop optimization) and a high strength operator. It may be noted that strength reduction should not be attempted on floating point expressions because the strength reduced program may produce different results than the original program. This may happen due to the finite precision of computer arithmetic. A repeated floating point operation may accummulate a good amount of error value as compared to the result of a multiplication.

6.5.6 Dead Code Elimination

Dead codes are the portions of the program that can never get executed for any control flow through the program. Thus, these codes can be eliminated from the program without affecting the program behaviour. For example,

1. A variable is said to be *dead* at a place in a program if the value contained in the variable at that place is not used anywhere in the program.

2. If an assignment is made to a variable v at a place where v is dead, then the assignment is a dead one.

Dead codes can get introduced in various manners. A typical example is the debugging information printed in the early phase of the program development. It is normally done like this,

```
#define DEBUG 1
...
#ifdef DEBUG
    print debugging information
...
```

Once the programmer is satisfied that the program is executing correctly, the first line is just changed to '#define DEBUG 0'. However, the statements to print debugging information remain there, which now become *dead code.*

EXAMPLE 6.23 Consider the flow graph shown in Fig. 6.28. The following observations can be made.

1. The assignment $a = c$ of block 1 is not dead, since a is used in the block 4.
2. The assignment $x = y - 5$ of block 5 is dead. The expression $y - 5$ can also be eliminated, since it is no longer meaningful. However, an expression capable of producing *side-effects* (for example, function calls) cannot be so simply eliminated.

6.5.7 Loop Optimization

Loops are very important candidates for optimization. Since the body of the loop is executed again and again, a small improvement in the execution of the loop body can result in a remarkable overall improvement in the performance of the program. Moreover, the loops may be nested. Thus, an improvement in the innermost loop body is always targeted by the optimizing compilers. In the following, we discuss about the commonly used loop optimization techniques.

Induction Variable Analysis. An induction variable v is an integer scalar variable which is only subjected to the following kinds of assignments in a loop:

$$v = v \; op \; constant$$

where the operator *op* can be addition or subtraction only. For example, $j = 4 * i + 1$. As shown in Example 6.22, it can be updated appropriately each time the loop variable is changed, resulting into a *strength reduction* transformation. This may even result into the elimination of certain portion of the code as *dead code.* Here i is an induction variable.

Loop Fission. Loop fission attempts to break a loop into multiple loops over the same index range, but each taking only a part of the loop's body. This can improve the *locality of reference.* For example, consider the code segment,

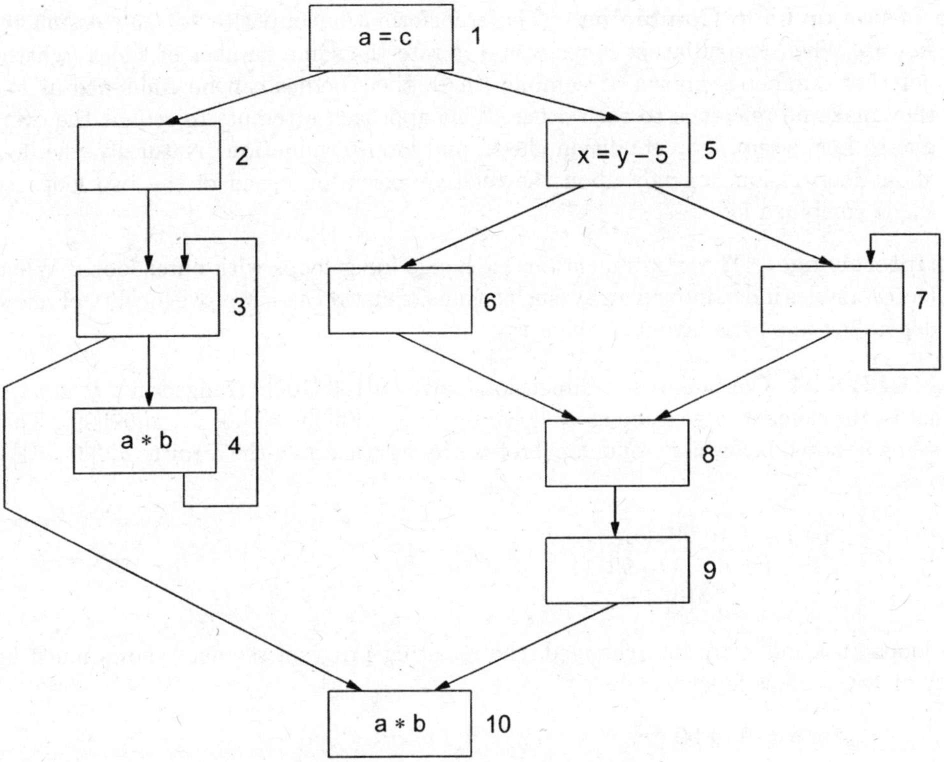

FIGURE 6.28 Dead code elimination.

for i = 1 to 100 do
  $a[i] = \ldots$
  $b[i] = \ldots$
end loop

Here, for each value of i, the program first refers to an element of the array a and then another element from the array b. If there is no data dependency between the two statements in the loop body, it can be broken down into two loops as shown below:

for i = 1 to 100 do
  $a[i] = \ldots$
end loop
for i = 1 to 100 do
  $b[i] = \ldots$
end loop

This version definitely shows better locality in the reference pattern, since in the first loop it accesses the memory locations corresponding to a only, and in the second loop, it accesses the area for b only.

Loop Fusion or Loop Combining. The transformation opposite to *loop fission* is *loop fusion.* When two adjacent loops would iterate the same number of times (whether or not that number is known at compile time), their bodies can be combined as long as they make no reference to each other. This approach attempts to reduce the overhead due to loop setup, loop condition check, and loop termination. Naturally, the decision about loop fusion depends upon the relative execution speed of the two loops versus single combined loop.

Loop Interchange. These optimizations exchange inner loops with outer loops. When the loop variables index into an array, such a transformation can improve locality of reference, depending upon the layout of the array.

EXAMPLE 6.24 Consider a two-dimensional array $a[100][100]$ arranged in a *row-major* order, that is, the elements are stored as $a[0][0], a[0][1], \ldots, a[0][99], a[1][0], \ldots, a[99][99]$. The program segment noted below makes nonlocal references as it accesses the array as $a[0][0], a[1][0], \ldots$, and so on.

```
for j = 0 to 99 do
    for i = 0 to 99 do
        a[i][j] = ...
```

If the loops on i and j are interchanged, the resulting program segment shows much better locality of reference as follows:

```
for i = 0 to 99 do
    for j = 0 to 99 do
        a[i][j] = ...
```

Loop Reversal. It reverses the order in which values are assigned to the index variable. This is a subtle optimization which can help eliminate dependencies and thus enable other optimizations.

EXAMPLE 6.25 Consider the problem of finding last occurrance of x in an integer array $a[100]$. The following is a code doing the same.

```
for i = 0 to 99 do
    k = 99 - i
    if a[k] = x then break
    ...
end loop
```

Here the expression $99 - i$ is computed for each iteration of i. Changing the order of index variable assignment, computation of k is not necessary, making it a dead code to be eliminated. The modified code is,

```
for i = 99 downto 0 do
    if a[i] = x then break
    ...
end loop
```

Loop Unrolling. It duplicates the body of the loop multiple times, in order to decrease the number of times the loop condition needs to be tested. It also reduces the number of jumps from end of the loop to the beginning. It may be noted that jump statements hurt performance by impairing the instruction pipeline. Completely unrolling a loop eliminates all overhead, but requires that the number of iterations be known at compile time. Moreover, if the loop body is big, unrolling may increase code size significantly, affecting performance.

Loop Splitting. Loop splitting attempts to simplify a loop or eliminate dependencies by breaking it into multiple loops which have the same bodies but iterate over different contiguous portions of the index range. For example, consider the code segment,

for $i = 1$ to 100 do
  if $i < 30$ then B_1
  if $30 \leq i < 60$ then B_2 else B_3
end loop

The loop can be split into three loops as follows:

for $i = 1$ to 29 do
  B_1
end loop
for $i = 30$ to 59 do
  B_2
end loop
for $i = 60$ to 100 do
  B_3
end loop

A useful special case is *loop peeling*, which can simplify a loop with a problematic first iteration by performing that iteration separately before entering the loop. For example, the code segment,

for $i = 1$ to 100 do
  if $i = 1$ then B_1 else B_2
end loop

can be modified as follows:

$i = 1$
B_1
for $i = 2$ to 100 do
  B_2
end loop

Unswitching. Unswitching moves a conditional inside a loop to outside of it by duplicating the loop's body and placing a version of it inside each of the *then* and *else* clauses of the conditional. For example, consider the code segment,

```
for i = 1 to 100 do
    if x > y then
        a[i] = b[i] + c
    else
        a[i] = b[i] - c
end loop
```

can be unswitched as,

```
if x > y then
    for i = 1 to 100 do
        a[i] = b[i] + c
    end loop
else
    for i = 1 to 100 do
        a[i] = b[i] - c
    end loop
```

Loop unswitching may increase the locality significantly.

Loop Test Replacement. This replaces a loop termination test phrased in terms of one variable, by a test phrased in terms of another variable. This may open up the possibilities of dead code elimination. It is typically useful following strength reduction.

EXAMPLE 6.26 Consider the following strength reduced program:

```
        temp = 5
        i = 1
loop :  x = temp
        i = i + 1
        temp = temp + 5
        if i ≤ 10 then goto loop
```

The program can be modified as,

```
        temp = 5
        i = 1
loop :  x = temp
        i = i + 1
        temp = temp + 5
        if temp ≤ 50 then goto loop
```

Here, the loop induction variable i is no longer meaningfully used in the program. Hence, it can be eliminated.

6.6 CONCLUSION

In this chapter, we have seen the design and implementation aspects of a *compiler*. A compiler generally consists of modules like *lexical analysis, syntax analysis, code generation* etc. which are intermixed with each other in the design process. A good compiler should do a good amount of program optimization as well. All these have been elaborated in different sections. In the next chapter, we will look into the design of a system utility—the *editor*.

EXERCISES

6.1 Write down the regular expressions for the following:

(a) identifiers of *C* language.

(b) binary strings such that a '0' is always followed by a '1'.

(c) to check an IP address for correct syntax, that is, four groups of 1-3 digits separated by periods.

(d) to check correct syntax for the E-mail address.

(e) a sentence (something that begins with a capital letter and ends with a full stop).

(f) any decimal number that is a multiple of 5.

(g) any string whose length is a multiple of 5.

6.2 What do the following regular expressions mean?

(a) $a(ab)^*a$

(b) [0-7][0-7]*

(c) (0|1)*0(0|1)(0|1)(0|1)

(d) $(a|b)^*abb$

(e) $(a|b)^*a(a|b)(a|b)(a|b)$

6.3 Construct NFAs for the regular expressions given in 6.2.

6.4 Convert the NFAs created in 6.3 to DFAs.

6.5 Write context free grammars to detect the following. Is your grammar ambiguous?

(a) occurrence of balanced parentheses.

(b) strings over the alphabet set $\{a, b\}$, such that every a is immediately followed by a b.

(c) strings over the alphabet set $\{a, b\}$, such that every pair of a (that is, aa) is immediately followed by a pair of b's (that is, bb).

(d) strings over the alphabet set $\{a, b\}$, having equal number of a's and b's.

(e) strings over the alphabet set $\{a, b\}$, having unequal number of a's and b's.

6.6 Consider the grammar

$$E \rightarrow E \,.\, i\,(\,E\,) \mid (\,E\,) \mid E \,?\, E \,:\, \mid i$$

where $\{E\}$ is the set of nonterminal symbols, E is the start symbol, and

$$\{.\ ?\ :\ (\ )\ \} \cup \{i \mid i \text{ is an identifier}\}$$

is the set of terminal symbols. Give a corresponding LL(1) grammar which generates the same language as the one above, show the First and Follow sets for each nonterminal symbol, and the predictive parsing table. Argue that the grammar is LL(1).

6.7 Consider the grammar

$$\begin{aligned} A &\rightarrow B\ C\ x \mid y \\ B &\rightarrow y\ A \mid \epsilon \\ C &\rightarrow A\ y \mid x \end{aligned}$$

where $\{A, B, C\}$ is the set of nonterminal symbols, A is the start symbol, $\{x, y\}$ is the set of terminal symbols. The grammar is not LL(1). Why? As part of your answer, show the First and Follow sets for each nonterminal symbol.

6.8 Consider the following grammar for regular expressions.

$$R \rightarrow R\,'|'\,R \mid RR \mid R^* \mid (R) \mid a \mid b$$

Modify the grammar to make it LL(1). Generate the predictive parsing table for the resulting grammar.

6.9 Construct SLR parsing tables for the grammars in 6.5, 6.6, 6.7, and 6.8.

6.10 Consider the grammar

$$\begin{aligned} E &\rightarrow E\ +\ T \mid T \\ T &\rightarrow T\ F \mid F \\ F &\rightarrow F^* \mid a \mid b \end{aligned}$$

Construct the SLR parsing table.

6.11 Extend the parsing table for the Boolean expression grammar to show error handling.

6.12 Show the annotated parse tree and code generation process for the following arithmetic expressions.

(a) $a + (b - c) * d$

(b) $-(a + b) * (c + d) + (a * b + c)$

6.13 Show the annotated parse tree and code generation process for the following Boolean expressions.

(a) *a and (b or c and not d)*
(b) *not (not (c and d) or a)*

6.14 Consider the following code fragment.

```
while a > b do
begin
    if x = y then c = a + b
    else d = a − b
    p = q + r
end
x = y + z
```

Show the annotated parse tree and the code generation process.

6.15 Study the program flow graph shown in Fig. 6.29 and indicate with justification whether any of the following optimizing transformations can be applied to it.

(a) common sub-expression elimination
(b) elimination of dead code
(c) constant propagation
(d) frequency reduction

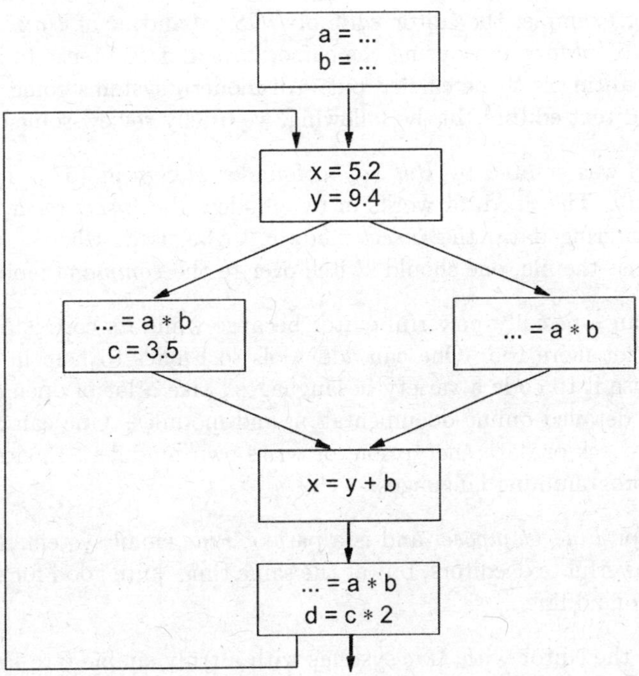

FIGURE 6.29 Program flow graph for 6.14.

Chapter 7

Text Editor

Editors are utilities to write programs in source languages. There are mainly two categories of such editors, namely,

1. line oriented editors
2. screen oriented editors.

The distinction between the two categories is made based upon the smallest unit that can be edited. In a *line editor*, the unit of editing consists of a full line. That is, to modify even a single character, the user has to modify/re-enter the complete line. These are very primitive type of editors. For example, the editor *edlin* of *DOS*, *ed* and *ex* of *Unix*, etc. On the other hand, *screen-oriented editors* allow using the cursor keys and/or mouse to point to a position at which the next editing is to be carried out. All modern systems come up with one/more such screen oriented text editors. In the following, we briefly review some of these.

vi: The editor *vi* was created by *Bill Joy*, cofounder of *Sun* in 1976. It is a considerably powerful utility. The *vi* editor works in two modes: the *insert mode* and the *command mode*. For entering data, the *insert* mode is to be used, whereas to copy, paste, or generally adjust the file, one should switch over to the *command* mode.

Emacs: This is an especially powerful editor because while its core is a plain text editor, it is a whole lot more too. One can add tools to Emacs to help in writing HTML or SGML, and use it to code a variety of languages. Like a lot of open source software, it has plenty of detailed online documentation and modules. One can add other features such as spell check or data encryption, or write own modules. Emacs also has support for different programming languages.

Pico: It stands for *Pine Composer* and is a part of *Pine* email system. It is much simpler than other powerful text editors, but at the same time quite good for writing quick code from the command line.

SimpleText: It is the editor with *Mac* systems with a truly simple interface. A nice feature is that one can view the clipboard while editing. For the portion of the text that is *cut*, SimpleText stores it for later review. It can also be used to view graphics and other binary files. It can play sounds, thus it can be made to read the text by adding *TextToSpeech* software from *Apple*.

Notepad: *Windows* Notepad is simpler than SimpleText. It offers many of the same features: the ability to cut, copy, paste, and find (but not replace). One can set fonts and styles within the document, but these are for display only, as the output is plain text, which means no document formatting code is created from within the program.

7.1 DESIGN OF A TEXT EDITOR

In this section, we will discuss the design of a text editor. Apparently, a text editor consists of a main window along with some edit controls. However, the other part of it is the text file being edited. The actual file resides in the disk in some format that may be totally different from the way it is shown in the edit window. As shown in Fig. 7.1, the key components of a text editor are the following:

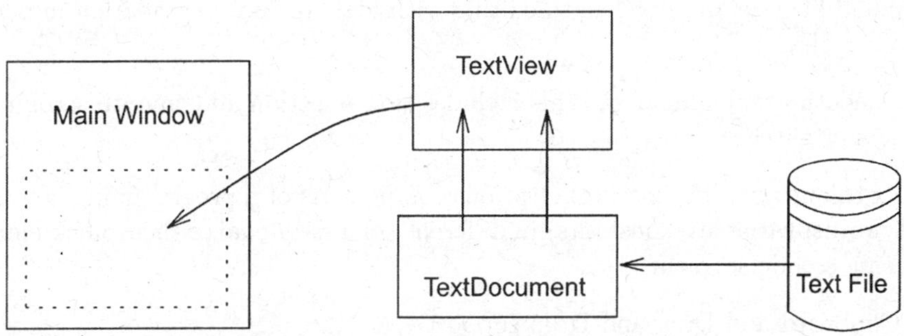

FIGURE 7.1 Components of a text editor.

1. *Main Window:* The top-level main window generally contains the title of the file being edited, menu, and status bars. It does not know how to edit text files, its only purpose is to provide an interface to the user.

2. *TextView:* TextView is the most important component of a text editor. It is generally designed as a separate window that is a child of the *Main Window*. The *TextView* is the visual component of a text editor. Its primary purpose is to display and edit text. However, it needs to do a number of other things, such as displaying scrollbars, process mouse and keyboard inputs, and support drag and drop.

3. *TextDocument:* It is not a visible component, but is used to store and manipulate a text file, once it has been loaded into the memory. It does not have any concept of windows, mice, drawing or painting. All that it knows is how to manipulate text, and supply text to the edit control when it wants to draw something.

4. *Text File:* Though it is not really a part of the text editor, it plays an important role nonetheless. It is the disk file that stores the text we want to edit. The TextDocument will interface directly with this text file, reading from and writing to it when it is time to load or save a new document.

It is important to note that separation of *TextView* from the data it stores (that is, *TextDocument*) provides the flexibility to modify the way we store and represent the actual data in the text file without impacting upon the design of visual component. Similarly, the visual component can be modified without any necessity to modify the storage organization of the text file. The interface between the components may also vary. For example, the *TextView* is a line-oriented, graphical entity. Most of the work performed by the edit-window will be updating the display. This will entail retrieving data from the *TextDocument* on a line-by-line basis. On the other hand, the *TextDocument* will either load the entire file into memory in one go, or access the file in manageable chunks.

7.1.1 Common Edit-Control Features

The edit-control features are the controls available to the user of the editor. Thus, before concentrating on the design of the editor, these features are to be fixed. The features present in most of the modern text editors include the following:

1. Unlimited file size and line length editing with little (or no) degradation in performance for larger files.

2. Fast, smooth graphic display. This includes text selection and smooth scrolling with no artifacts or glitches.

3. Syntax colouring. This shows the various components of a programming language (such as keywords, variables, constants) in different colours to enable their quick identification on seeing a code segment.

4. Full Clipboard and Drag-and-Drop support.

5. Single- or Multi-font display.

6. Complete Undo and Redo support.

7.2 DATA STRUCTURES FOR TEXT SEQUENCES

The central data structure in a text editor is the one that manages the *sequence* of characters that represents the current state of the file that is being edited. Every text editor requires such a data structure. In a *sequence*, reading an item (by position number) is extremely localized. There are several data structures that can be used to store sequences, starting from the most common ones like arrays, link list, etc. to complex ones that keep the *sequence* as a recursive sequence of spans of text. To judge the relative merits and demerits of these schemes, we have to first understand the type and frequency of operations carried out on such sequences.

- *NewSequence* operation is infrequent. Most sequence data structures require the *NewSequence* operation to scan the entire file and convert it to some internal form. This can be a problem with very large files, as to look through the large file, the entire file needs to be converted to the internal form first. Thus, editors not requiring this operation can interleave the file reading with text editing—the user need not worry how big a file is getting loaded into the memory.

- *Close* operation is also infrequent and not normally an important factor in comparing sequence data structures.
- *ItemAt* operation is of course very frequent, but it is also very localized due to the fact that text editors almost always access characters sequentially. When the screen is drawn (showing the file content on the window), the characters on the screen are accessed sequentially beginning with the first character on the screen. If the user pages forward or backward, the characters are accessed sequentially. Searches normally begin at current position and proceed forward or backward sequentially. Overall, there is almost no random access in a text editor.
- *Edits* (*inserts* and *deletes*) are the most important operations. The sequence data structures should be optimized for edits. In a typical text editing, the display is changed after each *insert* and *delete* and this requires a number of *ItemAts*, often just a few characters around the edit but possibly the whole rest of the window.

Next, we introduce a few terminologies that will be used hereafter.

1. An *item* is the basic element. Usually it will be a character.
2. A *sequence* is an ordered set of items.
3. Sequential items in a sequence are said to be *logically contiguous.*
4. Items of the sequence are kept in *buffers.* A buffer is a set of sequentially addressed memory locations. A buffer contains items from the sequence but not necessarily in the same order as they appear logically in the sequence.
5. Sequentially addressed items in a buffer are *physically contiguous.*
6. When a string of items is physically contiguous in a buffer and is also logically contiguous in the sequence, we call it a *span.*
7. A *descriptor* is a pointer to a span.

Sequence data structures keep spans in buffers and keep enough information (in terms of descriptors and sequences of descriptors) to piece together the spans to form the sequence. Buffers can be kept in memory but most sequence data structures allow buffers to get as large as necessary or allow an unlimited number of buffers. Thus, it is necessary to keep the buffers on disk in *disk files.* Many sequence data structures use buffers of unlimited size, that is, their size is determined by the file contents. This requires the buffer to be a disk file. With enough disk block caching, this can be made as fast as necessary.

7.2.1 Basic Sequence Data Structures

In this section, we will discuss about simple sequence data structures that use a fixed number of external descriptors.

The array method: one span in one buffer. This is the most obvious sequence data structure. In this method, there is one span and one buffer. Two descriptors are needed: one for the span and the other one for the buffer. The buffer contains the items of the sequence in a physically contiguous order. *Deletes* are handled by moving all items following the deleted item to fill in the hole left by the deleted item. *Inserts* are handled by moving all the items that will follow the item to be inserted in order to make room for the new item. *ItemAt* is an array reference. The buffer can be extended as much as necessary to hold the data. The array method has been shown in Fig. 7.2. Naturally, this would not be an efficient data structure if a lot of editing has to be done. However, its simplicity makes it a reasonable choice in situations where a few inserts and deletes are made (for example, read-only sequence), or the sequences are relatively small (for example, one-line text editor).

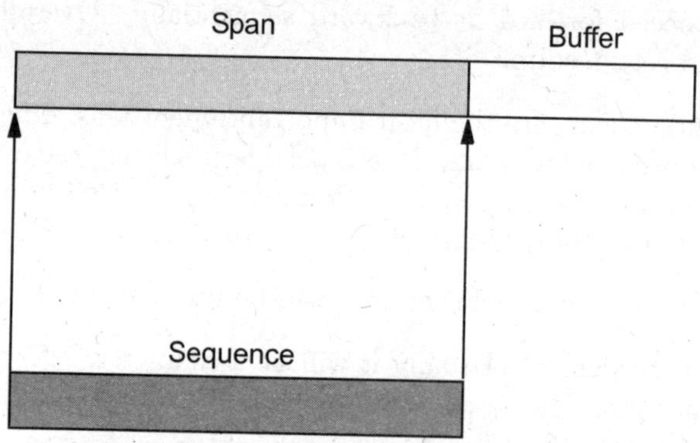

FIGURE 7.2 The array method.

The gap method: two spans in one buffer. This method is slightly more complex than the array method, however much more efficient. In this method, we have one large buffer that holds all the text, but there is a gap in the middle of the buffer that does not contain valid text. Three descriptors are needed: one for each span and one for the gap. The gap will be at the text "cursor" or "point" where all text editing operations take place. *Inserts* are handled by using up one of the places in the gap and incrementing the length of the first descriptor (or decrementing the begin pointer of the second descriptor). *Deletes* are handled by decrementing the length of the first descriptor (or incrementing the begin pointer of the second descriptor). *ItemAt* is a test (first or second span?) and an array reference. The structure has been shown in Fig. 7.3. When the cursor moves, the gap is also moved. Thus, if the cursor moves 100 items forward, then 100 items have to be moved from the second span to the first span (and the descriptors adjusted). Since most cursor moves are local, not that many items have to be moved in most cases. Moreover, the gap does not need to move every time the cursor is moved. Only when an editing operation is requested, the gap is moved. Thus, moving the cursor around the file while paging or searching will not cause unnecessary gap movements. If the gap fills up, the second span is moved in the buffer to create a new gap. Gap size is determined through some algorithm. In practice, it is usually increased by some fixed increment or by some fixed percentage of the current buffer size. With virtual memory, one can make the buffer so large that it is unlikely to fill up. The gap method is simple and surprisingly efficient. It is also known as the *split buffer* method.

The linked list method. This method has a span for each item in the sequence and the span is kept in the descriptor. This requires a large number of descriptors which must be sequenced. If the descriptors are linked together into a linked list, then only the

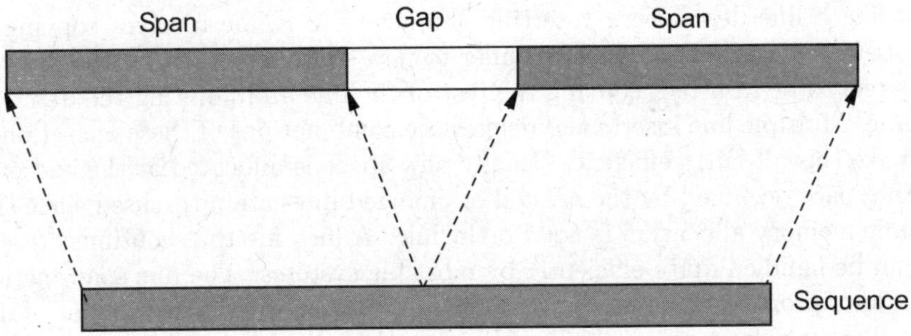

FIGURE 7.3 The gap method.

head of the list is needed to be remembered. *Inserts* and *deletes* are fast and easy (just move some pointers), but *ItemAt* is more expensive than the array or gap methods since several pointers may have to be followed. The structure has been shown in Fig. 7.4.

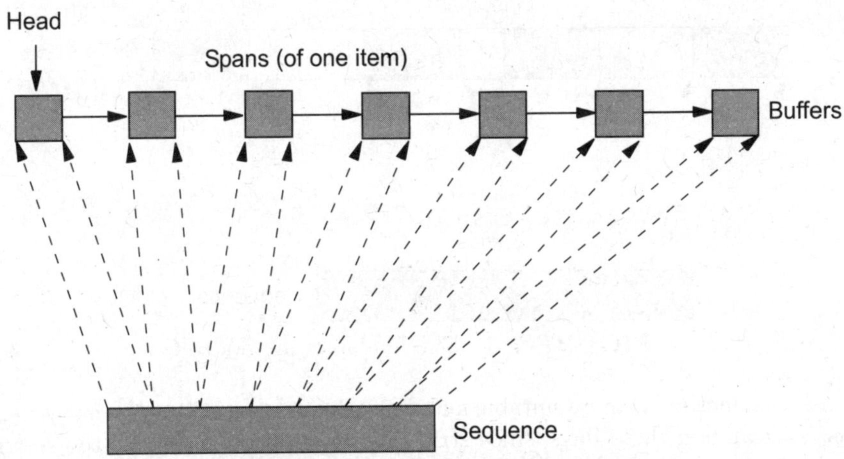

FIGURE 7.4 The linked list method.

7.2.2 Recursive Sequence Data Structures

In this section, we present a few data structures that use variable number of descriptors and so must be using a recursive structure.

The line span method: one span per line. Since most of the text editors do many operations on lines, it seems reasonable to use a data structure that is line oriented, so that line operations can be handled efficiently. The line span method uses a descriptor for each line. Often, one large buffer is used to hold all the line spans. New lines are appended to the end of the used part of the buffer. Figure 7.5 shows the line span method. Line deletes are handled by deleting the line descriptor. Deleting characters within a line involves moving the rest of the characters in the line up to fill the gap. Since any one line is probably not that long, this is reasonably efficient. Line inserts are handled by adding a line descriptor. Inserting characters in a line involves copying the initial part (before the insert) of the line buffer to new space allocated for the line, adding the characters to be inserted, copying the rest of the line and pointing the descriptor at the new line. Multiple line inserts and deletes are combinations of these operations. Caching can make this all fairly efficient. Usually new space is allocated at the end of the buffer and the space occupied by the deleted or changed lines are not reused since the effort of dynamic memory allocation is not worthwhile. A disk file that continues to grow at the end can be handled quite efficiently by most file systems. The line span method uses as many descriptors as there are lines in the file, that is, a variable number of descriptors, hence there is a recursive problem of keeping these descriptors in a sequence. Typically one of the basic data structures described in the previous section is used to maintain the sequence of line descriptors. These simpler methods are acceptable since the number of line descriptors is much smaller than the number of characters in the file being edited. The linked list method allows efficient insertions and deletions but requires the management of list nodes.

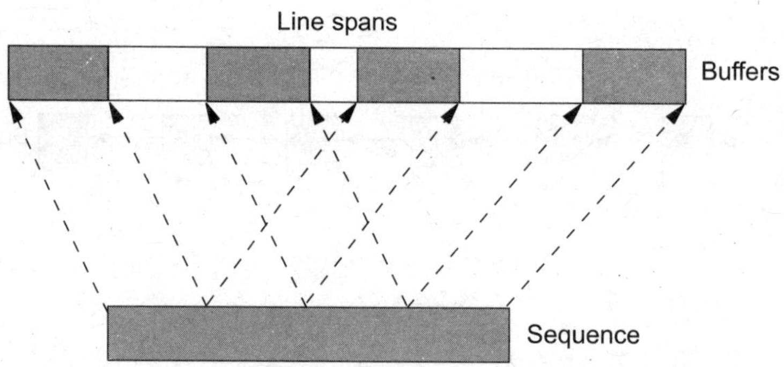

FIGURE 7.5 The line span method.

The line span method is more suitable for a line oriented text editor (for example, EDLIN) but is not common these days, since strict line orientation is seen as too restrictive. It does require preprocessing of the entire buffer before one can begin editing, since the line descriptors have to be set up.

Fixed size buffers. In the line span method, the partitioning of the sequence into spans is determined by the contents of the text file, in particular the line structure. Another approach is for the text editor to decide the partitioning of the sequence into spans based on the efficiency of buffer use. Since fixed size blocks are more efficient to deal with, the file can be divided into a sequence of fixed size buffers. Each block has a maximum size but will usually contain fewer actual items from the sequence so there is room for inserts and deletes, which will usually affect only one buffer. The scheme has been shown in Fig. 7.6.

The disk block size (or some multiple of the disk block size) is usually the most efficient choice for the fixed size buffers, since then the editor can do its own disk management more easily and not depend upon the virtual memory system or the file system for efficient use of the disk. Also, a lower bound on the number of items in a buffer is set (half the buffer size is a common choice). This requires moving items between buffers

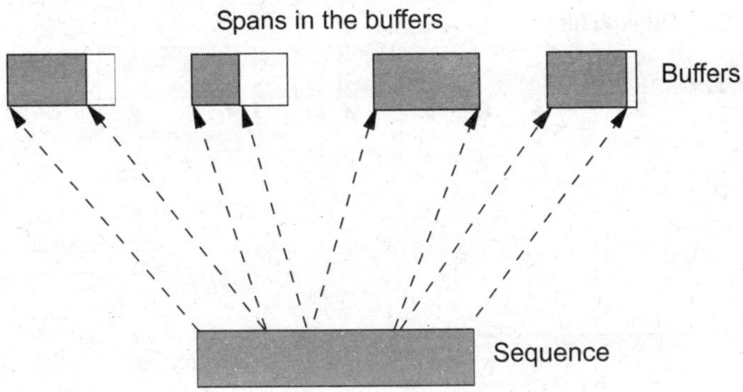

FIGURE 7.6 Fixed size buffers.

and occasionally merging two buffers to prevent the accumulation of large number of buffers. For example, assuming disk blocks to be 4K bytes long, each buffer will be 4K bytes long and will contain a span of length from 2K to 4K bytes. Each buffer is handled using the array method, that is, inserts and deletes are done by moving the items up or down in the buffer. Typically an edit will affect only one buffer, but if a buffer fills up, it is split into two buffers, and if the span in a buffer falls below 2K bytes, then items are moved into it from an adjacent buffer or it is coalesced with an adjacent buffer.

The piece table method. In this method, the sizes of the spans are as large as possible but are split as a result of the editing that is done on the sequence. The sequence starts out as one big span and that gets divided up as insertions and deletions are made. Each span is called a *piece* of the sequence, its descriptor is called a *piece descriptor*. The sequence of piece descriptors is called the *piece table*. The piece table uses the following two buffers.

1. *File buffer* contains the original content of the file being edited. It is of fixed size and is read-only.
2. *Add buffer* is another buffer that can grow without bound and is append-only. All new items are placed in this buffer.

Each piece descriptor points to a span in the file buffer or in the add buffer. Thus, a descriptor must contain three pieces of information: which buffer (a boolean), an offset into that buffer (a non-negative integer), and a length (a positive integer). Figure 7.7 shows a piece table structure. Initially, there is only one piece descriptor which points to the entire file buffer. A delete is handled by splitting a piece into two pieces. One of these pieces points to the items in the old piece before the deleted item and the other piece points to the items after the deleted item. A special case occurs when the deleted item is at the beginning or end of the piece, in which case we simply adjust the pointer or the piece length. On the other hand, an insert is handled by splitting the piece into three pieces. The first piece points to the items of the old piece before the inserted item. The third piece points to the items of the old piece after the inserted item. The inserted item is appended to the end of the add file and the second piece points to this item. Again there are special cases for insertion at the beginning or end of a piece. If several

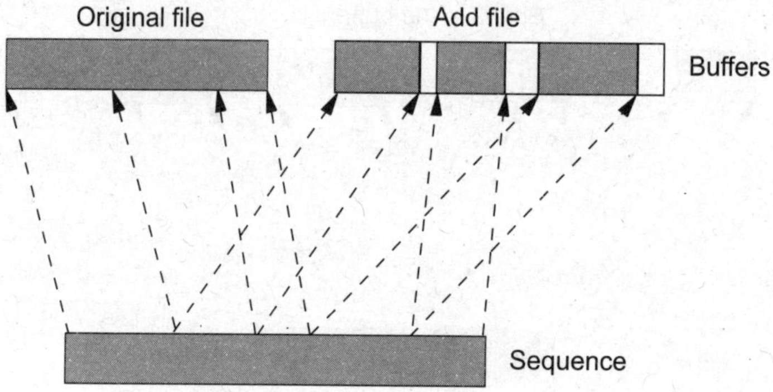

FIGURE 7.7 The piece table method.

items are inserted in a row, the inserted items are combined into a single piece rather than using a separate piece for each item inserted. Figure 7.8 shows the piece table after a file has been read initially. This is a very short file containing 20 characters. Figure 7.9 shows the piece table after the word "large" has been deleted. Figure 7.10 shows the piece table after the word "English" has been added. It may be noted that in general, a delete increases the number of pieces in the piece table by one and an insert increases the number of pieces in the piece table by two.

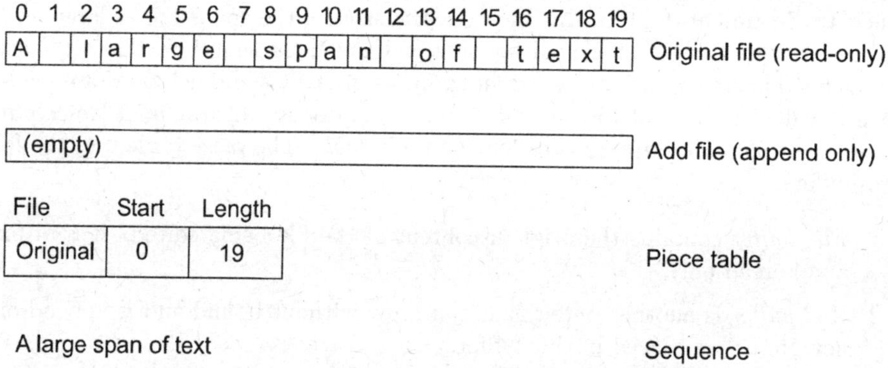

FIGURE 7.8 A piece table before any edits.

The piece table method has several advantages.

- The original file is never changed, so it can be a read-only file. This is advantageous for caching systems since the data never changes.
- The add file is append-only and so, once written, it never changes either.
- Items never move once they have been written into a buffer, so they can be pointed to by other data structures working together with the piece table.
- Undo is made much easier by the fact that items are never written over. It is never necessary to save deleted or changed items. Undo is just a matter of keeping the right piece descriptors around. Unlimited undos can be easily supported.

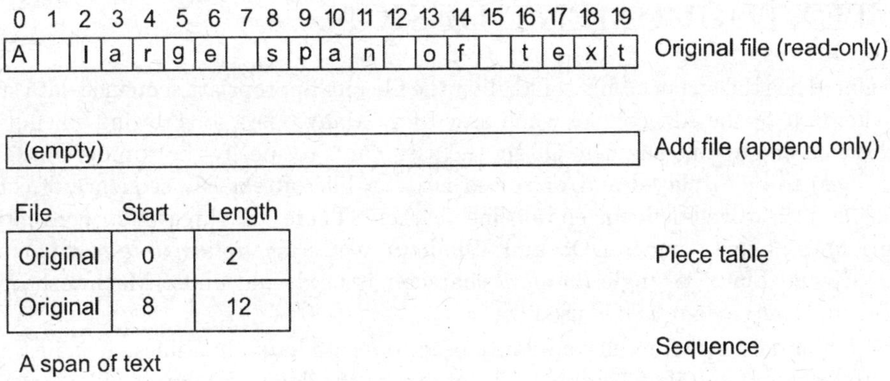

FIGURE 7.9 Piece table after deleting "large".

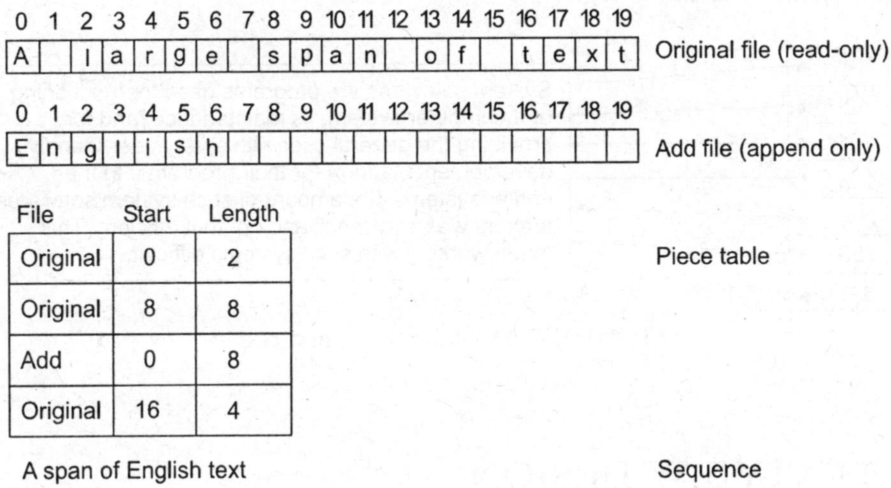

FIGURE 7.10 Piece table after deleting "large" and inserting "English".

- No file preprocessing is needed. The initial piece can be set up only knowing the length of the original file, information that can be quickly and easily obtained from the file system. Thus, the size of the file does not affect the startup time.
- The amount of memory used is a function of the number of edits, not the size of the file. Thus, edits on very large files will be quite efficient.
- Text editor is free to split pieces to suit its purposes. For example, a word processor needs to keep formatting information as well as the text sequence itself. The formatting information can be kept as a tree where the leaves of the tree are pieces. A word in bold face would be kept as a separate piece, so it could be pointed to by a "bold" format node in the format tree.

Overall, the piece table is an excellent data structure for sequences and is normally the data structure of choice. Caching can be used to speed up this data structure, so it is competitive with other data structures, for sequences.

7.3 TEXTDOCUMENT DESIGN

TextDocument has the responsibility of loading the file into appropriate sequence data structure and provide text to the edit-control when asked for. Many operations during editing need to access text in a line-by-line manner. Often, the user wants to specify the number of the line (or range of lines) to be displayed and/or edited next. A line of text is a sequence of characters within a file with a well-defined, end-of-line marker. There are three main conventions for delimiting lines of text—under DOS and Windows, a *carriage-return/line-feed* pair is used, under UNIX and Linux, a single *line-feed* character is used, and under Macintosh operating system, a single *carriage-return* is used.

A *line-buffer* data structure is commonly used to locate individual lines. It is just an array of integer offsets that specify where each line of text in the document starts. The array is filled up by processing the text—searching for *carriage-return/line-feed* sequences and recording the offset for each line as shown in Fig. 7.11.

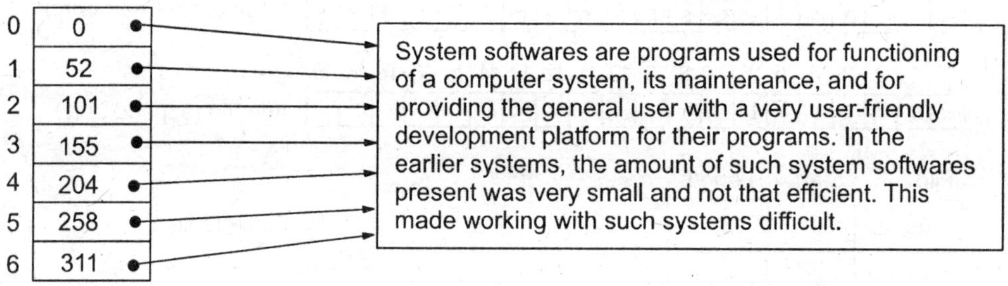

FIGURE 7.11 Line buffer and text.

7.4 TEXTVIEW DESIGN

TextView controls the way a document is displayed for editing to the user. The first major thing to do here is to draw the lines of text. Design of this drawing part is very much dependent on the underlying operating system. However, it basically consists of the following steps:

1. Create a basic drawing framework with a rectangular update area for displaying text.
2. Determine the *first* and *last* line of text that can be drawn in the update area by dividing the *top* and *bottom* co-ordinate (available as pixel) of the update window by the font height.
3. Now, the update area can be considered to be able to hold $(last - first + 1)$ lines of text, each line being drawn in a window of height equal to the font height. A basic drawing utility can thus be used to draw a line into its corresponding window.

It may be noted that the actual line of text that we want to draw is retrieved from *TextDocument* using some method to get a line of text. Thus, it does not matter if we change how to store the text file inside *TextDocument* as long as the interface to the *TextView* is not modified.

7.4.1 Scrolling

The *TextView* designed so far cannot handle *scrolling.* However, the scrollbars and the associated scrolling of text being displayed can be introduced easily into this design. It may be noted that all window systems come up with some technique to obtain the current position of the vertical scrollbar (say *m_nVScrollPos*) and of the horizontal scrollbar (say *m_nHScrollPos*). Moving the vertical scrollbar modifies the lines to be drawn. Thus, the *first* and *last* lines to be drawn can be computed as,

$$\begin{aligned} first &= m\_nVScrollPos + (top/FontHeight) \\ last &= m\_nVScrollPos + (bottom/FontHeight) \end{aligned}$$

where *top* and *bottom* are the window extents in pixels and *FontHeight* is also specified as number of vertical pixels needed to display a single character. Here, effectively we change the line index that we draw. Thus, as the scrollbar moves down, the lines of text effectively move up the display. We still draw lines at the same physical location within the window, but we draw *different* lines to give the illusion that we are scrolling through the document.

For horizontal scrolling, we consider the case of drawing a single line in its display window discussed earlier. We modify the *left, right, top,* and *bottom* extents of the window as follows:

$$\begin{aligned} left &= -m\_nHScrollPos * FontWidth \\ right &= right \\ top &= (nLineNo - m\_nVScrollPos) * FontHeight \\ bottom &= top + FontHeight \end{aligned}$$

When the horizontal scrollbar's position is increased (that is, we scroll to the right), we would expect a page to scroll to the left. So, as the scroll position increases, the text position must decrease. Hence "$m\_nHScrollPos$" has been used. This logical text position is then multiplied by the current font width to produce a pixel based co-ordinate that can be used for drawing. The right-most edge of the line of text must still be fixed to the right edge of the window, so this value is left unchanged. As we scroll to the right, the length of the text that we draw gets larger and larger because the starting x-co-ordinate becomes more and more negative. The display device-context will clip the negative part of the window to give the illusion of horizontal scrolling.

Another approach for horizontal scrolling can be to find out the correct place to draw within the line of buffered characters and do all the drawing from a fixed x-co-ordiante of zero.

As the scrollbars are moved, the *TextView* receives different types of messages to be handled. The messages correspond to various events occurring due to the user asking to scroll the text. The procedure to handle such messages for horizontal and vertical scrollbars is almost identical. Hence, we concentrate our discussion only on the vertical scrollbars.

- *TOP:* The window is scrolled to position zero and redrawn.

$$\begin{aligned} m\_nVScrollPos &= 0 \\ RefreshWindow() & \end{aligned}$$

- *BOTTOM:* The window is scrolled to the maximum position and redrawn.

$$\begin{aligned} m\_nVScrollPos &= m\_nVScrollMax \\ RefreshWindow() \end{aligned}$$

- *THUMB:* Here the user requests the window to be updated as the scrollbar is made to move up or down through some mechanism. The current scroll position is obtained via some tracking routine provided which is operating system specific.

$$\begin{aligned} m\_nVScrollPos &= TrackScrollBar() \\ RefreshWindow() \end{aligned}$$

- *LINEUP:* Scroll position is decremented by one.

$$\begin{aligned} m\_nVScrollPos - - \\ RefreshWindow() \end{aligned}$$

- *LINEDOWN:* Scroll position is incremented by one.

$$\begin{aligned} m\_nVScrollPos + + \\ RefreshWindow() \end{aligned}$$

- *PAGEUP:* Scroll up by entire page. Assuming that the variable *m_nWindowLines* holds the number of lines in current window, scroll position is updated by this amount.

$$\begin{aligned} m\_nVScrollPos &= m\_nVScrollPos - m\_nWindowLines \\ RefreshWindow() \end{aligned}$$

- *PAGEDOWN:* Scroll down by entire page. Assuming that the variable *m_nWindowLines* holds the number of lines in current window, scroll position is increased by this amount.

$$\begin{aligned} m\_nVScrollPos &= m\_nVScrollPos + m\_nWindowLines \\ RefreshWindow() \end{aligned}$$

7.4.2 Multicoloured Text

The text may need to be displayed in different colours. This is needed for *syntax colouring* and more often for *selection highlighting*—to distinguish between the selected and unselected text. Since colour and style information is not stored in the text file, character colours must be computed separately and applied to the displayed text at runtime.

7.4.3 Multifont Display

There are some added complications that arise from the use of multiple fonts.

1. Fonts can vary in width and height. The width does not create much of trouble; however, fonts of different heights must be aligned so that their bases are on the same horizontal line.
2. The height of a line of text is not based on a single font any more—it must be big enough to hold the tallest font currently in use.
3. Smaller fonts do not fill the vertical extents of the line when painted. This will require us to fill this extra *dead space* ourselves.

7.5 CONCLUSION

In this chapter, we have seen different types of editors and their design techniques. The data structures needed for the manipulation of text have been discussed. The *piece table* method seems to be a good structure for this purpose. The design of an editor is very much dependent upon the facilities provided by the underlying operating system. We have seen different utilities needed (particularly for text window manipulation) to implement various features in an editor. In the next chapter, we will discuss another program development aid—the debugger.

EXERCISES

7.1 Distinguish between the line editor and screen editor. Give examples of both categories.

7.2 Study the editors available in your computer system. Compare between them in terms of relative advantages and disadvantages.

7.3 What are the components of a text editor? Explain the role of individual components.

7.4 Describe the commonly available edit control features.

7.5 What are the operations performed on text sequences in the process of editing? Which of these needs more care to design an efficient editor?

7.6 Compare and contrast between the data structures available for the text sequences.

7.7 Show the piece tables after each of the following sequence of editing over the original string: "The distinction between the two categories is made based upon the smallest unit that can be edited".

(a) Delete the word "distinction".

(b) Insert the word "wonderful" between "two" and "categories".

(c) Delete the word "smallest".

(d) Insert the word "largest" at the place where "smallest" was stored earlier.

(e) Change word "edited" to "deleted".

7.8 Explain how vertical and horizontal scrolling are implemented in the display during editing.

Chapter 8

Debugger

Debugging is an essential step in the software development process. Unlike other utilities such as editor, compiler, assembler, etc., a debugger is not necessary to get the executable version of the program from the stage of entering the source language program. The usage of debugger comes once the program has been converted into the executable code and is being tested. Since it is almost impossible to write absolutely correct programs, there will remain a good number of *logical bugs* within it. These logical bugs manifest themselves in the form of runtime error (which may be as fatal as aborting the program or bringing the entire system into some undesirable state like system crash), or producing improper output. It is often very difficult to guess the root of the problem by just looking into the output. For example, if a program develops a *memory fault*, it may be due to the illegal access of the memory locations through any of its variables, pointer chains, or may be due to an array overflow. Though we can introduce some intermediate messages within the program to get an idea about how much of the program could proceed correctly, it is not a practical approach for programs with reasonable size and complexity. Moreover, the problem may be input data dependent, and thus very difficult to recreate. Debugger is particularly useful in such a scenario. Once the software has been specified and designed, it enters into a well-known *edit-compile-test-debug-repeat implementation* cycle. During this cycle, there is clearly a need for tools that aid debugging. A debugger provides the user with a controlled environment for program execution. The user can execute the program till certain predefined point, suspend its execution, check and possibly modify the contents of some of the variables and then resume execution. The program can be executed in steps of each line in the source program, thus providing information about the flow of logic through it.

The most widely available debuggers are known as *breakpoint debuggers.* They allow a programmer to suspend a program's execution at a particular point, inspect and possibly modify the program's state (values of the variables and registers) and then continue the program. In their usual form, breakpoint debuggers are adequate for a number of debugging tasks. However, they provide little support for particularly difficult bugs, such as those whose effects are not apparent until long after their erroneous action occurs. The degree to which hardware and operating system support debugging strongly influences the capabilities of a debugger.

8.1 OVERVIEW OF DEBUGGER FEATURES

In this section, we will discuss the commonly available features of breakpoint debuggers. It may be noted that, apart from these there may be some advanced or specific features available with particular debuggers. One such feature is the *graphical user interface* that may show the program code along with the execution trace as the program proceeds.

1. *Single-stepping:* It is the feature of executing one instruction, source-level statement, or procedure at a time.

2. *Conditional breakpoints:* As discussed earlier, breakpoints are set by the user to suspend execution of the program at some desirable point. A breakpoint may be set at a particular source-program statement, at invocation of a procedure, or at an exact address. A breakpoint may be conditional in that the breakpoint is triggered when the control reaches that point and the particular specified condition is true.

3. *Watchpoints:* These are data breakpoints. An expression involving program variables may be associated with a watchpoint. The breakpoint is triggered whenever the value of the expression changes.

4. *Teledebugging:* It refers to debugging the programs remotely—the debugger executes on one host while the debuggee executing on another.

5. *Attachment:* It refers to the ability of attaching a debugger to an already executing program.

6. *Meta-debugging:* These are the debuggers that can be used to debug themselves.

7. *Kernel debugging:* This advanced feature may be available with some debuggers enabling to debug the operating system.

8. *Checkpointing:* This takes a snapshot of the complete state of an executing program.

9. *Reverse execution:* This is the ability to roll back execution to a previous program state.

8.2 BREAKPOINT MECHANISMS

Breakpoints provide a fundamental type of support for debugging. They give a debugger the ability to suspend the debuggee when its thread of control reaches a particular point. The program's call stack and data values can then be examined, data values possibly modified, and program execution continued until the program encounters another breakpoint location, faults, or terminates.

Breakpoints are usually implemented by replacing the instruction (or instructions) at the desired location in the program with a *trap instruction.* The replaced instruction is remembered for later execution. When the trap instruction is executed, it causes a fault that is detected by the operating system. The operating system then informs the debugger (either via a message, or by completing a system call that the debugger is executing, or by a straight transfer of program control) that a fault has occurred. The debugger inspects the type of fault and reports it to the programmer. At this point, the programmer may wish to inspect or modify the debuggee's state. That is, the variables may be set to some values by the user, and so on. If the debugger shares its address space or part of its address space with the debuggee, the process is quite simple. If not, the debugger calls upon the operating system to provide a form of access to the debuggee's state.

When the programmer decides to continue execution, the program must be resumed starting at the instruction that was replaced by the trap instruction. Some systems provide a service to emulate the instruction; with others, the debugger must replace the trap instruction with the remembered instruction, single-step the debuggee, set the trap instruction again, and finally, continue the debuggee's execution.

Conditional breakpoints are usually implemented using nonconditional breakpoints. Each time the debuggee stops at a breakpoint, the debugger checks the condition associated with the breakpoint. If it is false, the debugger continues the debuggee without informing the programmer. If it is true, the programmer is so informed.

8.3 HARDWARE SUPPORT FOR DEBUGGING

Hardware support is essential for efficient implementation of debuggers. The hardware support can come in varying degrees.

1. At the minimum, some form of *trap* instruction is necessary for implementing breakpoints, and virtually all processors provide some form of it.
2. Instruction-level single-stepping is also often supported. Once such a mechanism exists for instruction-level stepping, statement-level stepping can be implemented by repeated instruction-level stepping. Though the procedure-level stepping can also be implemented by extending the concept, it is more simply implemented by breakpointing the return address of the procedure.
3. Beyond trap instructions, hardware can provide debugging support that has the major advantage of being non-intrusive: the debuggee runs wholly unmodified until the hardware detects a debugging-related event. This feature is particularly useful to eliminate *Heisenbugs*, which refers to memory problems that do occur in the normal execution of the program, but not in a controlled execution environment provided by the debuggers.
4. Most processors support single-stepping and instruction emulation by providing a bit in the *processor status word (PSW)* that indicates that a trap should be generated after the next instruction is executed.
5. On processors without the PSW-bit support (such as SPARC and R2000 architectures), the debugger must be able to decode the instruction to be single-stepped, compute its successor (or possible successors), breakpoint the successor (by modifying it with a trap), continue the program, trap the resulting breakpoint, and remove the successor breakpoint.
6. Hardware page protection can be used to implement *watchpoints* by making the pages read-only (to catch modifications) or inaccessible (to catch any form of access). This is particularly suitable for small page sizes (for example, 512 byte page of VAX). This is because the approach also generates a number of false alarms. For example, if we want to watch the variable x, we protect the page containing x. Now for access to any variable

in the page, it results in an exception. The debugger has to decide whether the access be permitted or not.

7. Availability of *hardware comparators* that trigger upon specific execution or memory access patterns and then record the present execution state can be used efficiently to implement various debugging features. Breakpoints can be implemented by using such comparators to trap when a particular address is about to be loaded into the instruction pointer register. Watchpoints can be realized similarly to trap reading, writing, or the writing of a particular value to a given address.

8. Another form of hardware debugging support is an *instruction counter.* The counter can be loaded with a particular value and decremented upon the execution of each instruction. When the counter reaches zero, an interrupt is generated. It can be used for various purposes:

   (a) It provides a simple mechanism to profile code by determining the number of instructions executed.

   (b) To implement conditional breakpoints, the debuggee can be periodically stopped and the breakpoint condition inspected. When the condition is found to be true, execution can be restarted from the beginning. If in the last time, the number of instructions executed was l, in the next execution, the number of instructions is set to $l/2$. This way, a binary search on the number of instructions executed can be used to find the exact point where the breakpoint condition becomes true.

   (c) Similarly, an instruction counter can be used for reverse execution by counting the number of instructions executed until a fault and then restarting and running for just a few instructions less, to achieve the state where the debuggee is about to fault but has not yet done so.

9. A much more expensive but powerful form of debugging support can be attained by using a *tagged* architecture, where each memory location has some information associated with it. It can be used to implement watchpoints, runtime type checking, catching access to uninitialized data, as well as many types of breakpoints (like trap before/after instruction execution, before successful branch, and on procedure entry and exit).

Hardware support can clearly yield substantial benefits in debugger support. However, if present trends towards RISC-style architecture continue, debugger support will probably remain spare—a trap instruction and perhaps a PSW trace bit—since most of the hardware supported debugging features can, with some effort and loss of performance, be done entirely in software. The fundamental tenet of RISC—that every feature supported by hardware be thoroughly justified—appears to require a greater emphasis on the importance of debugging than is now made.

8.4 CONTEXT OF DEBUGGER

A major issue in the debugger design is whether the debugger executes in the context of the same process as the debuggee or as a separate process (possibly from a remote machine). Both approaches are full of possibilities and limitations for debugging support.

8.4.1 Same-process Debugger

A *same-process debugger* is one that executes in the context of the same process as the debuggee. Consequently, the debugger also shares the debuggee's memory. The main advantages of same-process debuggers are as follows:

- They can directly access the debuggee's memory, making both setting breakpoints, examination and modification of the debuggee's state a simple matter. This eliminates the need for operating system support to provide these features, which can result in substantially better performance.

- The *context switch* from the debuggee to the debugger or vice versa can be extremely fast—as quick as a branch instruction. This can be especially valuable when faults are frequent, such as with programs that use floating-point emulation, since the performance degradation is much lower than when using a separate process debugger.

There are, however, some serious disadvantages of same-process debuggers.

- The debugger's presence deprives the debuggee of some of its resources (such as virtual memory or open files).

- A bug that causes the debuggee to scribble on arbitrary memory can wipe out the debugger, rendering it useless for finding the bug.

- Same-process debuggers cannot be attached to already-running processes, nor can they support kernel debugging, teledebugging, or meta-debugging.

- Finally, same-process debuggers are susceptible to *Heisenbugs*.

The modern examples of same-process debuggers tend to be those that run on microprocessors, such as *cdb, MD-16*, etc. Workstation and minicomputer debuggers tend to be a separate process, no doubt because operating system support is available for separate-process debugging. One well-known, same-process debugger that runs on minicomputers is *VAX DEBUG*, which provides many features including multilingual debugging, source-level debugging, and watchpoints.

8.4.2 Separate-process Debugger

Most debuggers are designed as processes separate from the debuggee. The challenge with separate-process debuggers is keeping the overhead of manipulating the debuggee low. Usually, such manipulation is done via operating system calls. On Unix systems, *ptrace* is used. This grab-bag system call provides mechanisms for processes to declare themselves as candidates for debugging as well as allowing a debugger to read and modify debuggee's memory and access additional state (such as registers and pending signals). A major problem with *ptrace* design is that all access and modification of debuggee state occurs one word or register at a time, and is done in the debuggee's context, so one system call plus two context switches are required for each word accessed.

Context switches can be greatly reduced by making the debuggee's state directly available via system calls. For example, */proc* mechanism supported in *System V Release 4 Unix* systems provides a virtual file system directory in which there is a file for each process. The "contents" of the file are the process's memory and system state. A particular part of the state can be read or modified by seeking to the appropriate address (offset) within the file and using the usual *read* and *write* system calls. No context switches are involved, only system calls are needed. While */proc* enhances the performance and simplifies access to debuggee's state, the system call overhead may well prove too high for state-access-intensive operations such as conditional breakpoints.

8.5 CHECKPOINTING AND REVERSE EXECUTION

A very powerful debugging tool is the ability to inspect the debuggee's previous states and possibly restart execution from one of them. Making a snapshot of a program's state at a particular point in its execution is *checkpointing*; "undoing" execution by returning to a previous state is *reverse execution*. For example, consider the debugging problem of a programmer discovering that a supposedly acyclic list contains a cycle—one of the elements points to a previous element. To find the bug responsible, the programmer would like to ask the debugger the question: "When did this tree first get an illegal cycle?" To answer this question, the debugger needs both to know how to recognize an illegal cycle (which might be specified by a program fragment) and to inspect previous checkpoints of the debuggee's execution until it finds the first one in which the tree contains an illegal cycle. The cycle must then first have appeared between that checkpoint and the previous one. By restarting the program from the previous checkpoint, the exact point at which the cycle was introduced can be found out. It can be implemented in the following ways:

1. A simple way to do this is to generate a code that maintains a *trace table* in which all assignments to variables are logged. However, the approach has got a severe performance problem.

2. Another technique is to generate checkpoints by writing the program state to disk at fixed intervals. The checkpoint includes those pages that have been modified since the last checkpoint along with the names, modes, and file pointers of all open files. The checkpoints can then be browsed, restarted with new functions dynamically bound to them, or executed by an object-code interpreter to find the exact point at which a bug occurs.

3. Another very simple yet intelligent way of implementing checkpoints in Unix systems is using the *fork* system call. It may be noted that in Unix, the *fork* call creates a child process with identical code, data, and stack segments as the parent. It can be utilized to implement checkpointing by keeping the forked child dormant. Thus it holds the entire execution state as it existed at that moment. The debuggee can be replayed by sending a signal to the appropriate forked child, which first forks another copy of itself so the debuggee can be restarted at that point again and then proceeds to continue execution.

8.6 CONCLUSION

In this chapter, we have seen different types of debuggers and their features. The supports needed from both software and hardware to implement such features have also been discussed. The design of a good debugger is a challenging task; however, having a good debugger makes the life of the programmer easy by providing an efficient environment to catch logical bugs easily.

EXERCISES

8.1 Explain why debugging is an essential step in program development and thus establish the necessity to have a good debugger.

8.2 What is a breakpoint? What are the normal program points at which breakpoint can be set?

8.3 What are the commonly available features of debuggers?

8.4 Study any debugger available in your system and use it to debug an erroneous program.

8.5 How can breakpoints be implemented within a program?

8.6 What are the common hardware features available for efficient implementation of debuggers?

8.7 What are checkpointing and reverse execution? How are these implemented?

8.8 Why is it necessary to compile the program with certain options for program debugging?

8.9 Compare and contrast between the contexts in which a debugger can execute.

Appendix

The Netwide Assembler: NASM

A.1 WHAT IS NASM

The *Netwide Assembler, NASM* is an 80x86 assembler designed for portability and modularity. It supports a range of object file formats, including *a.out, ELF, COFF, Microsoft 16-bit OBJ,* and *WIN32*. It also outputs plain binary files. Its syntax is designed to be simple and easy-to-understand. It supports *Pentium, P6, MMX, 3Dnow!, SSE* and *SSE2* opcodes, and has macro capability. It is available at *http://sourceforge.net/projects/nasm.*

A.2 INSTALLATION

A.2.1 Under MS-DOS or Windows

Once you have obtained the DOS archive for NASM, *nasmXXX.zip* (where *XXX* denotes the version number of NASM contained in the archive), unpack it into its own directory.

The archive will contain four executable files: the NASM executable files *nasm.exe* and *nasmw.exe*, and NDISASM executable files *ndisasm.exe* and *ndisasmw.exe*. In each case, the file whose name ends in *w* is a *Win32* executable, designed to run under *Windows*, and the other one is a 16-bit *DOS* executable. *nasm* is the assembler and *ndisasm* is the disassembler. Copy the appropriate files to a directory on your PATH. If you have downloaded the DOS source archive *nasmXXXs.zip*, the *nasm* directory will also contain the full NASM source code, and a selection of Makefiles you can use to rebuild your copy of NASM from scratch.

A.2.2 Under Linux

Once you have obtained the UNIX source archive for NASM *nasm-X.XX.tar.gz* (where *X.XX* denotes the version number of NASM contained in the archive), unpack it into a directory such as */usr/local/src*. The archive, when unpacked, will create its own subdirectory *nasm-X.XX*.

NASM is an auto-configuring package: once you have unpacked it, *cd* to the directory it has been unpacked into and type *./configure*. This shell script will find the best C compiler to use for building NASM and setup Makefiles accordingly.

Once NASM has auto-configured, you can type *make* to build the *nasm* and *ndisasm* binaries, and then *make install* to install them in */usr/local/bin* and install the man pages *nasm.l* and *ndisasm.l* in */usr/local/man/man1*. Alternatively, you can give options such as *−−prefix* to the configure script.

A.3 ASSEMBLYING WITH NASM

- To get command line help, type:

  nasm -h

- To assemble into an ELF object file .o, type:

  nasm -f elf myfile.asm

- To create a listing file, type:

  nasm -f elf myfile.asm -l myfile.lst

Bibliography

[1] A. Blauensteiner, "METSIM—A General Assembler," *North-Holland Microprocessing and Microprogramming*, vol. 14, pp. 201–203, 1984.

[2] S. W. Conley, "Portable Microcomputer Cross-Assemblers in Basic," *Computer*, vol. 8, pp. 32–42, Oct. 1975.

[3] S. Fujita and K. Yoshida, "A General-Purpose Cross-Assembler for Microprocessors," *Euromicro Newsletter*, vol. 3, no. 4, pp. 88–89, 1977.

[4] J. R. Heath and S. M. Patel, "How to Write Universal Cross-Assembler," *IEEE Micro*, vol. 1, pp. 45–66, Aug. 1981.

[5] E. Skordalakis, "Meta-assemblers," *IEEE Micro*, pp. 6–16, April 1983.

[6] K. R. Tavernier and P. H. Notredame, "Micro-based Cross-Assemblers," *IEEE Trans. on Software Engineering*, vol. SE-6, no. 4, pp. 334–340, 1980.

[7] J. Tiberghien and J. Taeymans, "CAS88: A Cross-Assembler Suitable for Most of the 8-bit Microprocessors," *Euromicro Newsletter*, vol. 3, no. 2, pp. 80–83, 1977.

[8] M. Watanabe *et al.*, "The Macro-Assembler Generator for Microcomputers," *Euromicro Newsletter*, vol. 3, no. 4, pp. 83–85, 1977.

[9] H. Wu and Y. Jin, "Gpasm: A general purpose cross-assembler for microprocessors," in *IEEE Asian Electronics Conference*, pp. 470–472, 1987.

[10] C. Crowley, "The point text editor for x," tech. rep., CS91-3, University of New Mexico, 1991.

[11] C. C. Charlton and P. H. Leng, "Editors: Two for the Price of One," *Software—Practice and Experience*, vol. 11, pp. 195–202, 1981.

[12] B. Elliot, "Design of a Simple Screen Editor," *Software—Practice and Experience*, vol. 12, pp. 375–384, 1982.

[13] C. W. Fraser and B. Krishnamurthy, "Live Text," *Software—Practice and Experience*, vol. 20, pp. 851–858, Aug. 1990.

[14] J. Gutknecht, "Concepts of Text Editor Lara," *Communications of the ACM*, vol. 28, pp. 942–960, Sept. 1985.

[15] I. A. MacLeod, "Design and Implementation of a Display Oriented Text Editor," *Software—Practice and Experience*, vol. 7, pp. 771–778, 1977.

[16] R. Pike, "The Text Editor sam," *Software—Practice and Experience*, vol. 17, pp. 813–845, Nov. 1987.

[17] C. Crowley, "Data structures for text sequences," tech. rep., University of New Mexico, 1998.

[18] M. A. Linton, "The Evolution of DBX," in *Usenix Summer Conference, Anaheim, CA*, June 1990.

[19] E. Adams and S. S. Muchnick, "DBXTOOL: A Window-based Symbolic Debugger for Sun Workstations," *Software—Practice and Experience*, vol. 16, pp. 653–659, July 1986.

[20] P. Maybee, "PDB: A Network Oriented Symbolic Debugger," in *Usenix Winter Conference,* Washington, D.C., Jan. 1990.

[21] J. Hennessy, "Symbolic Debugging of Optimized Programs," *ACM Transactions on Programming Languages and Systems*, vol. 4, no. 3, pp. 323–344, 1982.

[22] T. A. Cargill, "Implementation of the BLIT Debugger," *Software—Practice and Experience*, vol. 15, pp. 153–168, Feb. 1985.

[23] M. Farley and T. Thompson, "A C Language Debugger," in *Usenix Summer Conference,* Toronto, Ontario, Canada, July 1983.

[24] J. J. Donovan, *Systems Programming.* McGraw-Hill, 1972.

[25] D. H. Marcellus, *System Programming for Small Computers.* Prentice-Hall, 1984.

[26] L. L. Beck, *System Software—An Introduction to Systems Programming.* Addison-Wesley.

[27] L. Presser and J. R. White, "Linkers and loaders," *Computing Surveys*, vol. 4, pp. 149–167, Sept. 1972.

[28] M. E. Benitez and J. W. Davidson, "A portable global optimizer and linker," in *Proceedings of the SIGPLAN'88 Conference on Programming Language Design and Implementation,* (Atlanta, GA, USA), pp. 329–338, June 1988.

[29] C. W. Fraser and D. R. Hansson, "A machine-independent linker," *Software—Practice and Experience*, vol. 12, pp. 351–366, 1982.

[30] R. Kieburtz, W. Barabash, and C. Hill, "A type-checking program linkage system for Pascal," in *3rd International Conference on Software Engineering,* (Atlanta, GA, USA), pp. 23–28, May 1978.

[31] A. Rudmik and B. G. Moore, "An efficient separate compilation strategy for very large programs," *SIGPLAN Notices*, pp. 301–307, June 1982.

[32] H. Barringer, P. Capon, and R. Philips, "The portable compiling systems of MUSS," *Software—Practice and Experience*, vol. 9, pp. 645–655, 1979.

[33] M. Ancona, L. D. Floriani, D. Dodero, and P. Thea, "Program development by using a source linker," in *4th Jerusalem Conference on Information technology (JCIT). Next Decade in Information Technology*, (Jerusalem, Israel), pp. 251–259, May 1984.

[34] C. S. Collberg and M. G. Krampell, "Pasters: Linkers in a modular world," Technical Report CODEN: LUNDFD6/(NFCS-7002)/(1-27)(1986), Department of Computer Sciences, Lund University, 1986.

[35] C. S. Collberg and M. G. Krampell, "Design and implementation of modular languages supporting information hiding," in *Proceedings of the Sixth International Phoenix Confernece on Computers and Communications*, (Scottsdale, AZ, USA), pp. 224–228, Feb. 1987.

[36] D. W. Wall, "Global register allocation at link time," in *Proceedings of the SIGPLAN'86 Symposium on Compiler Construction*, (New York), pp. 264–275, 1986.

[37] M. Eulenstein, "An extension to Pascal for modular programming and a proposal of a conceptionally machine independent linker," in *Implementierung Pascal-artiger Programmiersprachen* (H. Langmaack, B. Schlender, and J. Schmidt, eds.), Stuttgart: B.G. Teubner, 1982.

[38] A. Celentano, P. Vigna, C. Ghezzi, and D. Mandrioli, "Modularization of block-structured languages: The case of pascal," in *Workshop on Reliable Software*, (Bonn, Germany), pp. 167–79, Sept. 1978.

[39] A. Celentano, P. Vigna, C. Ghezzi, and D. Mandrioli, "Separate compilation and partial specification in pascal," vol. 6, pp. 320–328, July 1980.

[40] J. McCarthy, J. C. Fernando, and M. D. Marjorie, "The Linking Segment Subprogram Language and Linking Loader," *Comm. of the ACM*, vol. 6, no. 7, pp. 391–395, 1963.

[41] W. C. McGee, "On Dynamic Program Relocation," *IBM Systems Journal*, vol. 4, no. 3, pp. 184–199, 1965.

Index

Acceptor states, 105
Addressing modes, 19
  based indexed relative, 21
  boased relative, 21
  direct, 20
  immediate, 20
  indexed relative, 21
  register, 20
  register indirect, 20
Application software, 1
Argument List Array (ALA), 90, 91
Array method, 169–170
Assembler, 2, 4, 29, 36
  input-output of, 5
Assembler design process, 40
Assembler directives, 29, 40
  bits, 29
  common, 30
  extern, 29
  global, 30
  section, 29

Backpatching, 54
Binary image, 81
  components, 81
Boolean expressions, 135, 138
Bootstrap loader, 82
Breakpoint debuggers, 180
  features, 181

Checkpointing, 181, 185
Code optimization, 4, 102
Code space reduction, 155
Combined Section Table (CST), 66, 69
Common table, 47
Compiler, 3, 102
  phases of, 103
    code optimization, 4, 102
    error handling and recovery, 4
    intermediate code generation, 4, 132
    lexical analysis, 3, 102
    semantic analysis, 3, 103
    symbol table management, 4
    syntax analysis, 3, 102, 114
    target code generation, 4, 144
Constant propagation, 151–152, 165
Context free languages, 115
Cross-assembler, 5

Debugger, 7, 180, 184
Derivation, 115
  leftmost deviation, 115
  rightmost deviation, 115
Descriptor tables, 17
  type of, 18
    Global Descriptor Table (GDT), 18
    Local Descriptor Table (LDT), 18
Dynamic Link Library (DLL), 77
  hell, 77, 80
Dynamic linking, 65

Emacs, 166
Error handling and recovery, 4
Error recovery, 131–132
Execution frequency reduction, 155

Finite automata, 105–106
  deterministic, 106
  nondeterministic, 106

Fixed size buffers, 172
Folding, 151
Forward reference, 54
Forward reference list, 55, 56, 59

Gap method, 170–171

Hand assembly, 5, 36
Hash table, 42, 46
Heisenbugs, 182, 184

Inputs of a linker, 63, 64
  object files, 63
  shared library stubs, 64
  static libraries, 63
Instruction format, 25
Instruction set, 22, 147
Intermediate code, 4, 132–133
Intermediate code generation, 4, 132

Language sensitive editors, 7
Left recursion, 118
  general, 118–119
  immediate, 118–119
Left recursive parsing, 123
  advantages, 123
  algorithm, 124
  bottomup, 123
  methods, 123
  tables, 124, 125, 130
  topdown, 119
Left sentential forms, 115
Lexeme, 103
Lexical analysis, 3, 102
Lexical analyzer, 102–103, 114
Line buffer, 176
Line editor, 7, 166
Line oriented editors, 166
Linear table, 45
Linked list method, 170–171
Linker, 5, 63
  input-output of, 6, 63–64
  objectives, 63
Linking, 63
  objectives, 63
  pass I of linking, 66
  pass II of linking, 69, 72

Load-and-go assembler, 58–59
  drawbacks, 59
Loading, 6, 80
  definition, 6

Machine Opcode Table (MOT), 37, 41
  organization of MOT, 41
Macro call nesting, 88
Macro definition nesting, 87
Macro Definition Table (MDT), 89
Macro Name Table (MNT), 89
Memory models, 14, 16
  flat mode, 14
  real address mode, 14
  segmented mode, 14
Multicoloured text, 178
Multifont display, 178

Nested macros, 87, 90
Netwide assembler (NASM), 27, 187
Notepad, 167

Object file formats, 60
  Aout, 61
  coff, 61
  elf, 61
  intel hex, 60
  obj, 61
  win32, 61
Operating system, 2, 3
  modules of, 2
    memory management, 2, 14
    process management, 2
    resource management, 2
    secondary storage management, 3
    security management, 3
    user management, 3
Optimizing transformations, 150, 165
  code movement optimization, 155
  common sub-expression elimination, 152, 165
  compile time evaluation, 151
  dead code elimination, 157, 159
  loop optimization, 156, 158
    induction variable analysis, 158
    loop fission, 158
    loop fusion, 160
    loop interchange, 160

loop reversal, 160
loop splitting, 161
loop test replacement, 162
loop unrolling, 161
unswitching, 161
strength reduction, 157
variable propagation, 153-154
Ordered list, 45, 46
Outputs of a linker, 64
executable file, 64
external table, 64

Parse tree, 3, 115, 116–117, 136
Parsing, 114, 119
Pico, 166
Piece table method, 173–174
add buffer, 173
advantages, 174
file buffer, 173
Position Independent Code (PIC), 77
advantages, 78
drawbacks, 79
Procedure Linkage Table (PLT), 79
Public definition table (PDT), 66, 69

Registers, 11
EFLAS register, 12, 14
EIP, 12
general purpose register, 12, 13
uses of, 13
segment register, 12, 13
Regular expression, 104–107, 111–113
Reject states, 105
Relocation, 69
bitmap, 70
table, 70, 72
Reverse execution, 181, 185
Right sentential forms, 116

Same-process debugger, 184
advantages, 184
disadvantages, 184
Scaling factors, 22
Screen editors, 7
Screen oriented editors, 166
Scrolling, 177
Segment overrides, 22, 25
Semantic analysis, 3, 103
Separate-process debuggers, 184
Simpletext, 166
Single-pass assembler, 54, 55
Split buffer method, 170
Static linking, 65
Symbol table, 4, 38, 41, 44, 46, 79
Symbol table (SYMTAB), 4, 44, 45, 46
Symbol table management, 4
Syntax analysis, 3, 102, 114
System software, 1, 2, 7

Target code generation, 4, 144
Text editor, 7, 166, 175
components, 167
main window, 167
Text file, 167
TextDocument, 167-168, 176
TextView, 167, 176
design, 176
steps, 176
Thompson's construction, 111
Three-address code, 133–136
Tokens, 102, 105
attributes, 104
specification, 104
Two-pass assembler, 46
Pass I, 47
Pass II, 50, 52
Types of loaders, 81
absolute, 81
linking, 82
relocating, 81

Versioning, 80
Vi, 166